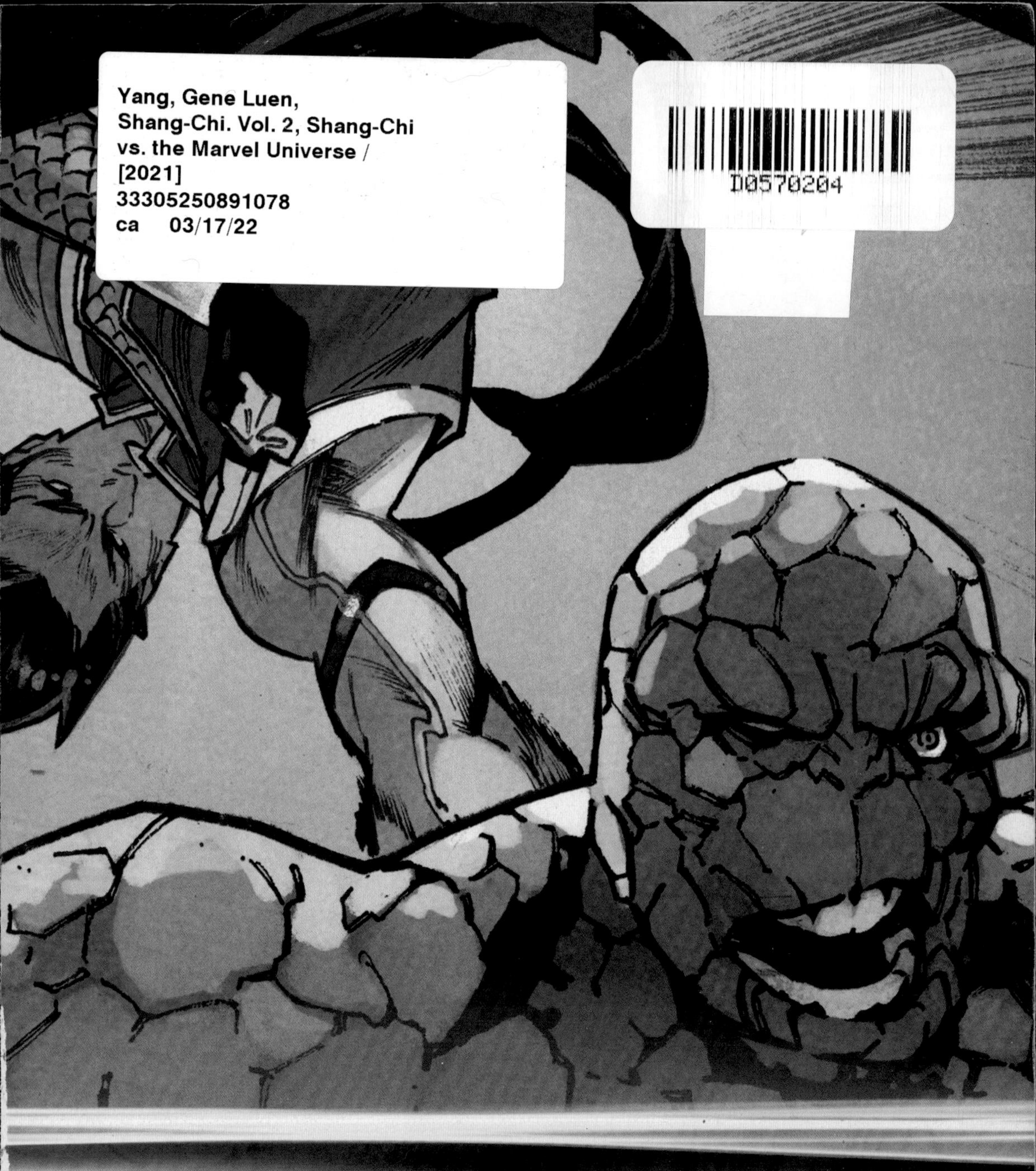

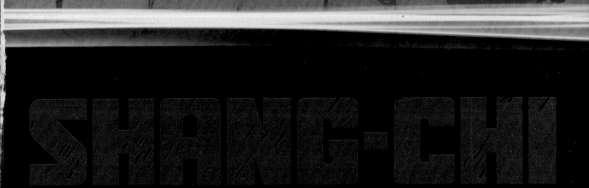

SHANG-CHI

SHANG-CHI VS. THE MARVEL UNIVERSE

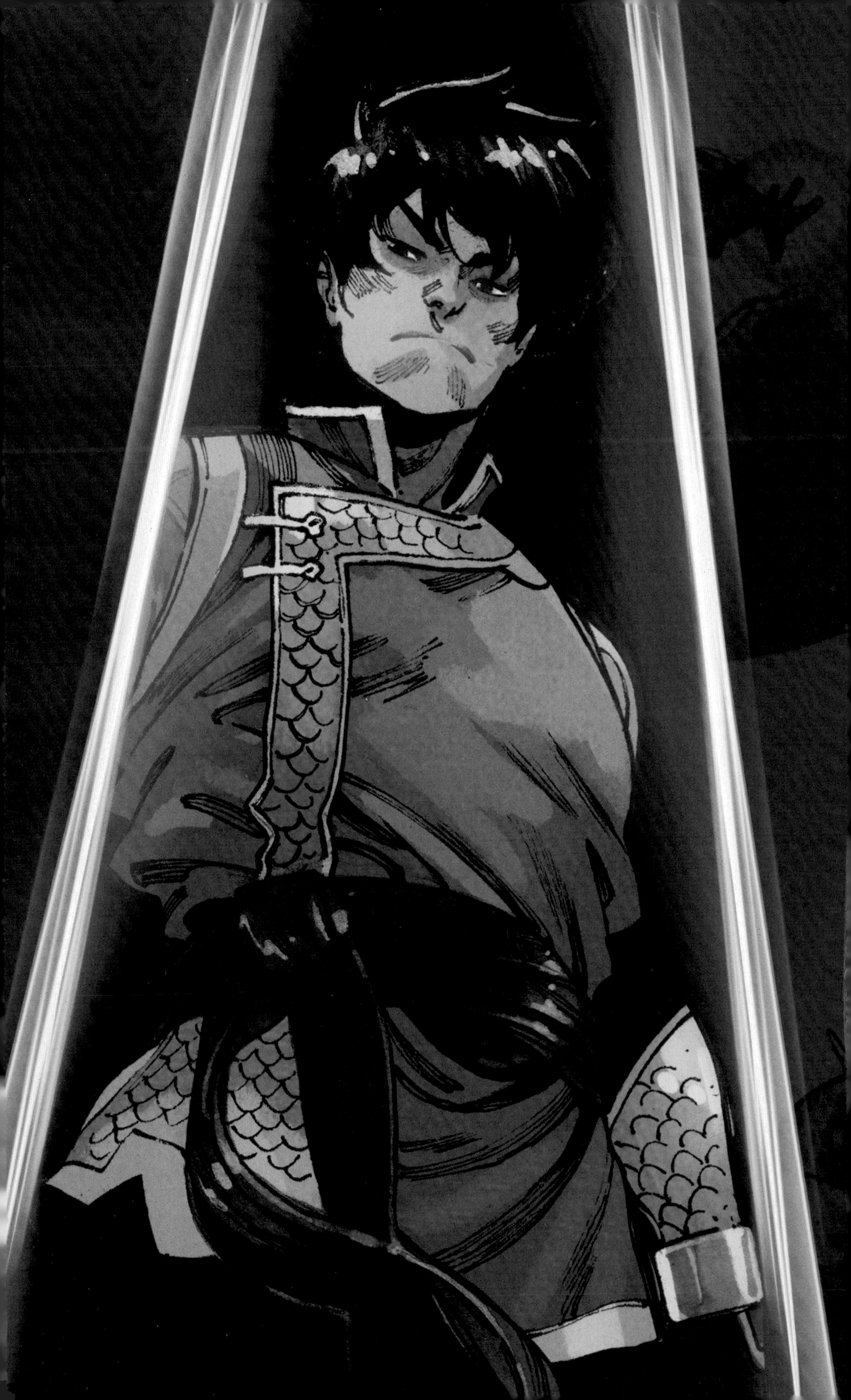

FROM THE DAY HE WAS BORN, HIS EVIL FATHER TRAINED HIM TO BE A LIVING WEAPON. HIS MIND, BODY, AND SPIRIT HONED TO A RAZOR'S EDGE, HE NOW USES HIS ABILITIES TO STRIKE DOWN INJUSTICE AND ATONE FOR HIS FAMILY'S MISDEEDS. HE IS...

SHANG-CHI

SHANG-CHI VS. THE MARVEL UNIVERSE

A FEW MONTHS AGO, SHANG-CHI DISCOVERED HIS FATHER'S CULT-LIKE ORGANIZATION, THE FIVE WEAPONS SOCIETY, WAS STILL ACTIVE. EVEN MORE SURPRISING WAS THE APPEARANCE OF HIS LONG-LOST SIBLINGS, WHO PROCLAIMED HIM THEIR NEW LEADER! NOW SHANG-CHI HAS INHERITED HIS FATHER'S LEGACY, BUT CHANGING THE SOCIETY'S EVIL WAYS WON'T BE EASY...

WRITER **GENE LUEN YANG**

ARTIST **DIKE RUAN**

COLOR ARTIST **TRÍONA FARRELL**

LETTERERS VC's **TRAVIS LANHAM** WITH **JOE CARAMAGNA** [#4]

COVER ART **LEINIL FRANCIS YU** & **SUNNY GHO**

ASSISTANT EDITOR **KAT GREGOROWICZ**

EDITOR **DARREN SHAN**

COLLECTION EDITOR **JENNIFER GRÜNWALD**   JEFF YOUNGQUIST VP PRODUCTION & SPECIAL PROJECTS
ASSISTANT EDITOR **DANIEL KIRCHHOFFER**   ADAM DEL RE WITH SALENA MAHINA BOOK DESIGNERS
ASSISTANT MANAGING EDITOR **MAIA LOY**   DAVID GABRIEL SVP PRINT, SALES & MARKETING
ASSISTANT MANAGING EDITOR **LISA MONTALBANO**   C.B. CEBULSKI EDITOR IN CHIEF

SHANG-CHI BY GENE LUEN YANG VOL. 2: SHANG-CHI VS. THE MARVEL UNIVERSE. Contains material originally published in magazine form as SHANG-CHI (2021) #1-6. First printing 2021. ISBN 978-1-302-93023-3. Published by MARVEL WORLDWIDE, INC., a subsidiary of MARVEL ENTERTAINMENT, LLC. OFFICE OF PUBLICATION: 1290 Avenue of the Americas, New York, NY 10104. © 2021 MARVEL. No similarity between any of the names, characters, persons, and/or institutions in this book with those of any living or dead person or institution is intended, and any such similarity which may exist is purely coincidental. **Printed in Canada.** KEVIN FEIGE, Chief Creative Officer; DAN BUCKLEY, President, Marvel Entertainment; JOE QUESADA, EVP & Creative Director; DAVID BOGART, Associate Publisher & SVP of Talent Affairs; TOM BREVOORT, VP, Executive Editor; NICK LOWE, Executive Editor, VP of Content, Digital Publishing; DAVID GABRIEL, VP of Print & Digital Publishing; JEFF YOUNGQUIST, VP of Production & Special Projects; ALEX MORALES, Director of Publishing Operations; DAN EDINGTON, Managing Editor; RICKEY PURDIN, Director of Talent Relations; JENNIFER GRÜNWALD, Senior Editor, Special Projects; SUSAN CRESPI, Production Manager; STAN LEE, Chairman Emeritus. For information regarding advertising in Marvel Comics or on Marvel.com, please contact Vit DeBellis, Custom Solutions & Integrated Advertising Manager, at vdebellis@marvel.com. For Marvel subscription inquiries, please call 888-511-5480. **Manufactured between 10/29/2021 and 11/30/2021 by SOLISCO PRINTERS, SCOTT, QC, CANADA.**

10 9 8 7 6 5 4 3 2 1

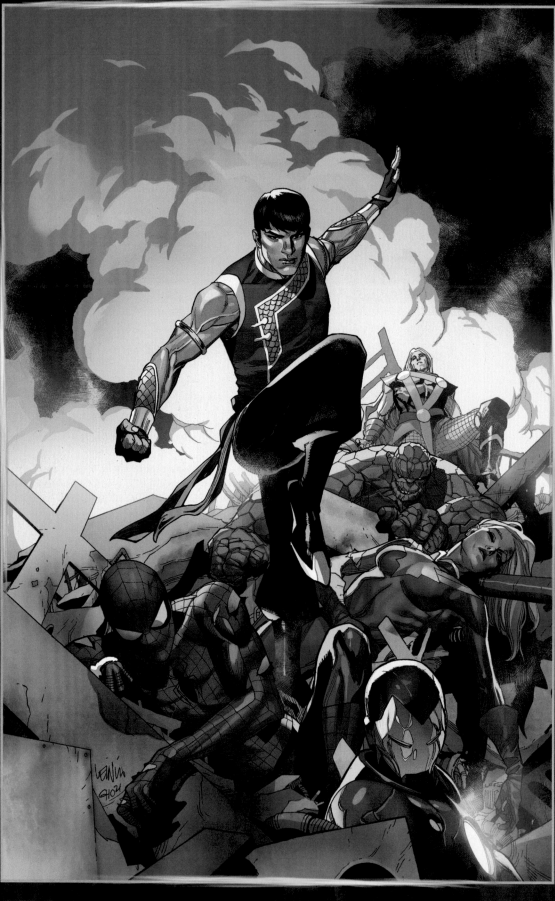

ONE

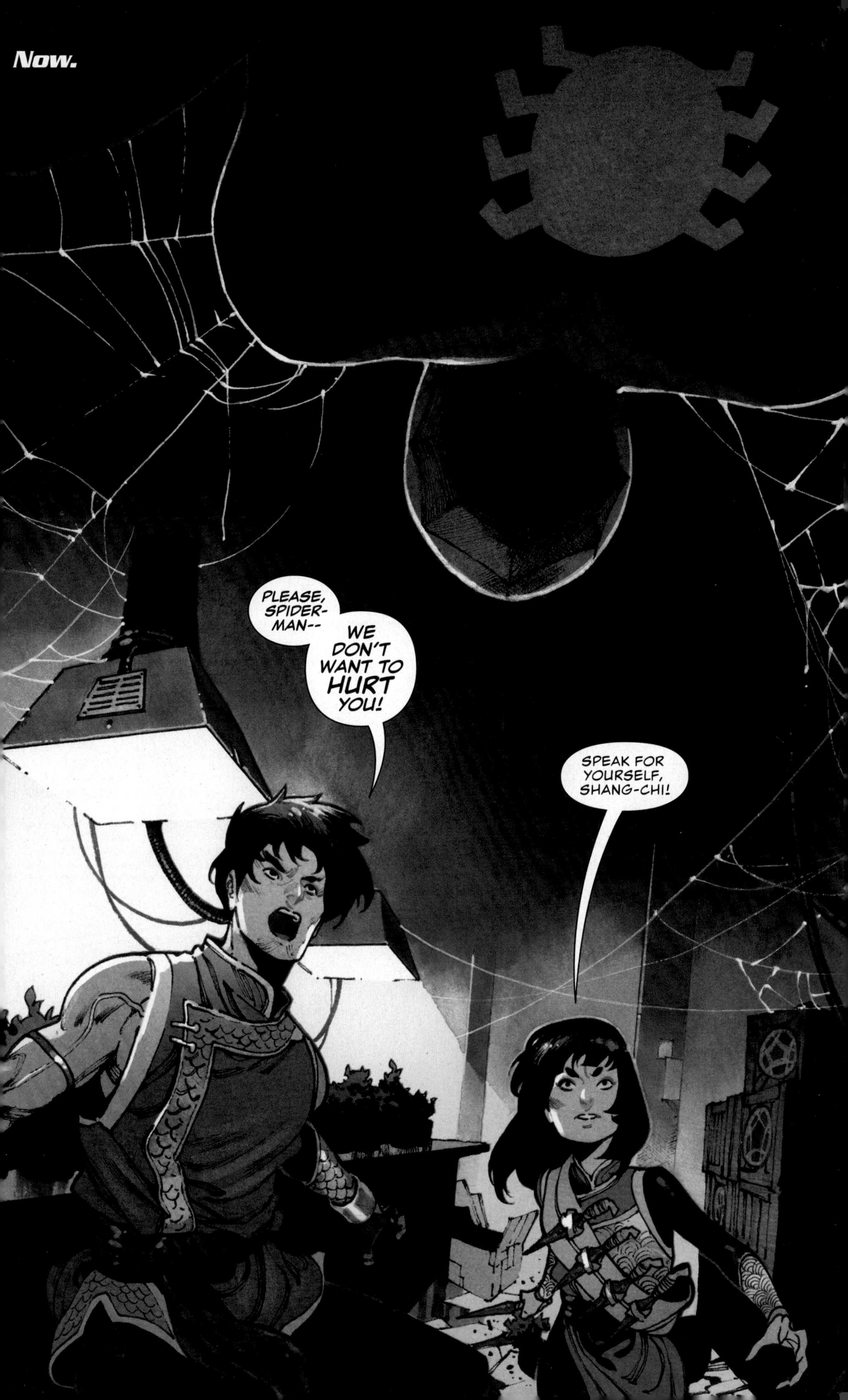
Now.
PLEASE, SPIDER-MAN--
WE DON'T WANT TO HURT YOU!
SPEAK FOR YOURSELF, SHANG-CHI!

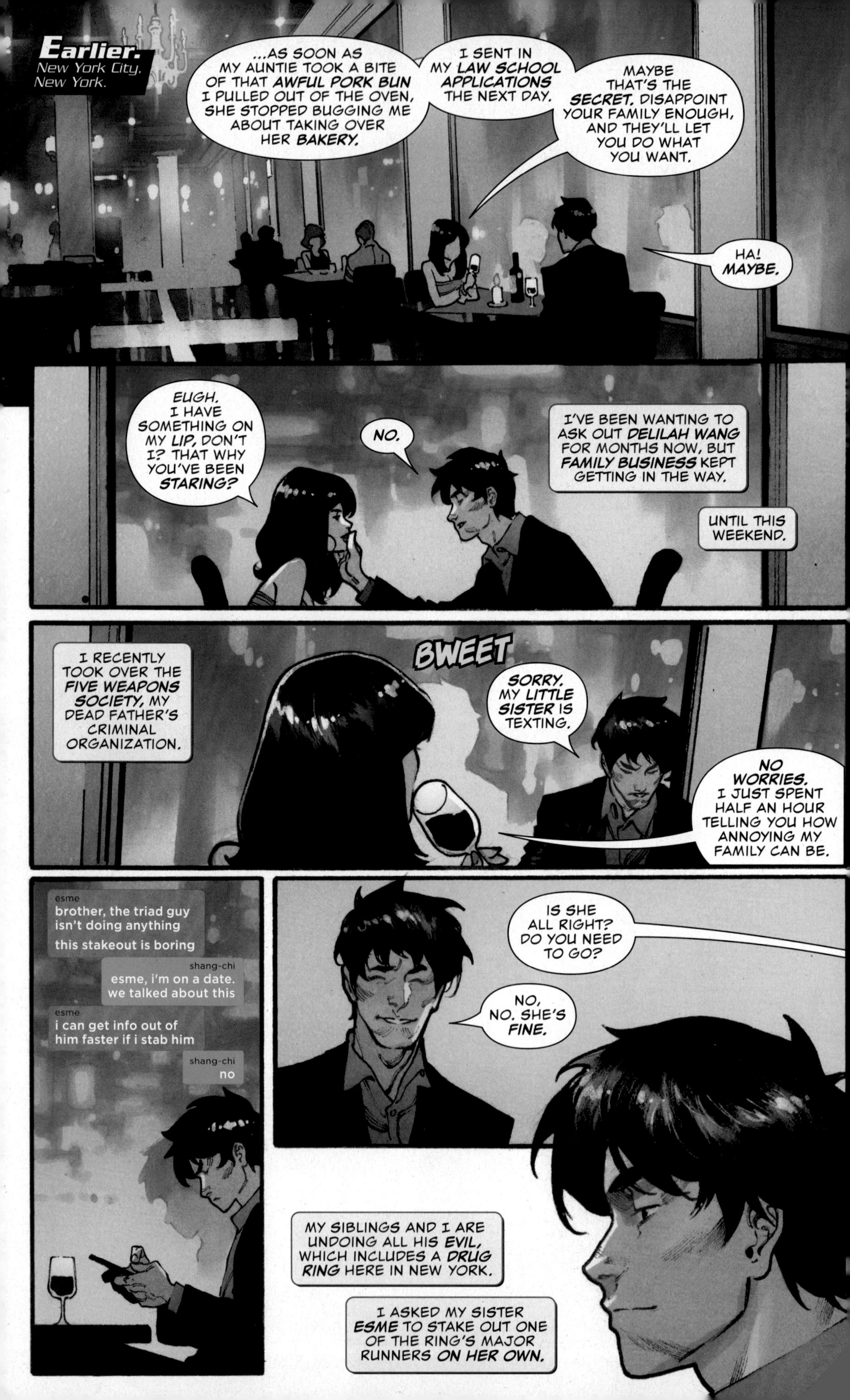
Earlier.
New York City. New York.
...AS SOON AS MY AUNTIE TOOK A BITE OF THAT AWFUL PORK BUN I PULLED OUT OF THE OVEN, SHE STOPPED BUGGING ME ABOUT TAKING OVER HER BAKERY.
I SENT IN MY LAW SCHOOL APPLICATIONS THE NEXT DAY.
MAYBE THAT'S THE SECRET. DISAPPOINT YOUR FAMILY ENOUGH, AND THEY'LL LET YOU DO WHAT YOU WANT.
HA! MAYBE.
EUGH. I HAVE SOMETHING ON MY LIP, DON'T I? THAT WHY YOU'VE BEEN STARING?
NO.
I'VE BEEN WANTING TO ASK OUT DELILAH WANG FOR MONTHS NOW, BUT FAMILY BUSINESS KEPT GETTING IN THE WAY.
UNTIL THIS WEEKEND.
I RECENTLY TOOK OVER THE FIVE WEAPONS SOCIETY, MY DEAD FATHER'S CRIMINAL ORGANIZATION.
BWEET
SORRY. MY LITTLE SISTER IS TEXTING.
NO WORRIES. I JUST SPENT HALF AN HOUR TELLING YOU HOW ANNOYING MY FAMILY CAN BE.
esme
brother, the triad guy isn't doing anything
this stakeout is boring
shang-chi
esme, i'm on a date. we talked about this
esme
i can get info out of him faster if i stab him
shang-chi
no
IS SHE ALL RIGHT? DO YOU NEED TO GO?
NO, NO. SHE'S FINE.
MY SIBLINGS AND I ARE UNDOING ALL HIS EVIL, WHICH INCLUDES A DRUG RING HERE IN NEW YORK.
I ASKED MY SISTER ESME TO STAKE OUT ONE OF THE RING'S MAJOR RUNNERS ON HER OWN.

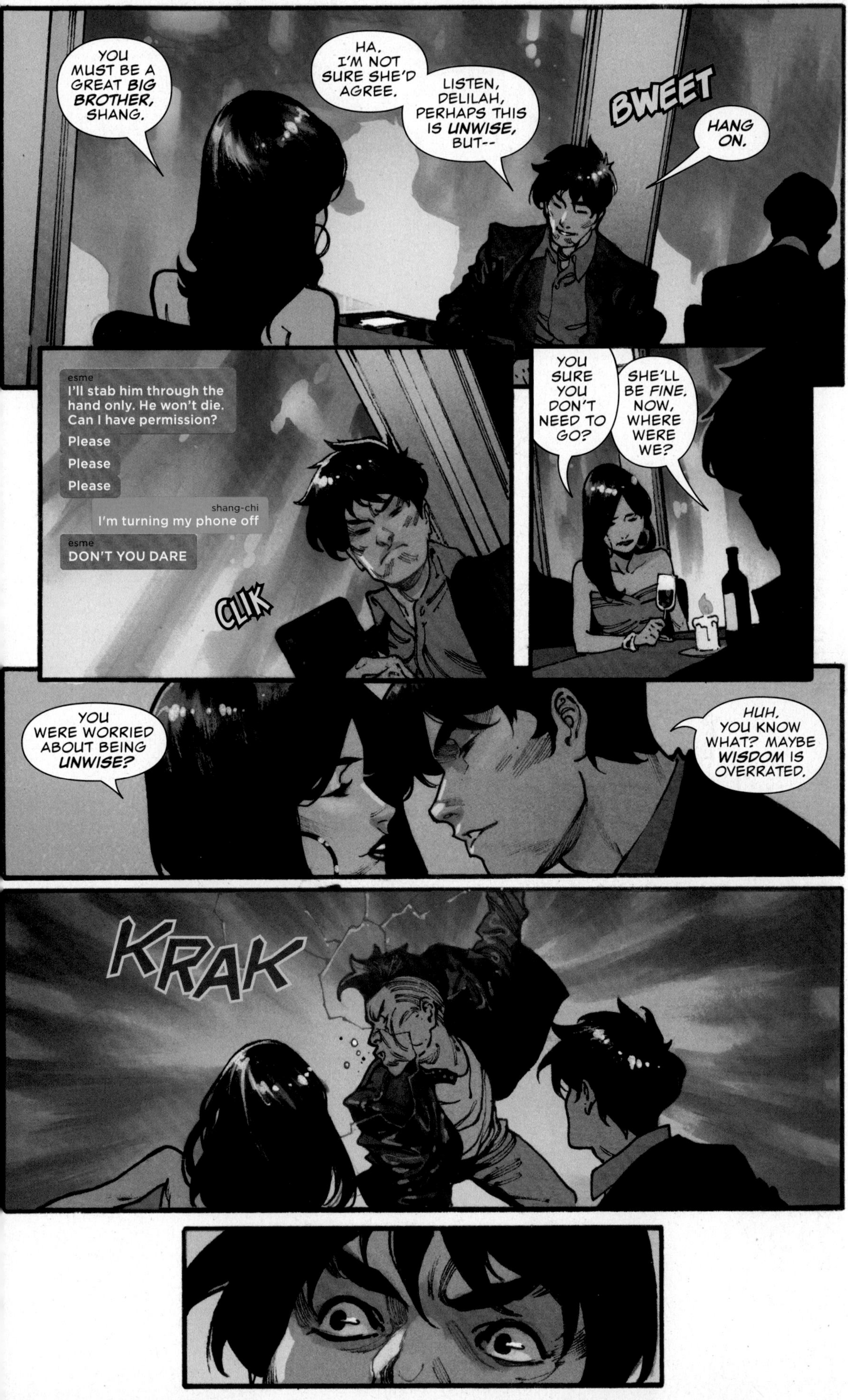
YOU MUST BE A GREAT BIG BROTHER, SHANG.
HA. I'M NOT SURE SHE'D AGREE.
LISTEN, DELILAH, PERHAPS THIS IS UNWISE, BUT--
BWEET
HANG ON.
esme
I'll stab him through the hand only. He won't die. Can I have permission?
Please
Please
Please
shang-chi
I'm turning my phone off
esme
DON'T YOU DARE
CLIK
YOU SURE YOU DON'T NEED TO GO?
SHE'LL BE FINE. NOW, WHERE WERE WE?
YOU WERE WORRIED ABOUT BEING UNWISE?
HUH. YOU KNOW WHAT? MAYBE WISDOM IS OVERRATED.
KRAK

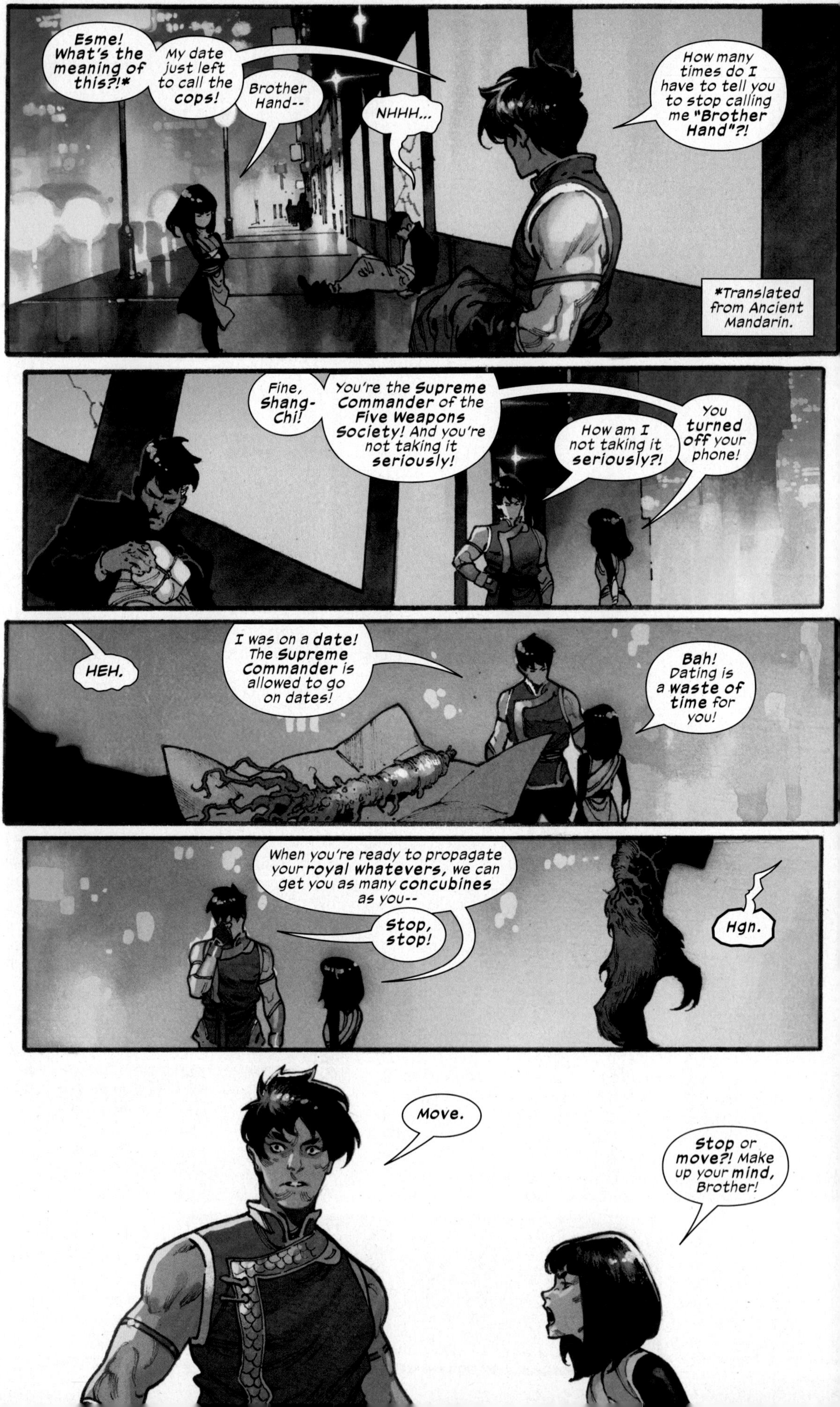
Esme! What's the meaning of this?!*
My date just left to call the cops!
Brother Hand--
NHHH...
How many times do I have to tell you to stop calling me "Brother Hand"?!
*Translated from Ancient Mandarin.
Fine, Shang-Chi!
You're the Supreme Commander of the Five Weapons Society! And you're not taking it seriously!
How am I not taking it seriously?!
You turned off your phone!
HEH.
I was on a date! The Supreme Commander is allowed to go on dates!
Bah! Dating is a waste of time for you!
When you're ready to propagate your royal whatevers, we can get you as many concubines as you--
Stop, stop!
Hgn.
Move.
Stop or move?! Make up your mind, Brother!

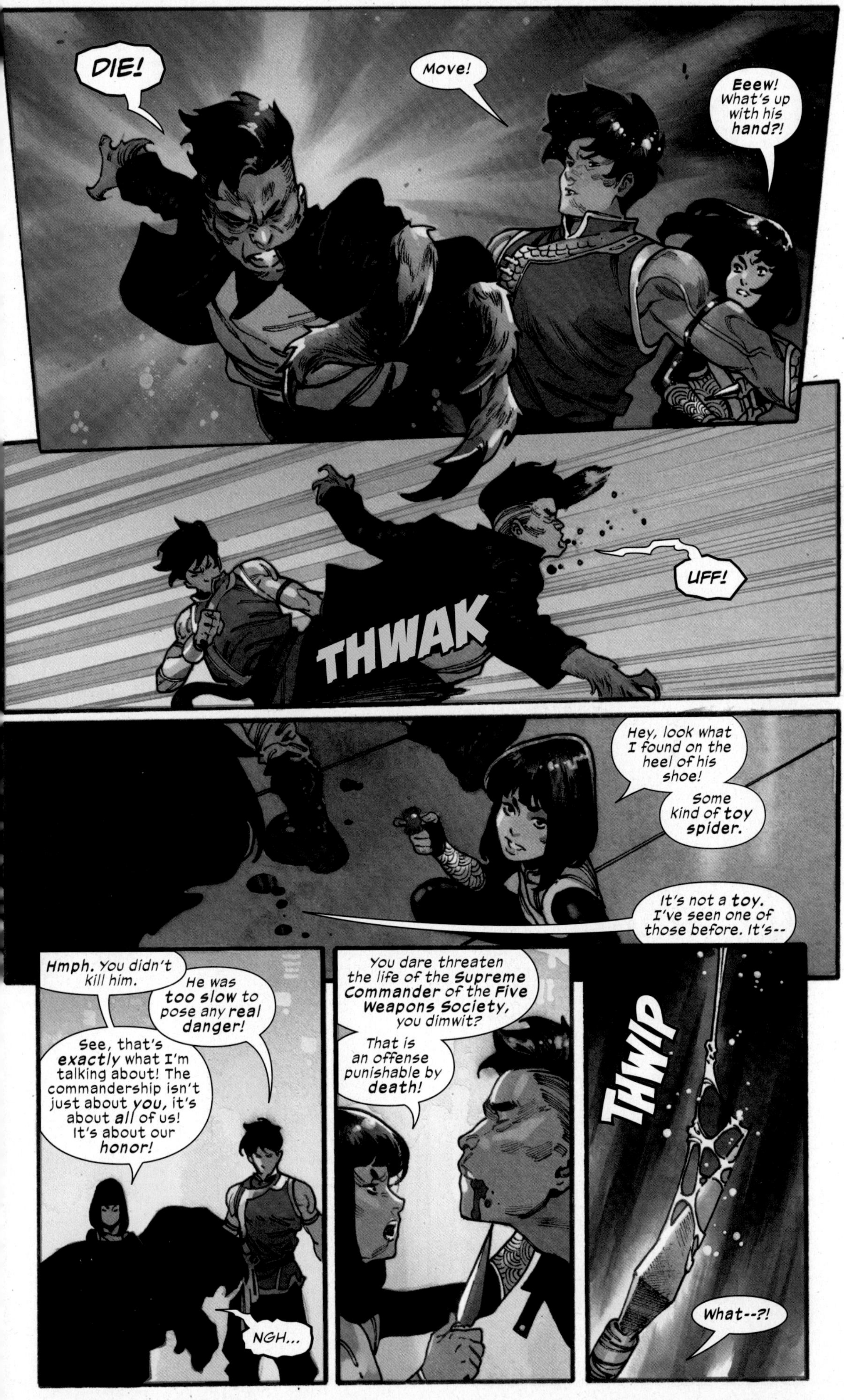
DIE!
Move!
Eeew! What's up with his hand?!
THWAK
UFF!
Hey, look what I found on the heel of his shoe!
Some kind of toy spider.
It's not a toy. I've seen one of those before. It's--
Hmph. You didn't kill him.
He was too slow to pose any real danger!
See, that's exactly what I'm talking about! The commandership isn't just about you, it's about all of us! It's about our honor!
NGH...
You dare threaten the life of the Supreme Commander of the Five Weapons Society, you dimwit?
That is an offense punishable by death!
THWIP
What--?!

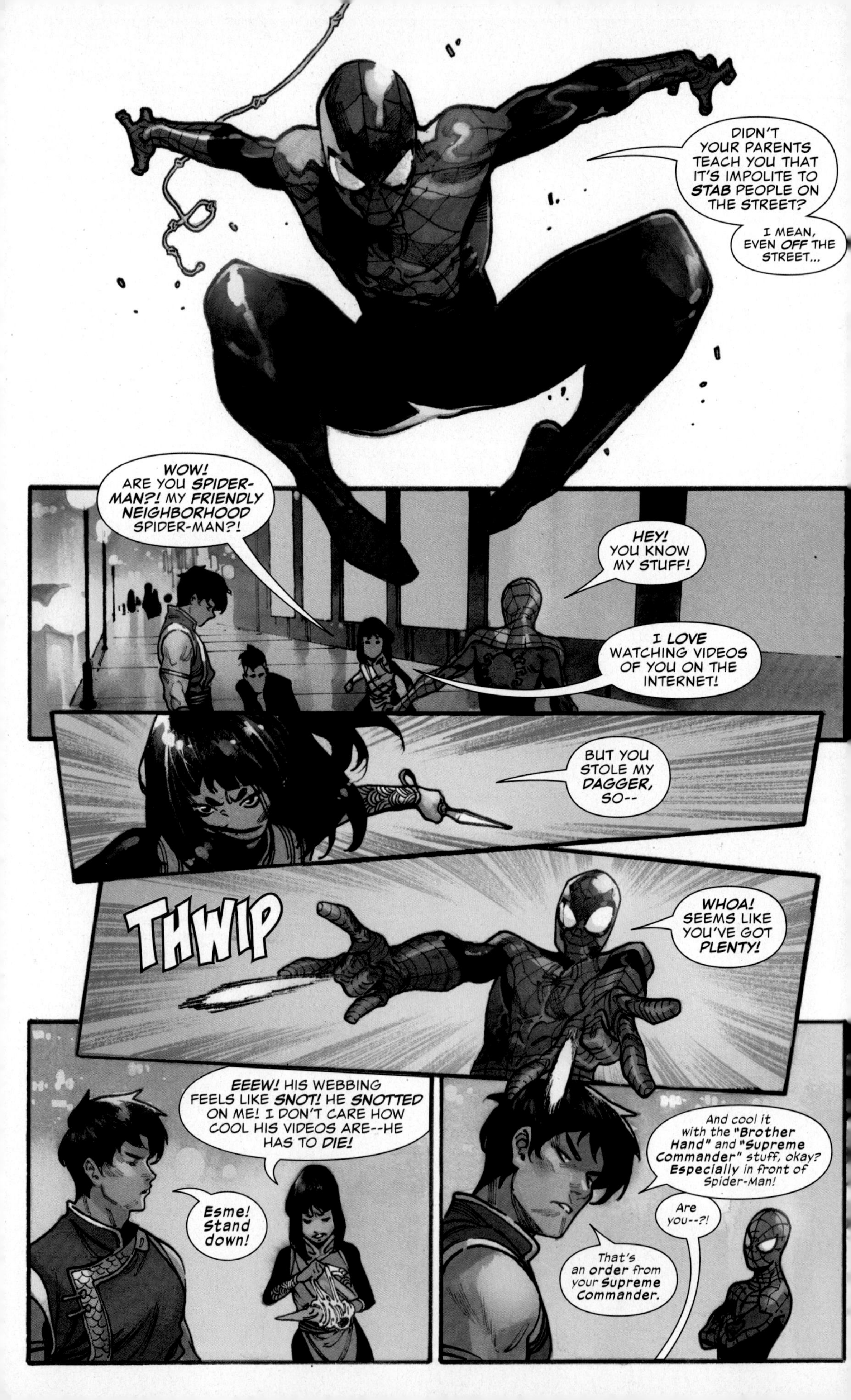

DIDN'T YOUR PARENTS TEACH YOU THAT IT'S IMPOLITE TO STAB PEOPLE ON THE STREET?
I MEAN, EVEN OFF THE STREET...
WOW! ARE YOU SPIDER-MAN?! MY FRIENDLY NEIGHBORHOOD SPIDER-MAN?!
HEY! YOU KNOW MY STUFF!
I LOVE WATCHING VIDEOS OF YOU ON THE INTERNET!
BUT YOU STOLE MY DAGGER, SO--
THWIP
WHOA! SEEMS LIKE YOU'VE GOT PLENTY!
EEEW! HIS WEBBING FEELS LIKE SNOT! HE SNOTTED ON ME! I DON'T CARE HOW COOL HIS VIDEOS ARE--HE HAS TO DIE!
Esme! Stand down!
And cool it with the "Brother Hand" and "Supreme Commander" stuff, okay? Especially in front of Spider-Man!
Are you--?!
That's an order from your Supreme Commander.

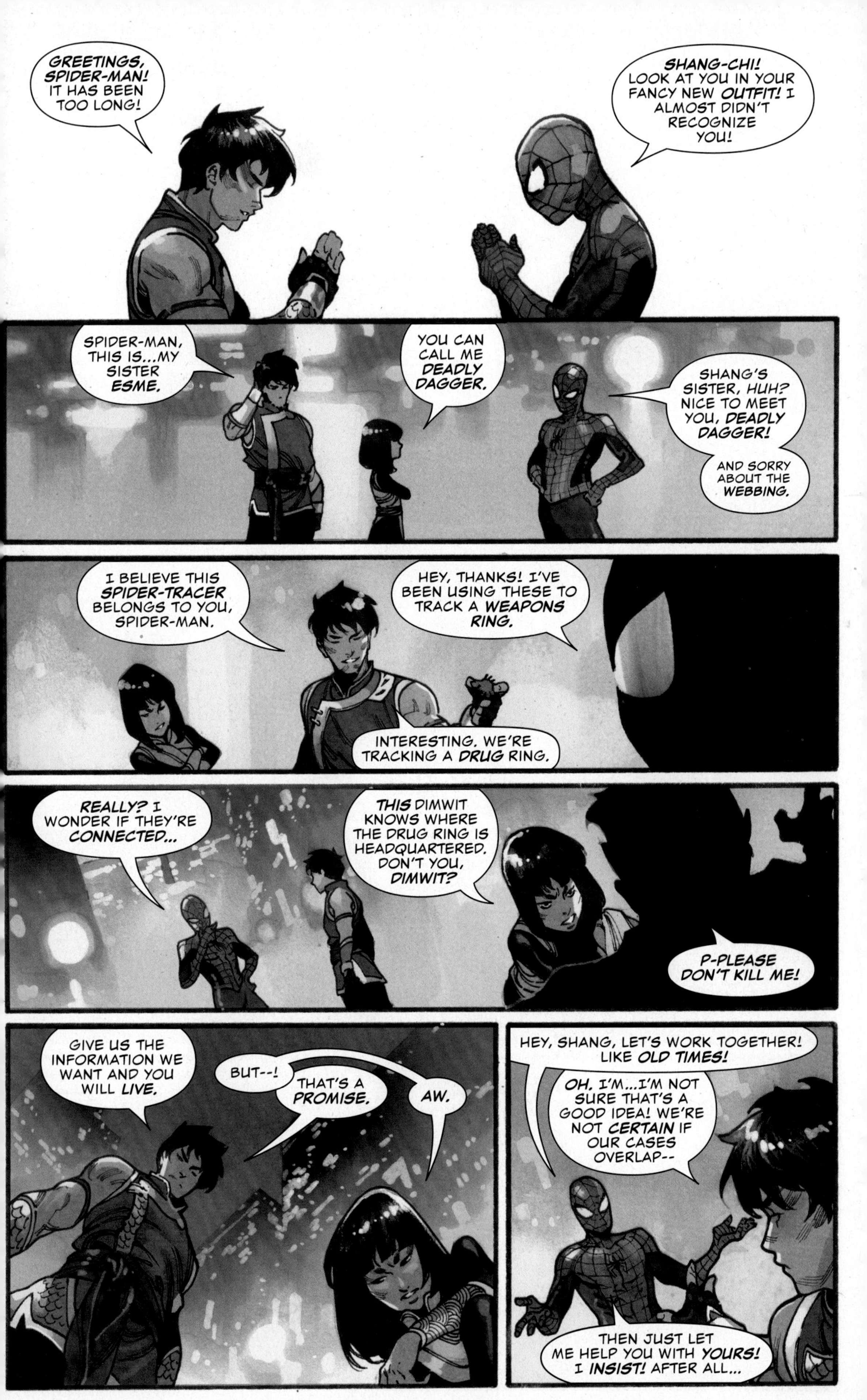
GREETINGS, SPIDER-MAN! IT HAS BEEN TOO LONG!
SHANG-CHI! LOOK AT YOU IN YOUR FANCY NEW OUTFIT! I ALMOST DIDN'T RECOGNIZE YOU!
SPIDER-MAN, THIS IS...MY SISTER ESME.
YOU CAN CALL ME DEADLY DAGGER.
SHANG'S SISTER, HUH? NICE TO MEET YOU, DEADLY DAGGER!
AND SORRY ABOUT THE WEBBING.
I BELIEVE THIS SPIDER-TRACER BELONGS TO YOU, SPIDER-MAN.
HEY, THANKS! I'VE BEEN USING THESE TO TRACK A WEAPONS RING.
INTERESTING. WE'RE TRACKING A DRUG RING.
REALLY? I WONDER IF THEY'RE CONNECTED...
THIS DIMWIT KNOWS WHERE THE DRUG RING IS HEADQUARTERED. DON'T YOU, DIMWIT?
P-PLEASE DON'T KILL ME!
GIVE US THE INFORMATION WE WANT AND YOU WILL LIVE.
BUT--!
THAT'S A PROMISE.
AW.
HEY, SHANG, LET'S WORK TOGETHER! LIKE OLD TIMES!
OH. I'M...I'M NOT SURE THAT'S A GOOD IDEA! WE'RE NOT CERTAIN IF OUR CASES OVERLAP--
THEN JUST LET ME HELP YOU WITH YOURS! I INSIST! AFTER ALL...

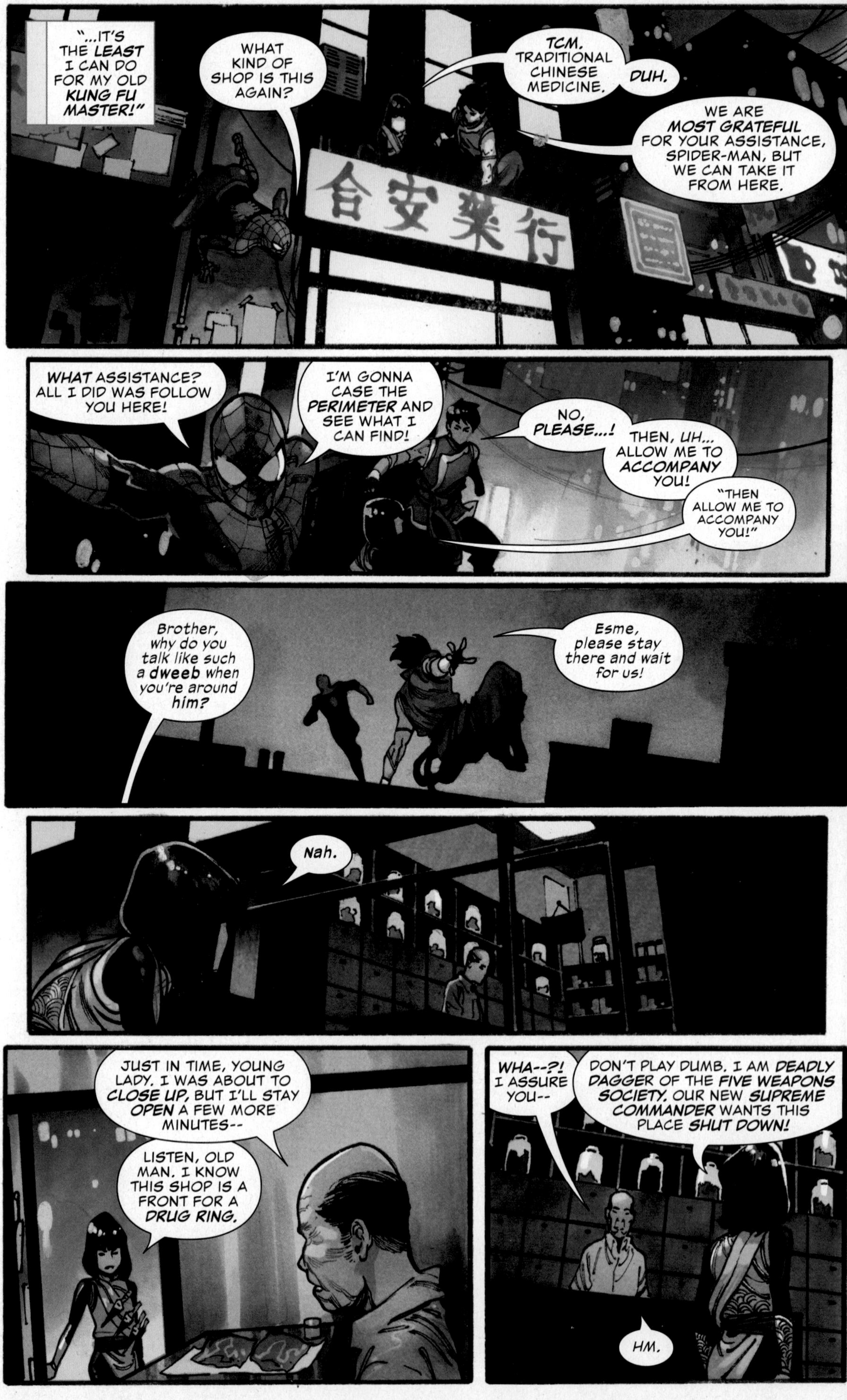
"...IT'S THE LEAST I CAN DO FOR MY OLD KUNG FU MASTER!"
WHAT KIND OF SHOP IS THIS AGAIN?
TCM. TRADITIONAL CHINESE MEDICINE.
DUH.
WE ARE MOST GRATEFUL FOR YOUR ASSISTANCE, SPIDER-MAN, BUT WE CAN TAKE IT FROM HERE.
合安藥行
WHAT ASSISTANCE? ALL I DID WAS FOLLOW YOU HERE!
I'M GONNA CASE THE PERIMETER AND SEE WHAT I CAN FIND!
NO, PLEASE...!
THEN, UH... ALLOW ME TO ACCOMPANY YOU!
"THEN ALLOW ME TO ACCOMPANY YOU!"
Esme, please stay there and wait for us!
Brother, why do you talk like such a dweeb when you're around him?
Nah.
JUST IN TIME, YOUNG LADY. I WAS ABOUT TO CLOSE UP, BUT I'LL STAY OPEN A FEW MORE MINUTES--
LISTEN, OLD MAN. I KNOW THIS SHOP IS A FRONT FOR A DRUG RING.
WHA--?! I ASSURE YOU--
DON'T PLAY DUMB. I AM DEADLY DAGGER OF THE FIVE WEAPONS SOCIETY. OUR NEW SUPREME COMMANDER WANTS THIS PLACE SHUT DOWN!
HM.

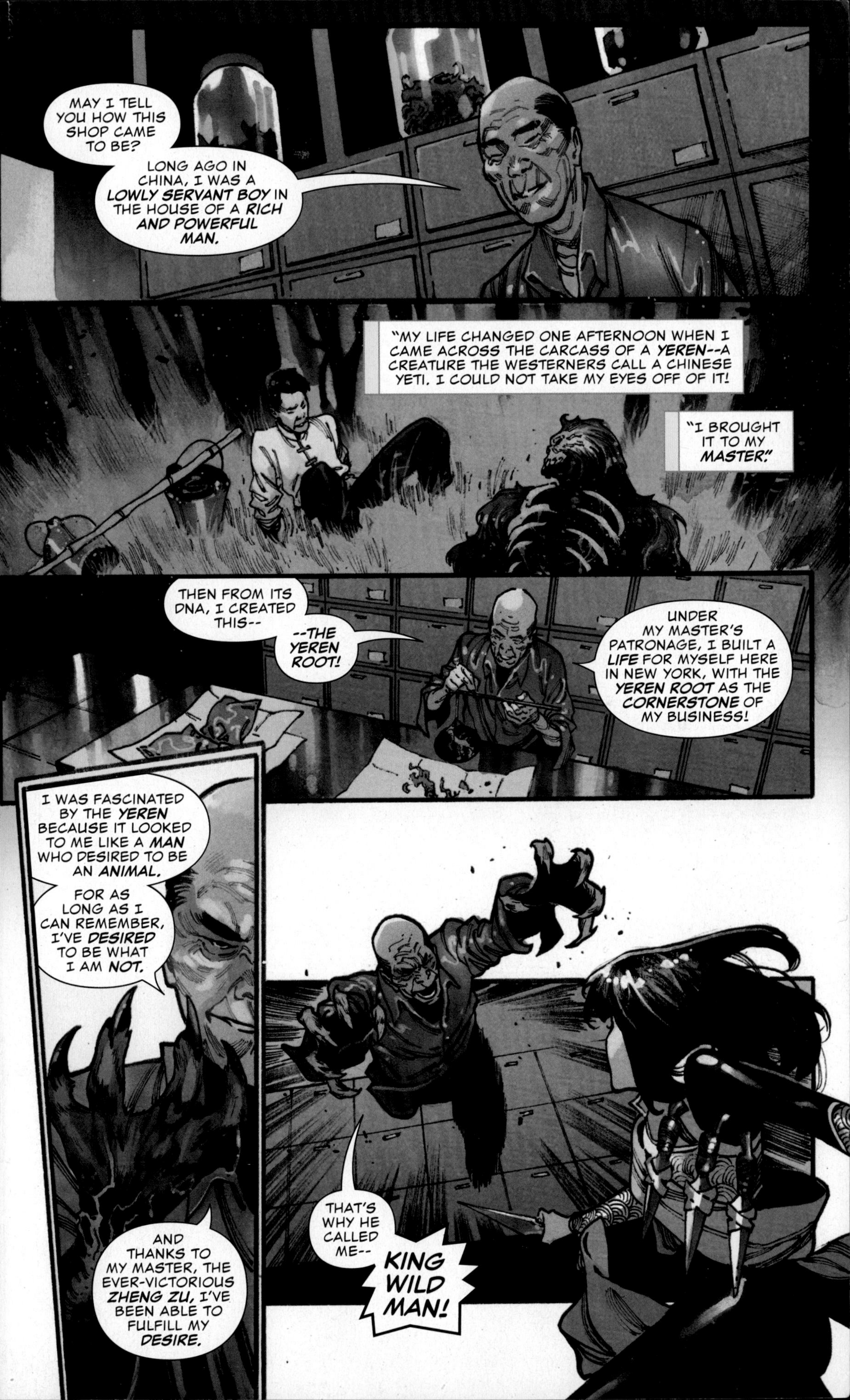
MAY I TELL YOU HOW THIS SHOP CAME TO BE?
LONG AGO IN CHINA, I WAS A LOWLY SERVANT BOY IN THE HOUSE OF A RICH AND POWERFUL MAN.
"MY LIFE CHANGED ONE AFTERNOON WHEN I CAME ACROSS THE CARCASS OF A YEREN--A CREATURE THE WESTERNERS CALL A CHINESE YETI. I COULD NOT TAKE MY EYES OFF OF IT!
"I BROUGHT IT TO MY MASTER."
THEN FROM ITS DNA, I CREATED THIS--
--THE YEREN ROOT!
UNDER MY MASTER'S PATRONAGE, I BUILT A LIFE FOR MYSELF HERE IN NEW YORK, WITH THE YEREN ROOT AS THE CORNERSTONE OF MY BUSINESS!
I WAS FASCINATED BY THE YEREN BECAUSE IT LOOKED TO ME LIKE A MAN WHO DESIRED TO BE AN ANIMAL.
FOR AS LONG AS I CAN REMEMBER, I'VE DESIRED TO BE WHAT I AM NOT.
AND THANKS TO MY MASTER, THE EVER-VICTORIOUS ZHENG ZU, I'VE BEEN ABLE TO FULFILL MY DESIRE.
THAT'S WHY HE CALLED ME--
KING WILD MAN!

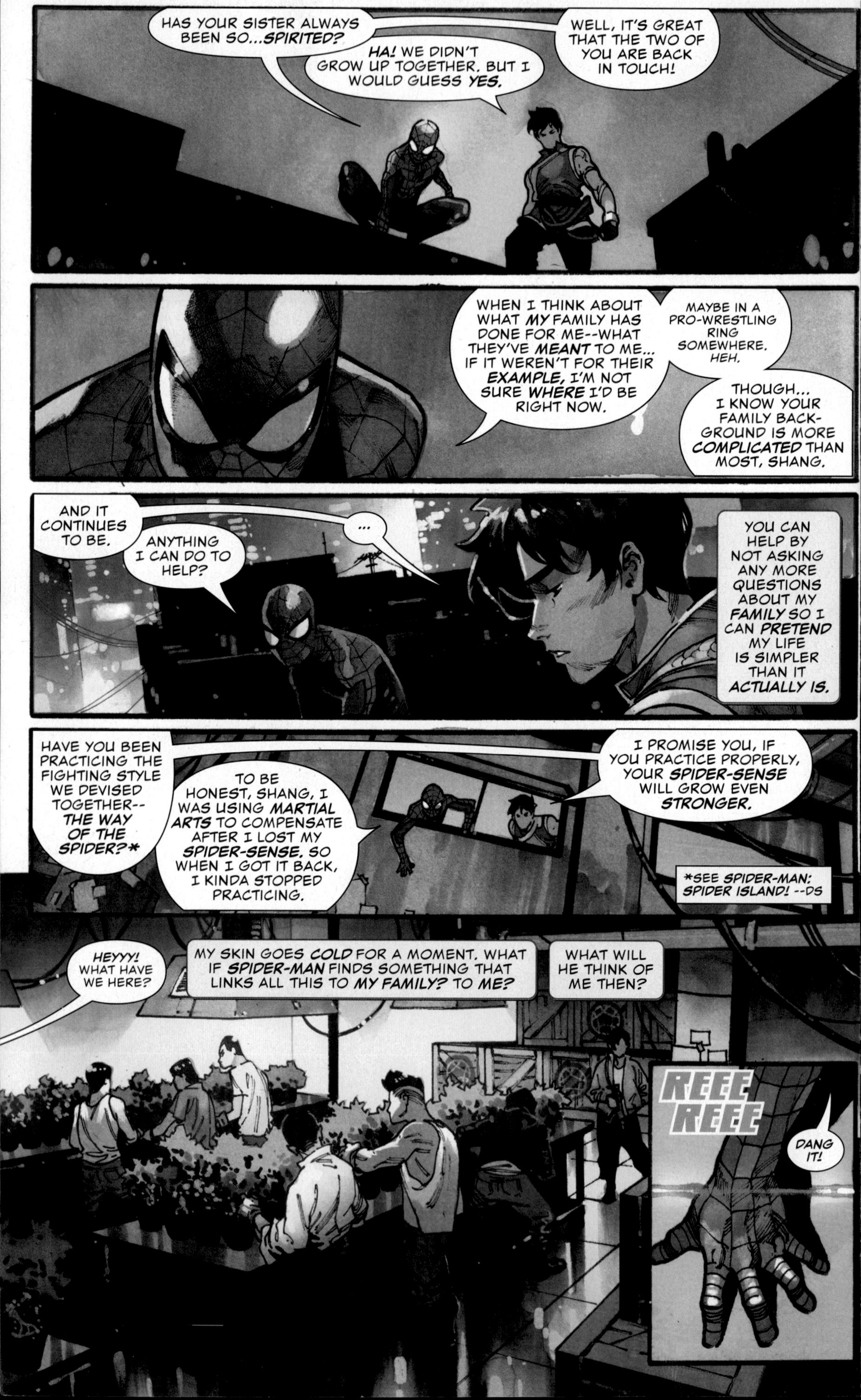
HAS YOUR SISTER ALWAYS BEEN SO...SPIRITED?
HA! WE DIDN'T GROW UP TOGETHER. BUT I WOULD GUESS YES.
WELL, IT'S GREAT THAT THE TWO OF YOU ARE BACK IN TOUCH!
WHEN I THINK ABOUT WHAT MY FAMILY HAS DONE FOR ME--WHAT THEY'VE MEANT TO ME... IF IT WEREN'T FOR THEIR EXAMPLE, I'M NOT SURE WHERE I'D BE RIGHT NOW.
MAYBE IN A PRO-WRESTLING RING SOMEWHERE. HEH.
THOUGH... I KNOW YOUR FAMILY BACKGROUND IS MORE COMPLICATED THAN MOST, SHANG.
AND IT CONTINUES TO BE.
...
ANYTHING I CAN DO TO HELP?
YOU CAN HELP BY NOT ASKING ANY MORE QUESTIONS ABOUT MY FAMILY SO I CAN PRETEND MY LIFE IS SIMPLER THAN IT ACTUALLY IS.
HAVE YOU BEEN PRACTICING THE FIGHTING STYLE WE DEVISED TOGETHER--THE WAY OF THE SPIDER?*
TO BE HONEST, SHANG, I WAS USING MARTIAL ARTS TO COMPENSATE AFTER I LOST MY SPIDER-SENSE. SO WHEN I GOT IT BACK, I KINDA STOPPED PRACTICING.
I PROMISE YOU, IF YOU PRACTICE PROPERLY, YOUR SPIDER-SENSE WILL GROW EVEN STRONGER.
*SEE SPIDER-MAN: SPIDER ISLAND! --DS
HEYYY! WHAT HAVE WE HERE?
MY SKIN GOES COLD FOR A MOMENT. WHAT IF SPIDER-MAN FINDS SOMETHING THAT LINKS ALL THIS TO MY FAMILY? TO ME?
WHAT WILL HE THINK OF ME THEN?
REEE REEE
DANG IT!

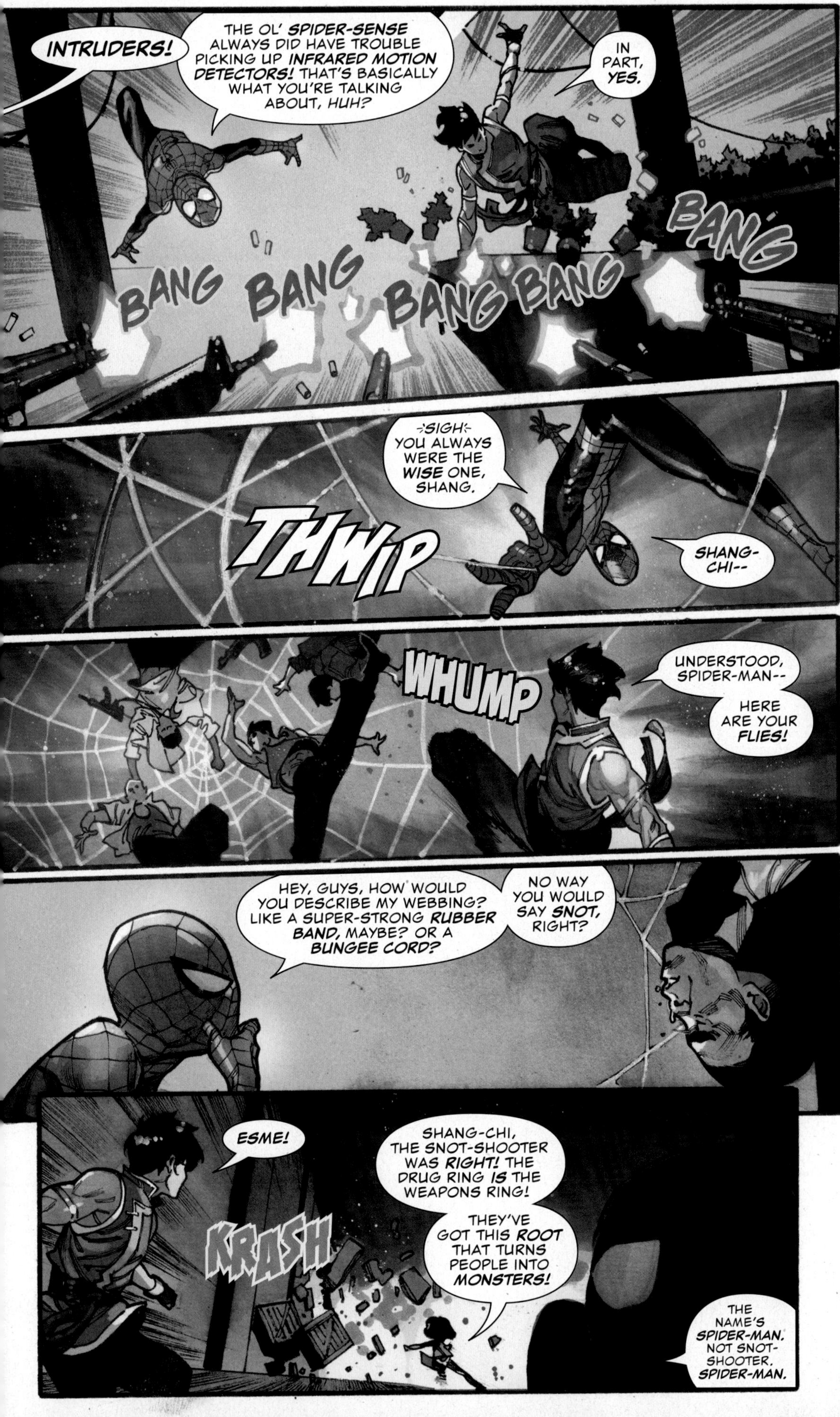
INTRUDERS!
THE OL' SPIDER-SENSE ALWAYS DID HAVE TROUBLE PICKING UP INFRARED MOTION DETECTORS! THAT'S BASICALLY WHAT YOU'RE TALKING ABOUT, HUH?
IN PART, YES.
BANG BANG BANG BANG BANG
SIGH YOU ALWAYS WERE THE WISE ONE, SHANG.
THWIP
SHANG-CHI--
WHUMP
UNDERSTOOD, SPIDER-MAN--
HERE ARE YOUR FLIES!
HEY, GUYS, HOW WOULD YOU DESCRIBE MY WEBBING? LIKE A SUPER-STRONG RUBBER BAND, MAYBE? OR A BUNGEE CORD?
NO WAY YOU WOULD SAY SNOT, RIGHT?
ESME!
SHANG-CHI, THE SNOT-SHOOTER WAS RIGHT! THE DRUG RING IS THE WEAPONS RING!
KRASH
THEY'VE GOT THIS ROOT THAT TURNS PEOPLE INTO MONSTERS!
THE NAME'S SPIDER-MAN. NOT SNOT-SHOOTER. SPIDER-MAN.

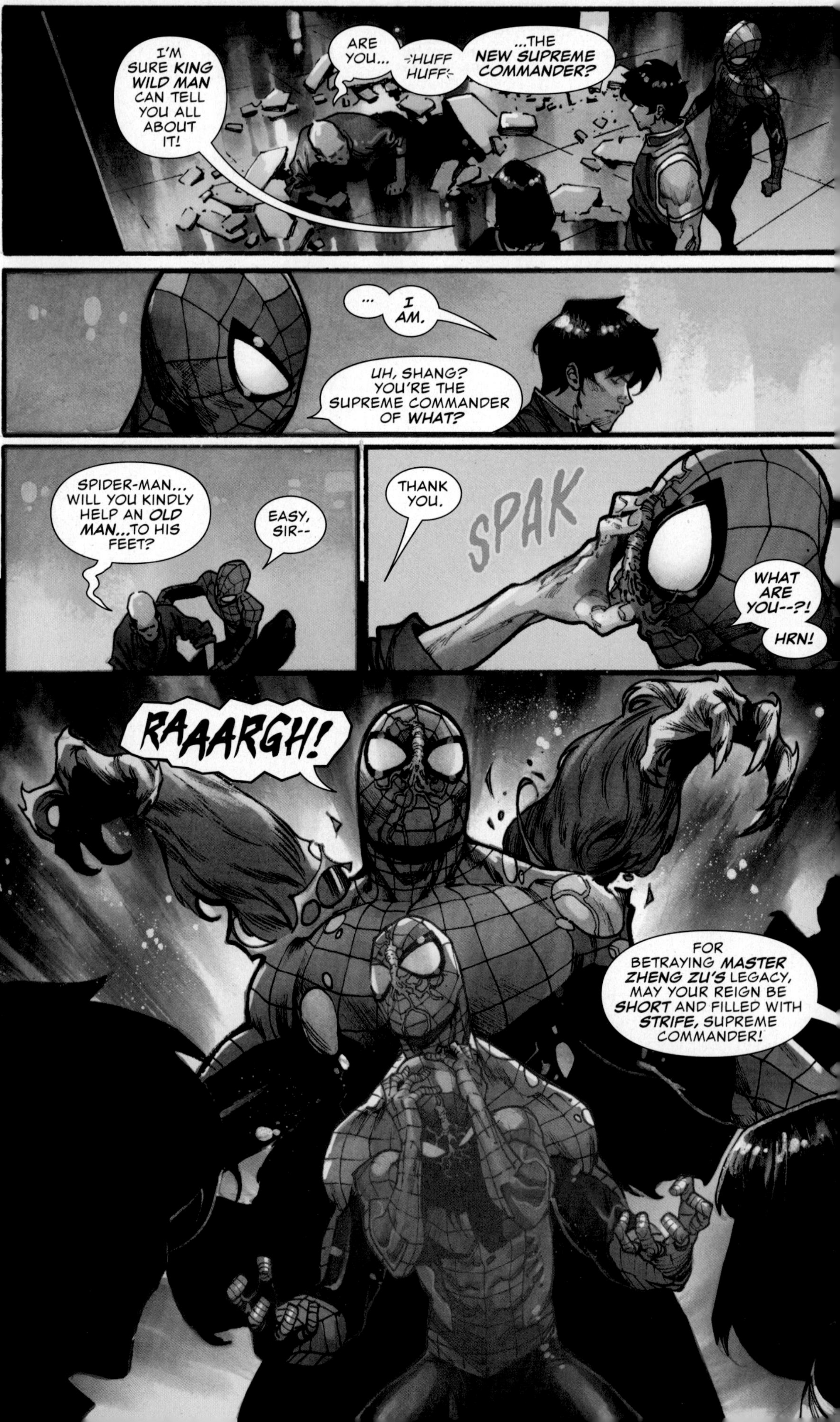

I'M SURE KING WILD MAN CAN TELL YOU ALL ABOUT IT!
ARE YOU...
HUFF HUFF
...THE NEW SUPREME COMMANDER?
... I AM.
UH, SHANG? YOU'RE THE SUPREME COMMANDER OF WHAT?
SPIDER-MAN... WILL YOU KINDLY HELP AN OLD MAN...TO HIS FEET?
EASY, SIR--
THANK YOU.
SPAK
WHAT ARE YOU--?!
HRN!
RAAARGH!
FOR BETRAYING MASTER ZHENG ZU'S LEGACY, MAY YOUR REIGN BE SHORT AND FILLED WITH STRIFE, SUPREME COMMANDER!

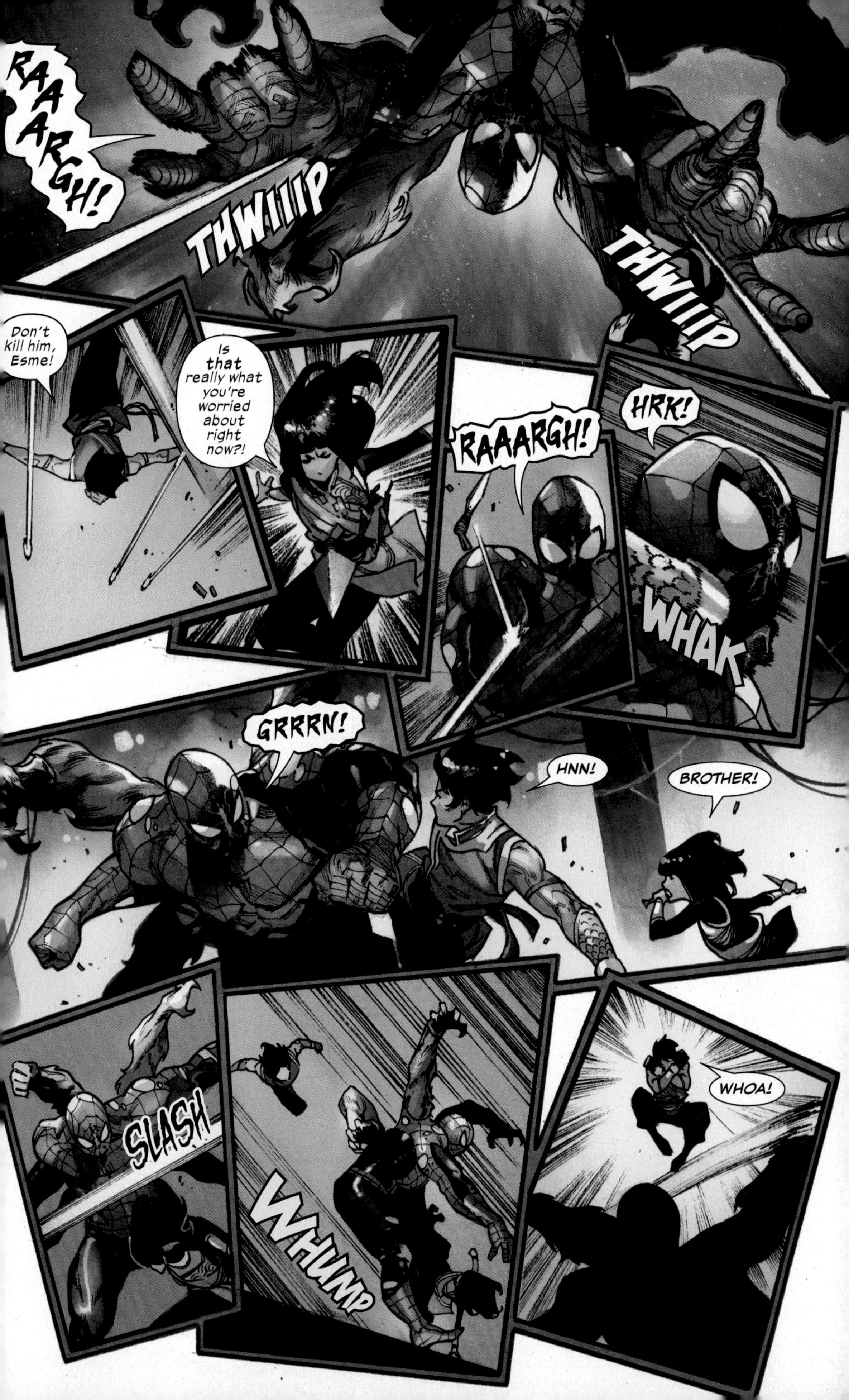
RAAARGH!
THWIIIP
THWIIIP
Don't kill him, Esme!
Is that really what you're worried about right now?!
RAAARGH!
HRK!
WHAK
GRRRN!
HNN!
BROTHER!
SLASH
WHUMP
WHOA!

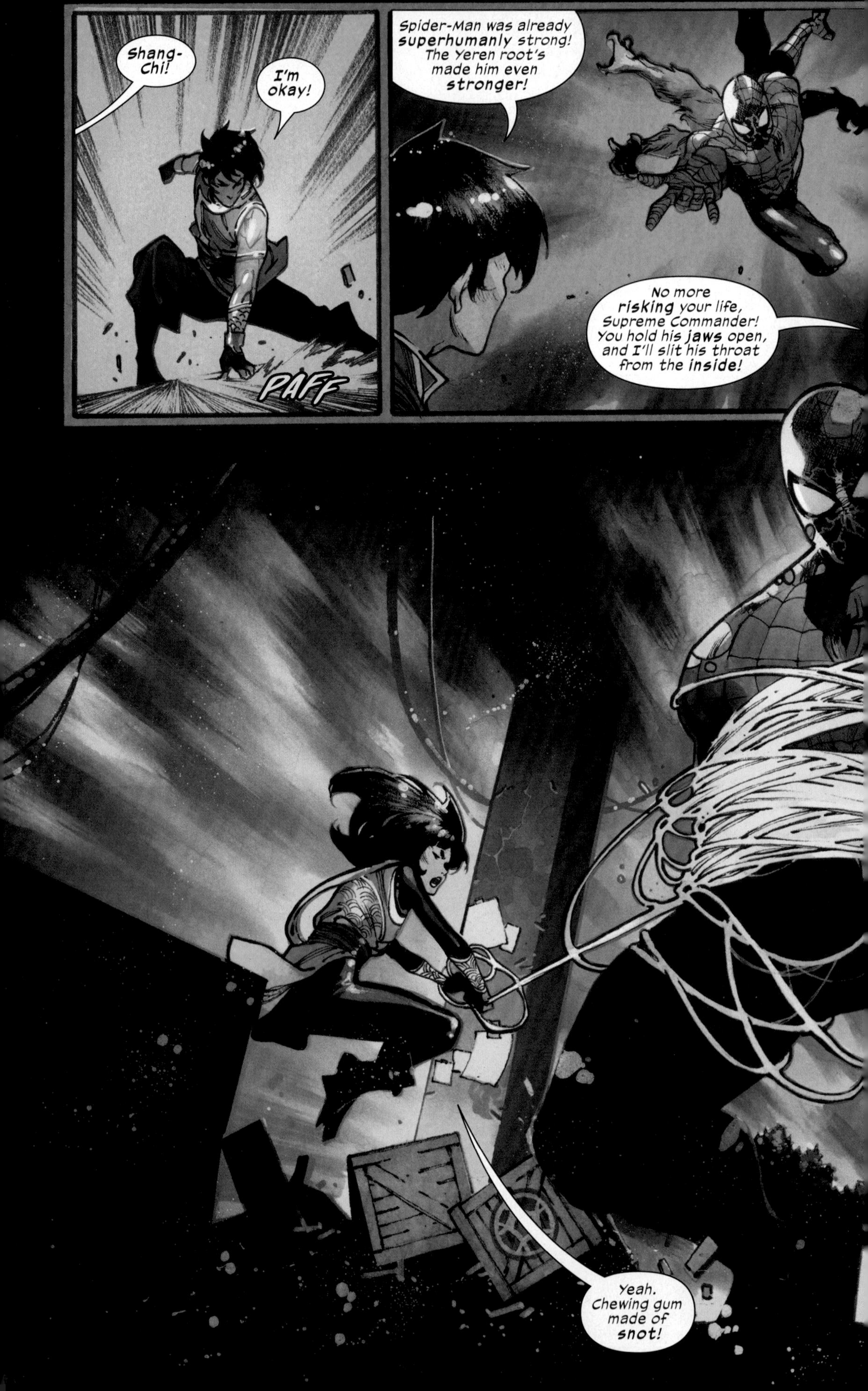
Shang-Chi!
I'm okay!
PAFF
Spider-Man was already superhumanly strong! The Yeren root's made him even stronger!
No more risking your life, Supreme Commander! You hold his jaws open, and I'll slit his throat from the inside!
Yeah. Chewing gum made of snot!

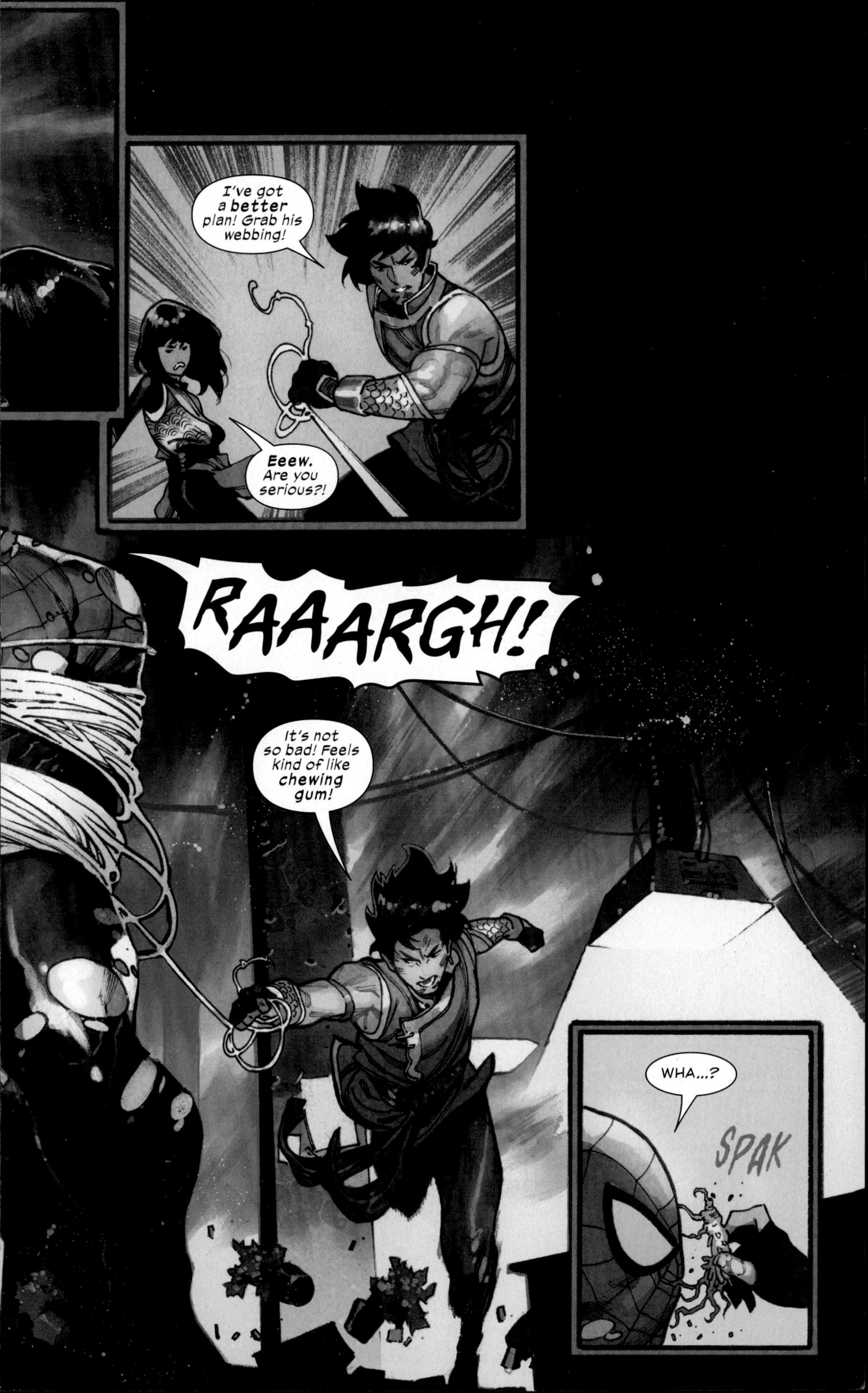
I've got a better plan! Grab his webbing!
Eeew. Are you serious?!
RAAARGH!
It's not so bad! Feels kind of like chewing gum!
WHA...?
SPAK

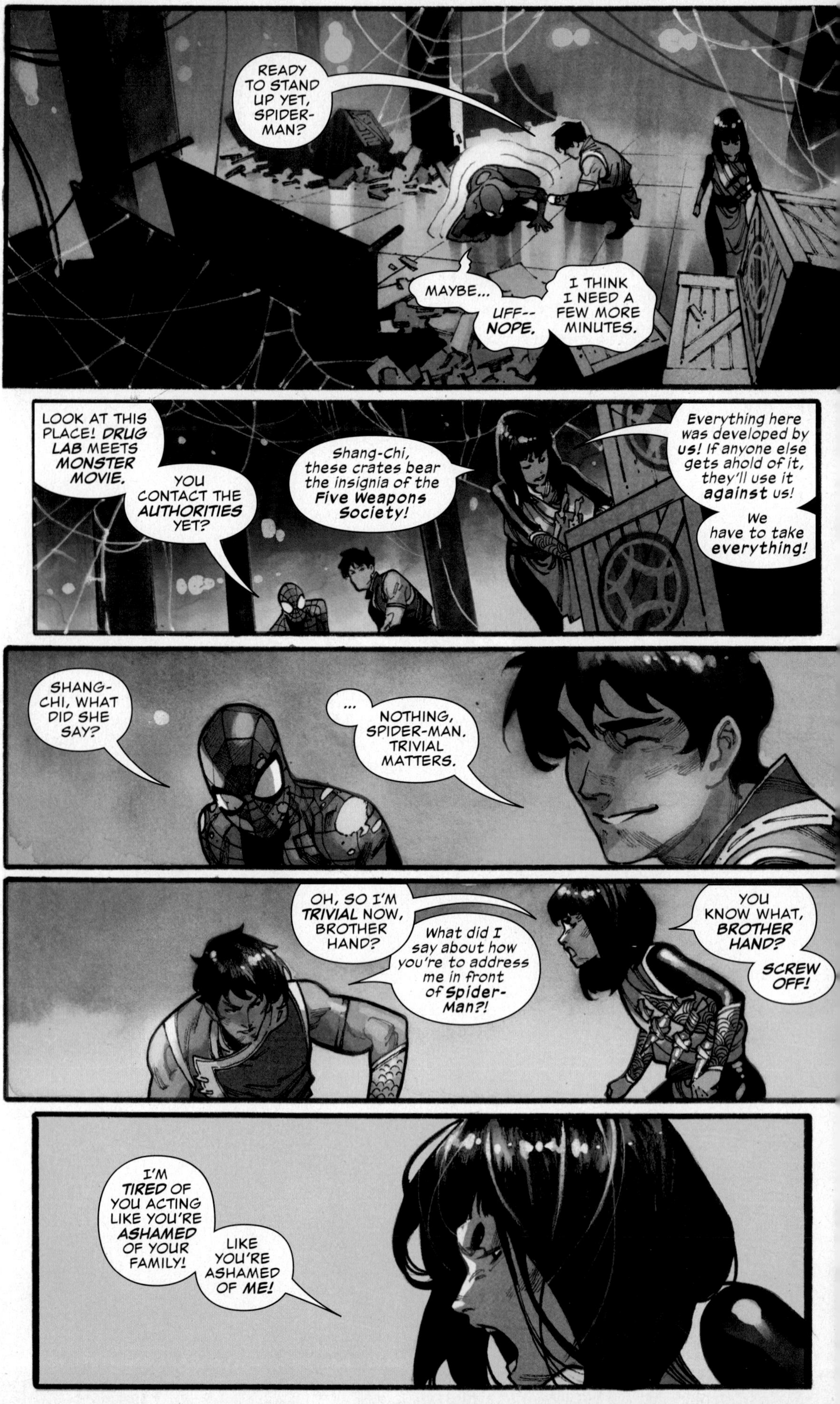
READY TO STAND UP YET, SPIDER-MAN?
MAYBE... UFF-- NOPE.
I THINK I NEED A FEW MORE MINUTES.
LOOK AT THIS PLACE! DRUG LAB MEETS MONSTER MOVIE.
YOU CONTACT THE AUTHORITIES YET?
Shang-Chi, these crates bear the insignia of the Five Weapons Society!
Everything here was developed by us! If anyone else gets ahold of it, they'll use it against us!
We have to take everything!
SHANG-CHI, WHAT DID SHE SAY?
...
NOTHING, SPIDER-MAN. TRIVIAL MATTERS.
OH, SO I'M TRIVIAL NOW, BROTHER HAND?
What did I say about how you're to address me in front of Spider-Man?!
YOU KNOW WHAT, BROTHER HAND?
SCREW OFF!
I'M TIRED OF YOU ACTING LIKE YOU'RE ASHAMED OF YOUR FAMILY!
LIKE YOU'RE ASHAMED OF ME!

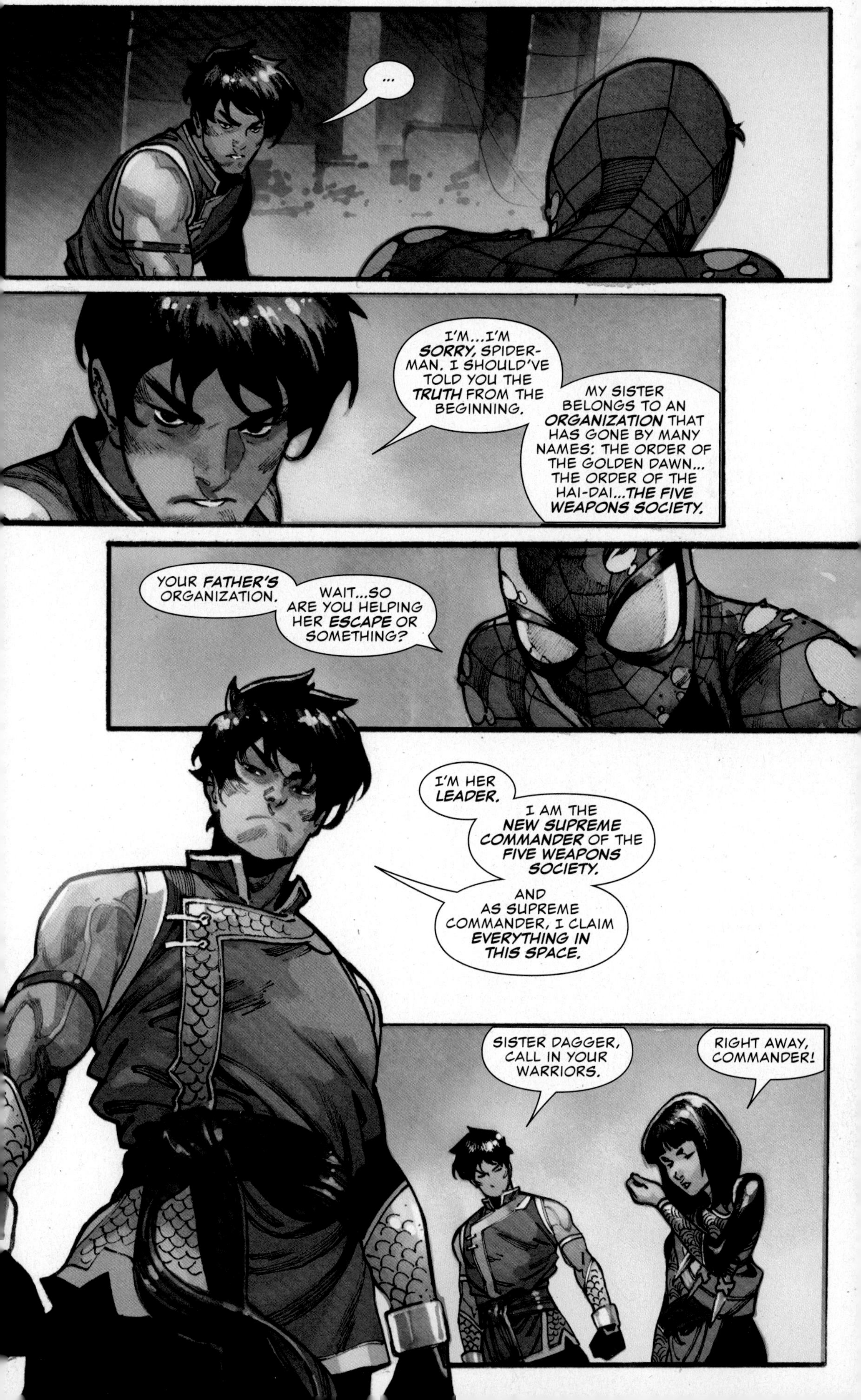
...
I'M...I'M SORRY, SPIDER-MAN. I SHOULD'VE TOLD YOU THE TRUTH FROM THE BEGINNING.
MY SISTER BELONGS TO AN ORGANIZATION THAT HAS GONE BY MANY NAMES: THE ORDER OF THE GOLDEN DAWN... THE ORDER OF THE HAI-DAI...THE FIVE WEAPONS SOCIETY.
YOUR FATHER'S ORGANIZATION.
WAIT...SO ARE YOU HELPING HER ESCAPE OR SOMETHING?
I'M HER LEADER.
I AM THE NEW SUPREME COMMANDER OF THE FIVE WEAPONS SOCIETY.
AND AS SUPREME COMMANDER, I CLAIM EVERYTHING IN THIS SPACE.
SISTER DAGGER, CALL IN YOUR WARRIORS.
RIGHT AWAY, COMMANDER!

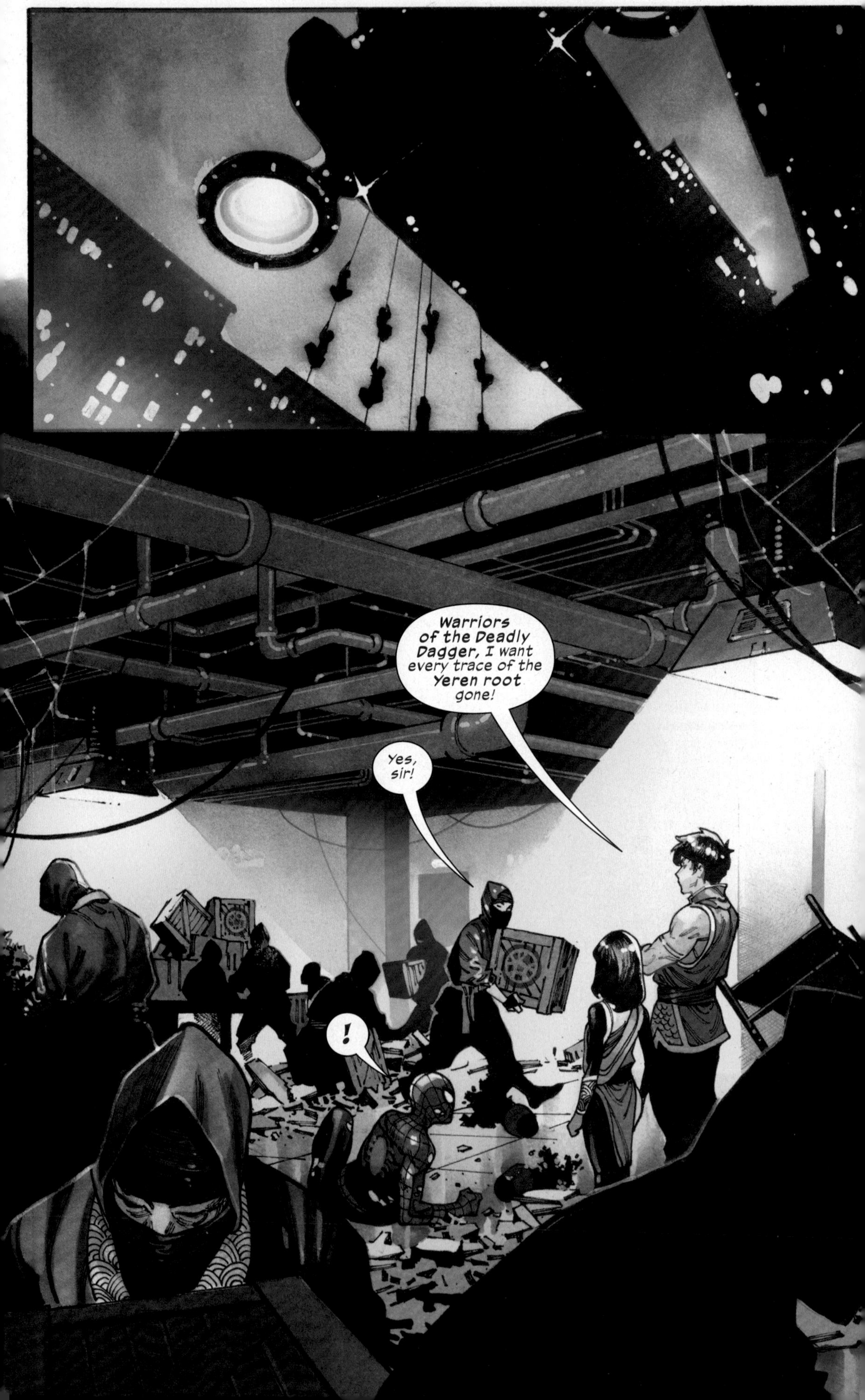
Warriors of the Deadly Dagger, I want every trace of the Yeren root gone!
Yes, sir!
!

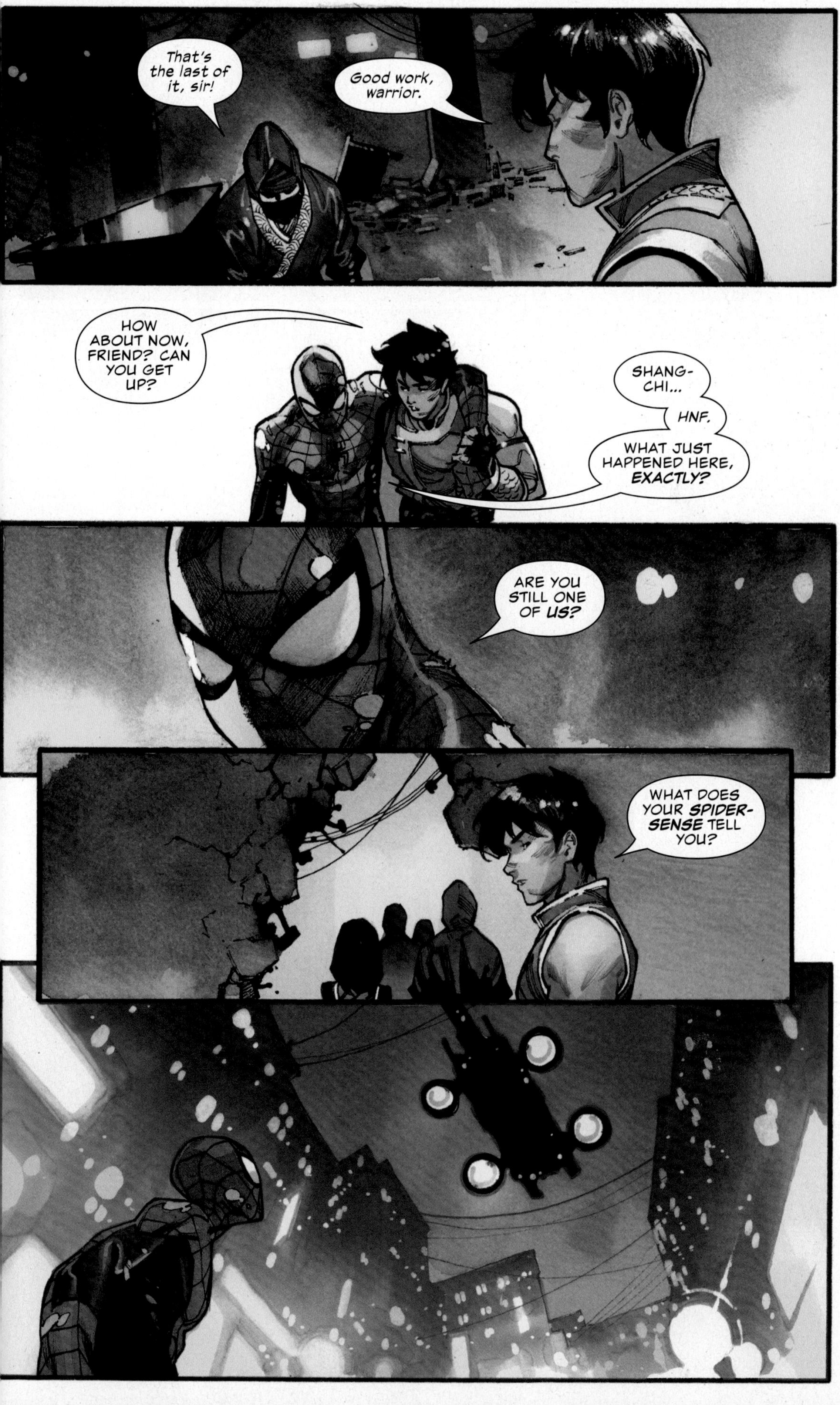

That's the last of it, sir!
Good work, warrior.
HOW ABOUT NOW, FRIEND? CAN YOU GET UP?
SHANG-CHI...
HNF.
WHAT JUST HAPPENED HERE, EXACTLY?
ARE YOU STILL ONE OF US?
WHAT DOES YOUR SPIDER-SENSE TELL YOU?

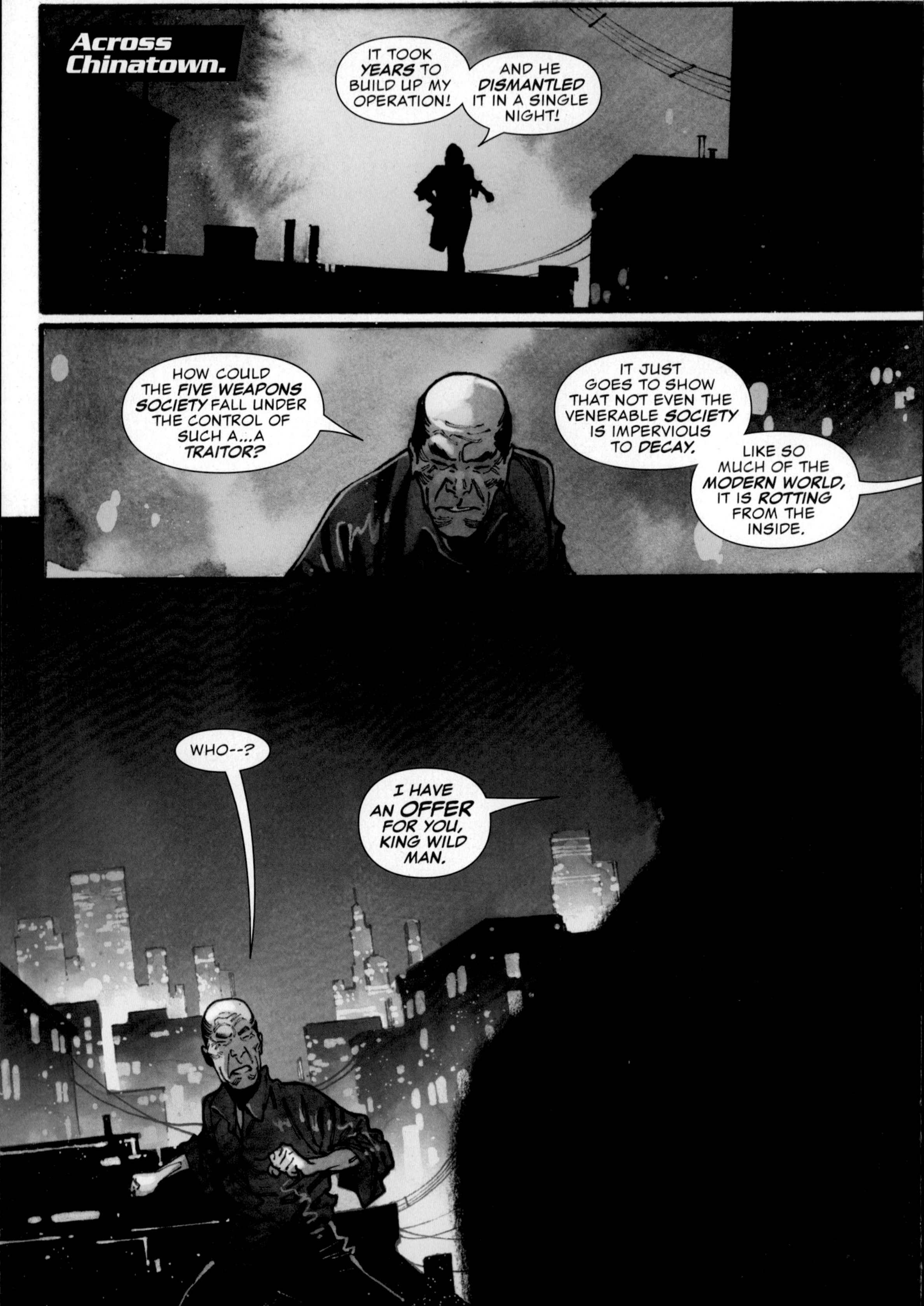
Across Chinatown.
IT TOOK YEARS TO BUILD UP MY OPERATION!
AND HE DISMANTLED IT IN A SINGLE NIGHT!
HOW COULD THE FIVE WEAPONS SOCIETY FALL UNDER THE CONTROL OF SUCH A...A TRAITOR?
IT JUST GOES TO SHOW THAT NOT EVEN THE VENERABLE SOCIETY IS IMPERVIOUS TO DECAY.
LIKE SO MUCH OF THE MODERN WORLD, IT IS ROTTING FROM THE INSIDE.
WHO--?
I HAVE AN OFFER FOR YOU, KING WILD MAN.

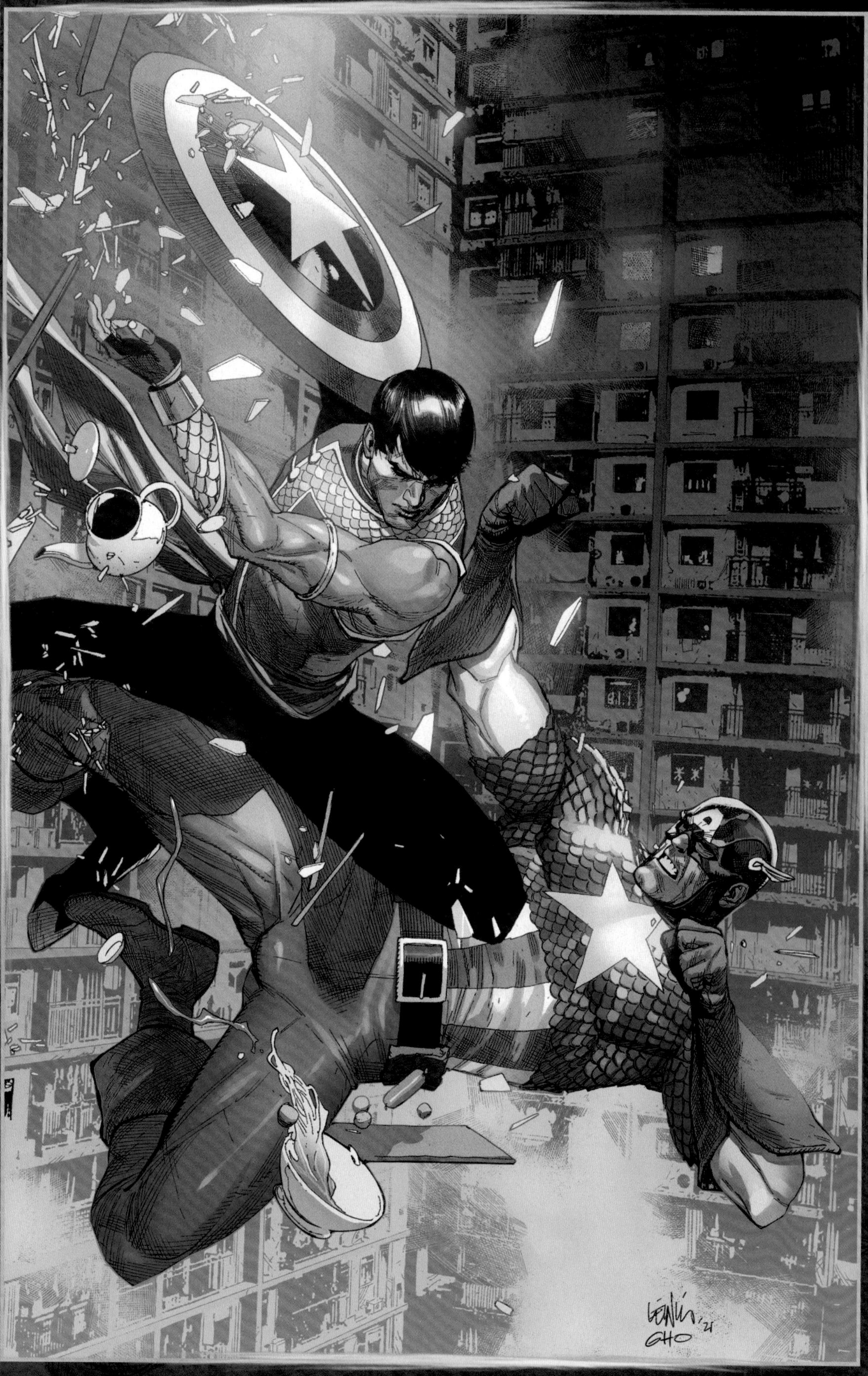

TWO

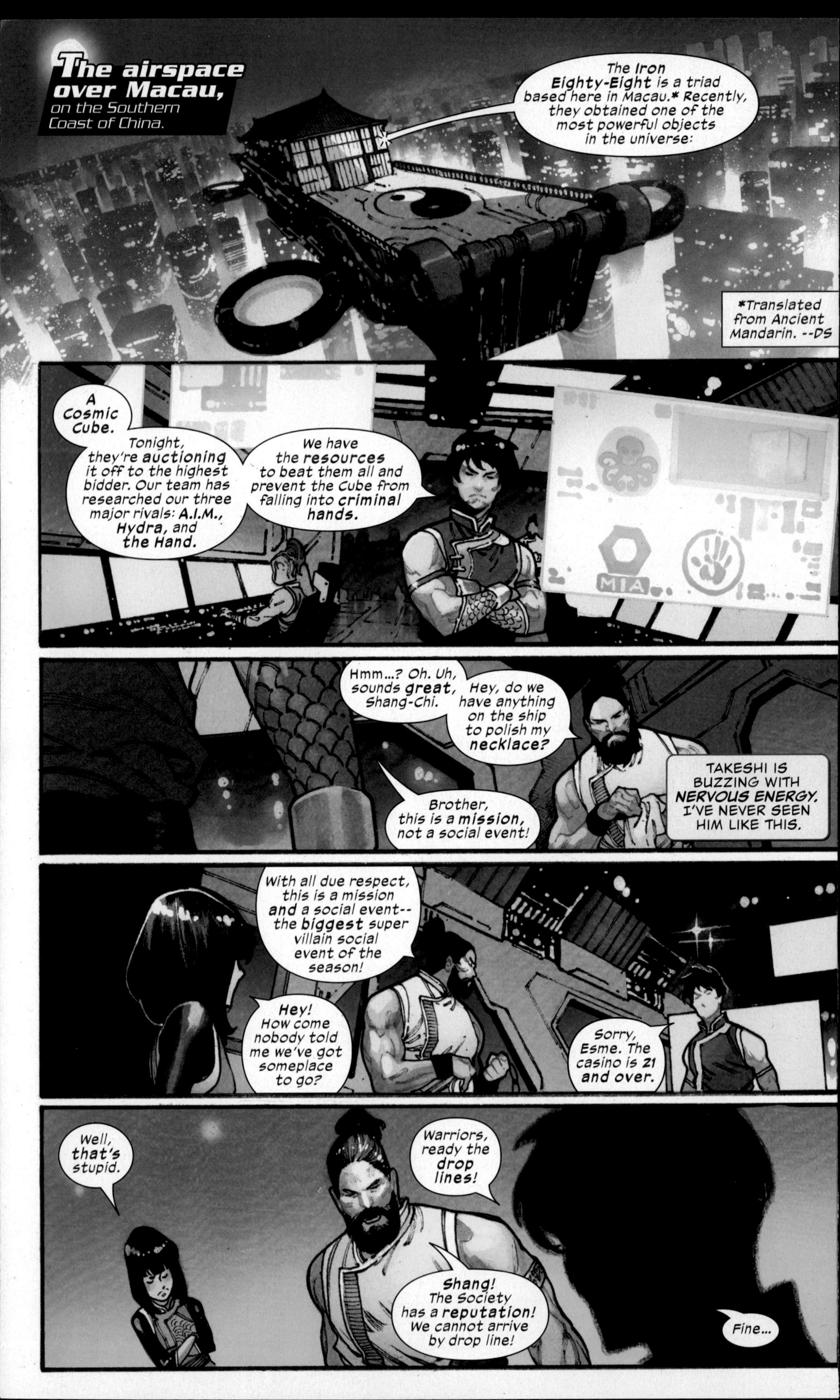

The airspace over Macau, on the Southern Coast of China.
The Iron Eighty-Eight is a triad based here in Macau.* Recently, they obtained one of the most powerful objects in the universe:
*Translated from Ancient Mandarin. --DS
A Cosmic Cube.
Tonight, they're auctioning it off to the highest bidder. Our team has researched our three major rivals: A.I.M., Hydra, and the Hand.
We have the resources to beat them all and prevent the Cube from falling into criminal hands.
MIA
Hmm...? Oh. Uh, sounds great, Shang-Chi.
Hey, do we have anything on the ship to polish my necklace?
Brother, this is a mission, not a social event!
TAKESHI IS BUZZING WITH NERVOUS ENERGY. I'VE NEVER SEEN HIM LIKE THIS.
With all due respect, this is a mission and a social event-- the biggest super villain social event of the season!
Hey! How come nobody told me we've got someplace to go?
Sorry, Esme. The casino is 21 and over.
Well, that's stupid.
Warriors, ready the drop lines!
Shang! The Society has a reputation! We cannot arrive by drop line!
Fine...

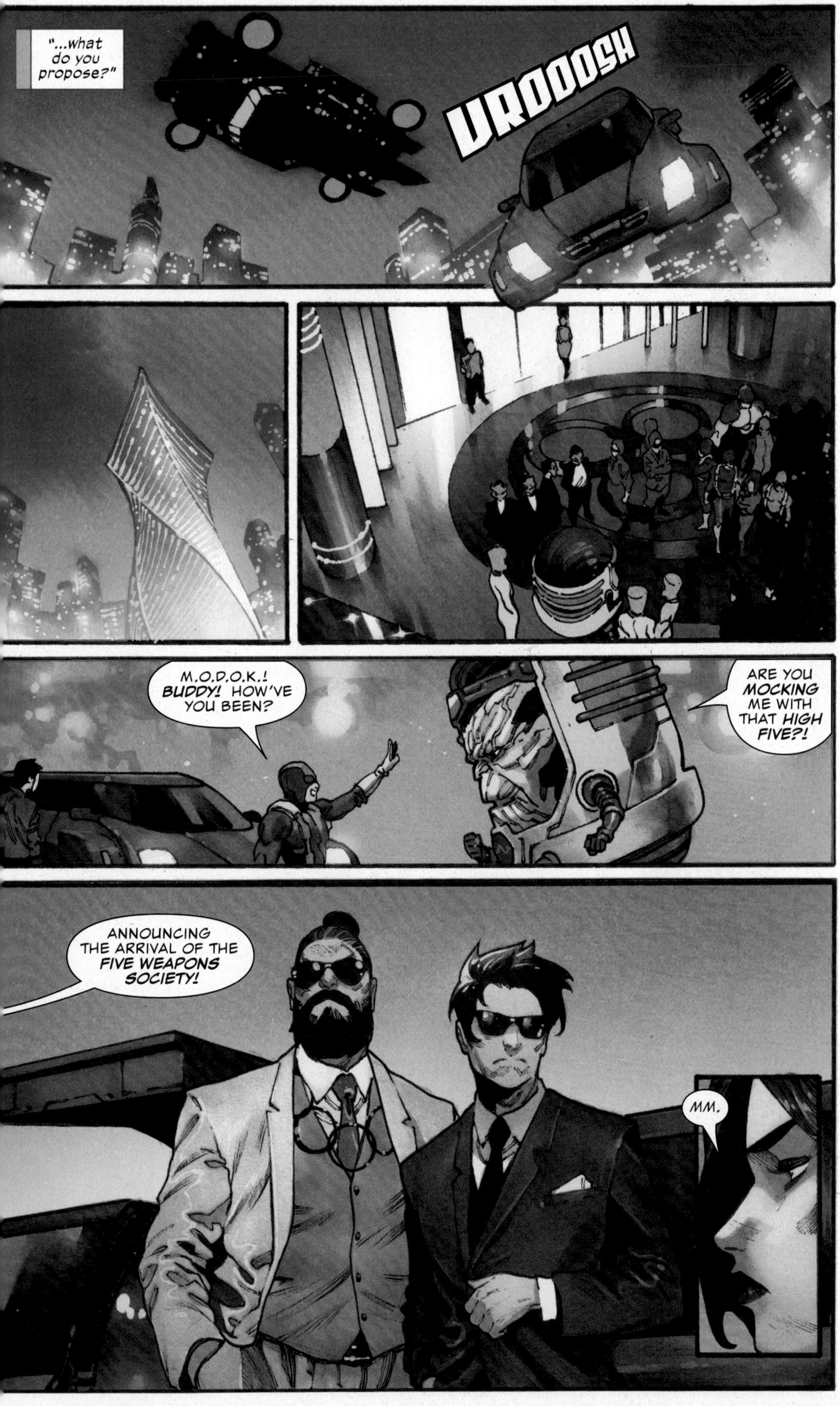
"...what do you propose?"
VROOOSH
M.O.D.O.K.! BUDDY! HOW'VE YOU BEEN?
ARE YOU MOCKING ME WITH THAT HIGH FIVE?!
ANNOUNCING THE ARRIVAL OF THE FIVE WEAPONS SOCIETY!
MM.

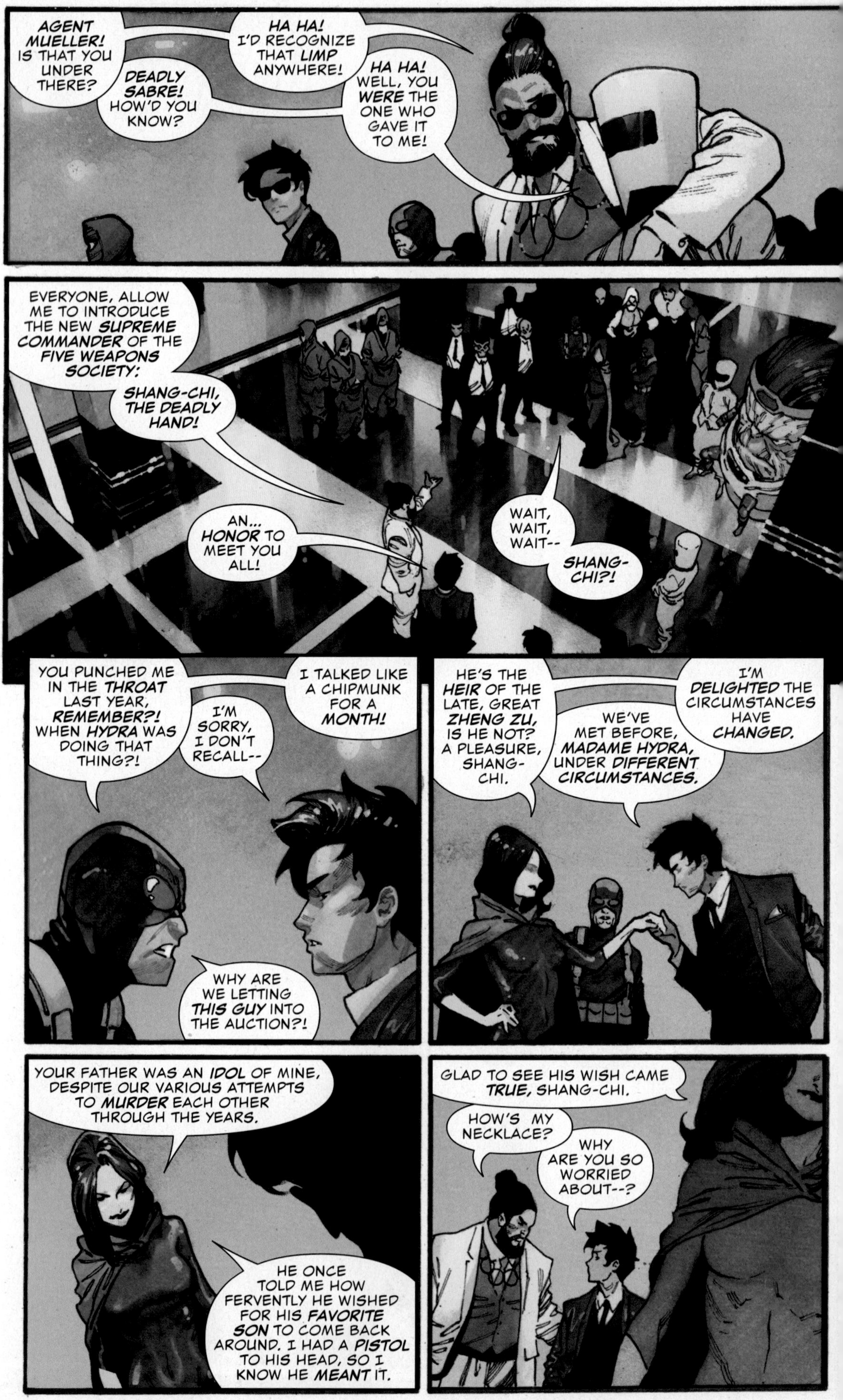
AGENT MUELLER! IS THAT YOU UNDER THERE?
HA HA! I'D RECOGNIZE THAT LIMP ANYWHERE!
DEADLY SABRE! HOW'D YOU KNOW?
HA HA! WELL, YOU WERE THE ONE WHO GAVE IT TO ME!
EVERYONE, ALLOW ME TO INTRODUCE THE NEW SUPREME COMMANDER OF THE FIVE WEAPONS SOCIETY:
SHANG-CHI, THE DEADLY HAND!
AN... HONOR TO MEET YOU ALL!
WAIT, WAIT, WAIT--
SHANG-CHI?!
YOU PUNCHED ME IN THE THROAT LAST YEAR, REMEMBER?! WHEN HYDRA WAS DOING THAT THING?!
I TALKED LIKE A CHIPMUNK FOR A MONTH!
I'M SORRY, I DON'T RECALL--
WHY ARE WE LETTING THIS GUY INTO THE AUCTION?!
HE'S THE HEIR OF THE LATE, GREAT ZHENG ZU, IS HE NOT? A PLEASURE, SHANG-CHI.
I'M DELIGHTED THE CIRCUMSTANCES HAVE CHANGED.
WE'VE MET BEFORE, MADAME HYDRA, UNDER DIFFERENT CIRCUMSTANCES.
YOUR FATHER WAS AN IDOL OF MINE, DESPITE OUR VARIOUS ATTEMPTS TO MURDER EACH OTHER THROUGH THE YEARS.
HE ONCE TOLD ME HOW FERVENTLY HE WISHED FOR HIS FAVORITE SON TO COME BACK AROUND. I HAD A PISTOL TO HIS HEAD, SO I KNOW HE MEANT IT.
GLAD TO SEE HIS WISH CAME TRUE, SHANG-CHI.
HOW'S MY NECKLACE?
WHY ARE YOU SO WORRIED ABOUT--?

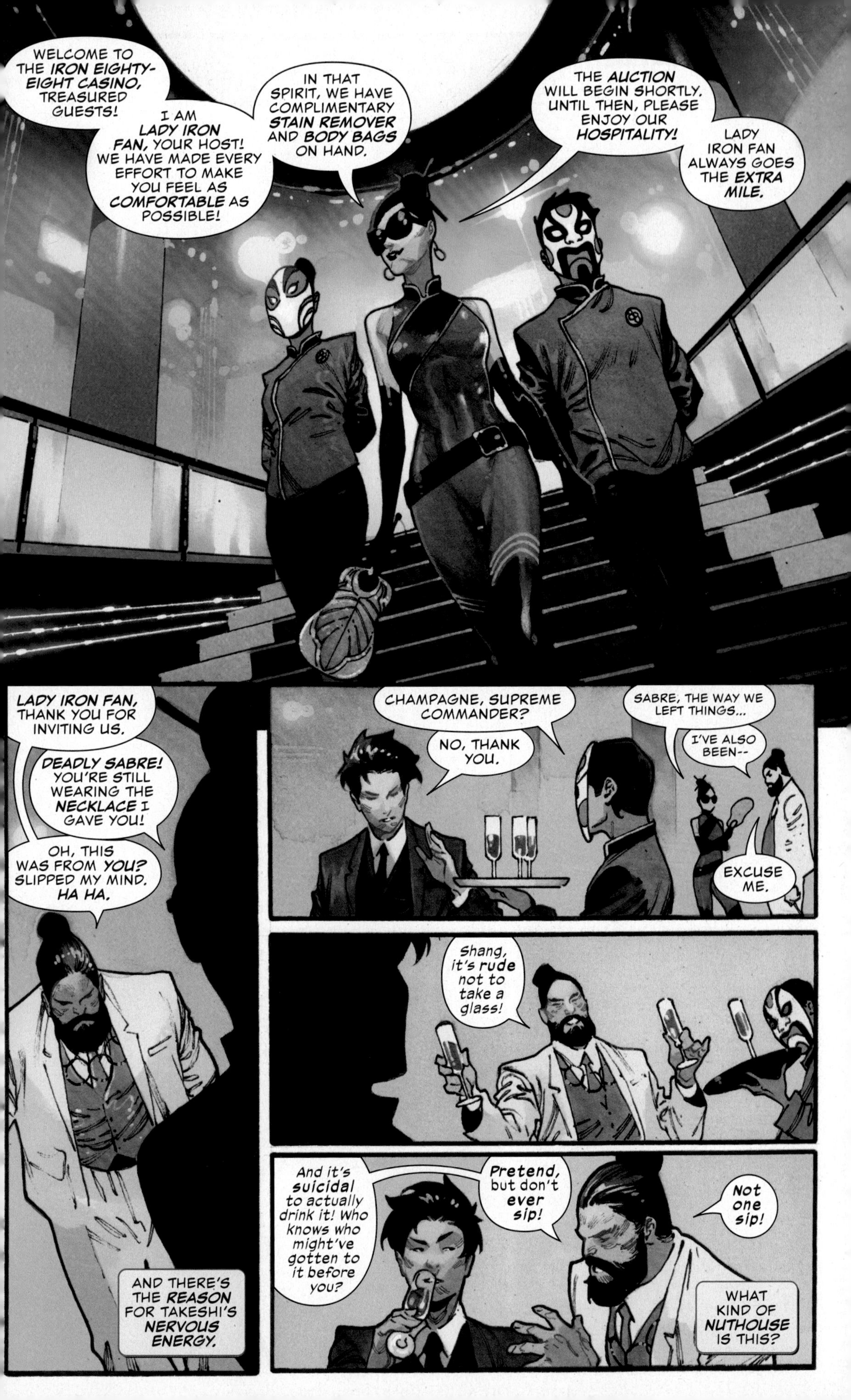

WELCOME TO THE IRON EIGHTY-EIGHT CASINO, TREASURED GUESTS!
I AM LADY IRON FAN, YOUR HOST! WE HAVE MADE EVERY EFFORT TO MAKE YOU FEEL AS COMFORTABLE AS POSSIBLE!
IN THAT SPIRIT, WE HAVE COMPLIMENTARY STAIN REMOVER AND BODY BAGS ON HAND.
THE AUCTION WILL BEGIN SHORTLY. UNTIL THEN, PLEASE ENJOY OUR HOSPITALITY!
LADY IRON FAN ALWAYS GOES THE EXTRA MILE.
LADY IRON FAN, THANK YOU FOR INVITING US.
DEADLY SABRE! YOU'RE STILL WEARING THE NECKLACE I GAVE YOU!
OH, THIS WAS FROM YOU? SLIPPED MY MIND. HA HA.
AND THERE'S THE REASON FOR TAKESHI'S NERVOUS ENERGY.
CHAMPAGNE, SUPREME COMMANDER?
NO, THANK YOU.
SABRE, THE WAY WE LEFT THINGS...
I'VE ALSO BEEN--
EXCUSE ME.
Shang, it's rude not to take a glass!
And it's suicidal to actually drink it! Who knows who might've gotten to it before you?
Pretend, but don't ever sip!
Not one sip!
WHAT KIND OF NUTHOUSE IS THIS?

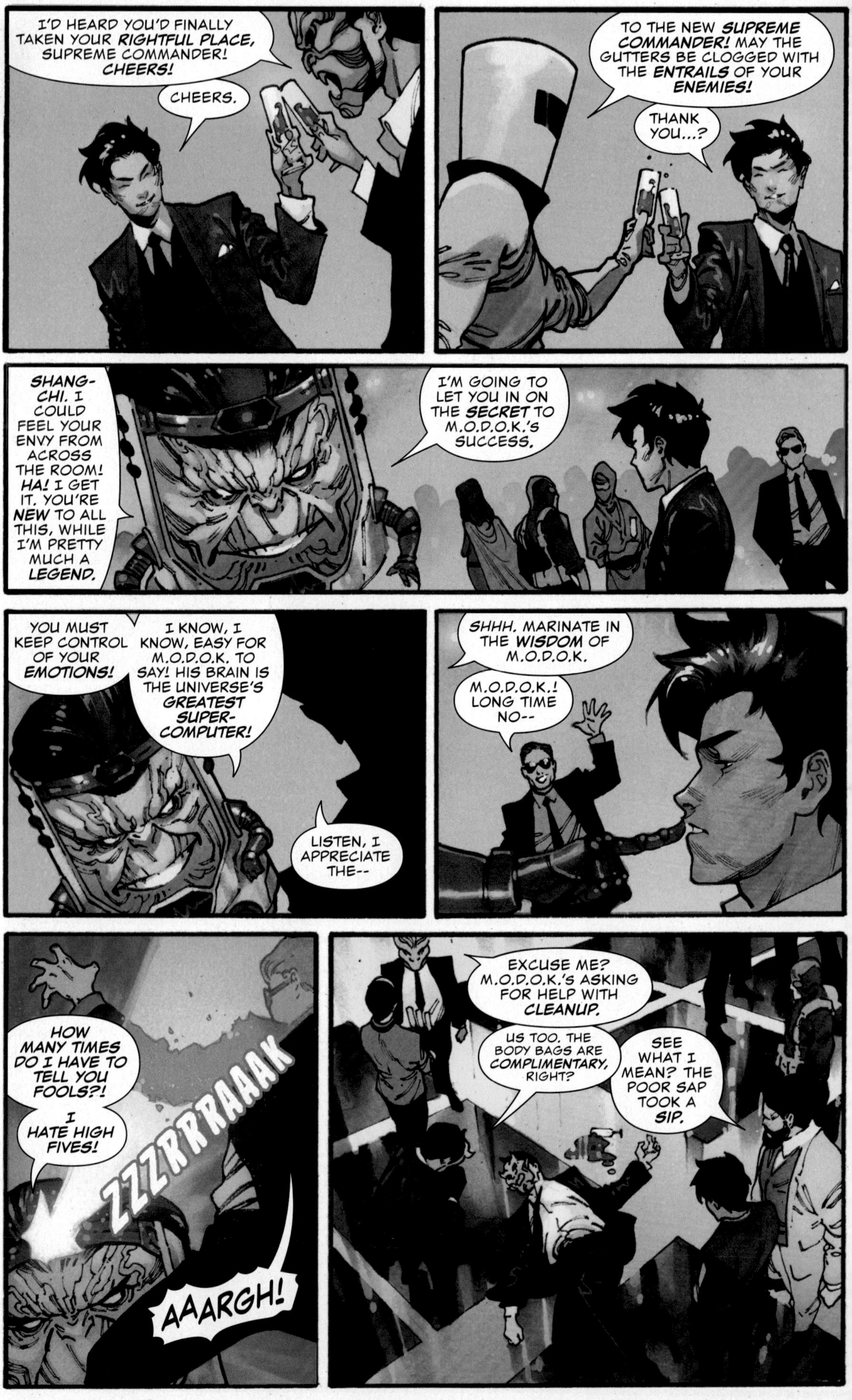

I'D HEARD YOU'D FINALLY TAKEN YOUR RIGHTFUL PLACE, SUPREME COMMANDER! CHEERS!
CHEERS.
TO THE NEW SUPREME COMMANDER! MAY THE GUTTERS BE CLOGGED WITH THE ENTRAILS OF YOUR ENEMIES!
THANK YOU...?
SHANG-CHI. I COULD FEEL YOUR ENVY FROM ACROSS THE ROOM! HA! I GET IT. YOU'RE NEW TO ALL THIS, WHILE I'M PRETTY MUCH A LEGEND.
I'M GOING TO LET YOU IN ON THE SECRET TO M.O.D.O.K.'s SUCCESS.
YOU MUST KEEP CONTROL OF YOUR EMOTIONS!
I KNOW, I KNOW, EASY FOR M.O.D.O.K. TO SAY! HIS BRAIN IS THE UNIVERSE'S GREATEST SUPER-COMPUTER!
LISTEN, I APPRECIATE THE--
SHHH. MARINATE IN THE WISDOM OF M.O.D.O.K.
M.O.D.O.K.! LONG TIME NO--
HOW MANY TIMES DO I HAVE TO TELL YOU FOOLS?!
I HATE HIGH FIVES!
ZZZRRRAAAK
AAARGH!
EXCUSE ME? M.O.D.O.K.'s ASKING FOR HELP WITH CLEANUP.
US TOO. THE BODY BAGS ARE COMPLIMENTARY, RIGHT?
SEE WHAT I MEAN? THE POOR SAP TOOK A SIP.

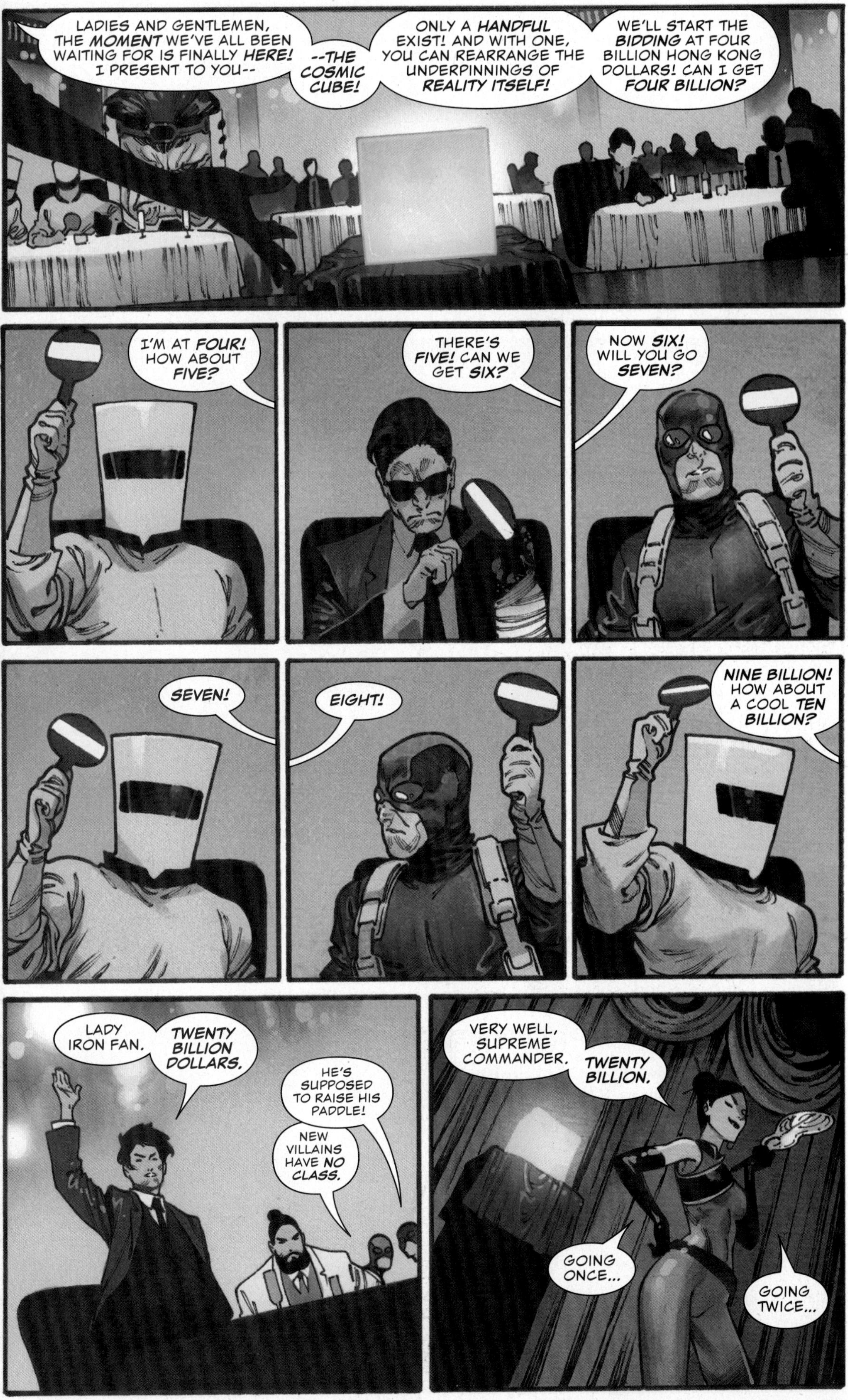
LADIES AND GENTLEMEN, THE MOMENT WE'VE ALL BEEN WAITING FOR IS FINALLY HERE! I PRESENT TO YOU--
--THE COSMIC CUBE!
ONLY A HANDFUL EXIST! AND WITH ONE, YOU CAN REARRANGE THE UNDERPINNINGS OF REALITY ITSELF!
WE'LL START THE BIDDING AT FOUR BILLION HONG KONG DOLLARS! CAN I GET FOUR BILLION?
I'M AT FOUR! HOW ABOUT FIVE?
THERE'S FIVE! CAN WE GET SIX?
NOW SIX! WILL YOU GO SEVEN?
SEVEN!
EIGHT!
NINE BILLION! HOW ABOUT A COOL TEN BILLION?
LADY IRON FAN.
TWENTY BILLION DOLLARS.
HE'S SUPPOSED TO RAISE HIS PADDLE!
NEW VILLAINS HAVE NO CLASS.
VERY WELL, SUPREME COMMANDER.
TWENTY BILLION.
GOING ONCE...
GOING TWICE...

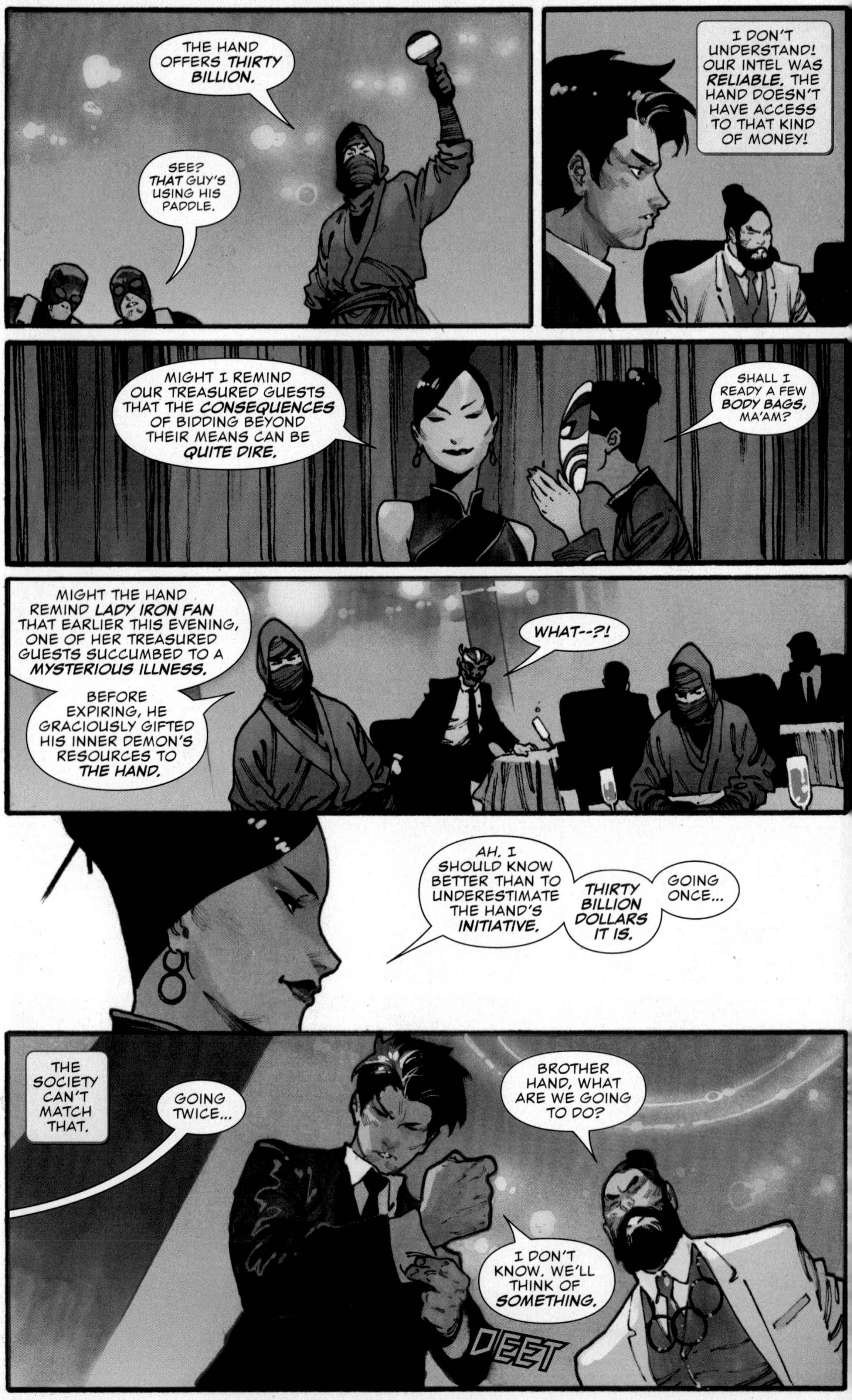
THE HAND OFFERS THIRTY BILLION.
SEE? THAT GUY'S USING HIS PADDLE.
I DON'T UNDERSTAND! OUR INTEL WAS RELIABLE. THE HAND DOESN'T HAVE ACCESS TO THAT KIND OF MONEY!
MIGHT I REMIND OUR TREASURED GUESTS THAT THE CONSEQUENCES OF BIDDING BEYOND THEIR MEANS CAN BE QUITE DIRE.
SHALL I READY A FEW BODY BAGS, MA'AM?
MIGHT THE HAND REMIND LADY IRON FAN THAT EARLIER THIS EVENING, ONE OF HER TREASURED GUESTS SUCCUMBED TO A MYSTERIOUS ILLNESS.
BEFORE EXPIRING, HE GRACIOUSLY GIFTED HIS INNER DEMON'S RESOURCES TO THE HAND.
WHAT--?!
AH. I SHOULD KNOW BETTER THAN TO UNDERESTIMATE THE HAND'S INITIATIVE.
THIRTY BILLION DOLLARS IT IS.
GOING ONCE...
THE SOCIETY CAN'T MATCH THAT.
GOING TWICE...
BROTHER HAND, WHAT ARE WE GOING TO DO?
I DON'T KNOW. WE'LL THINK OF SOMETHING.
DEET

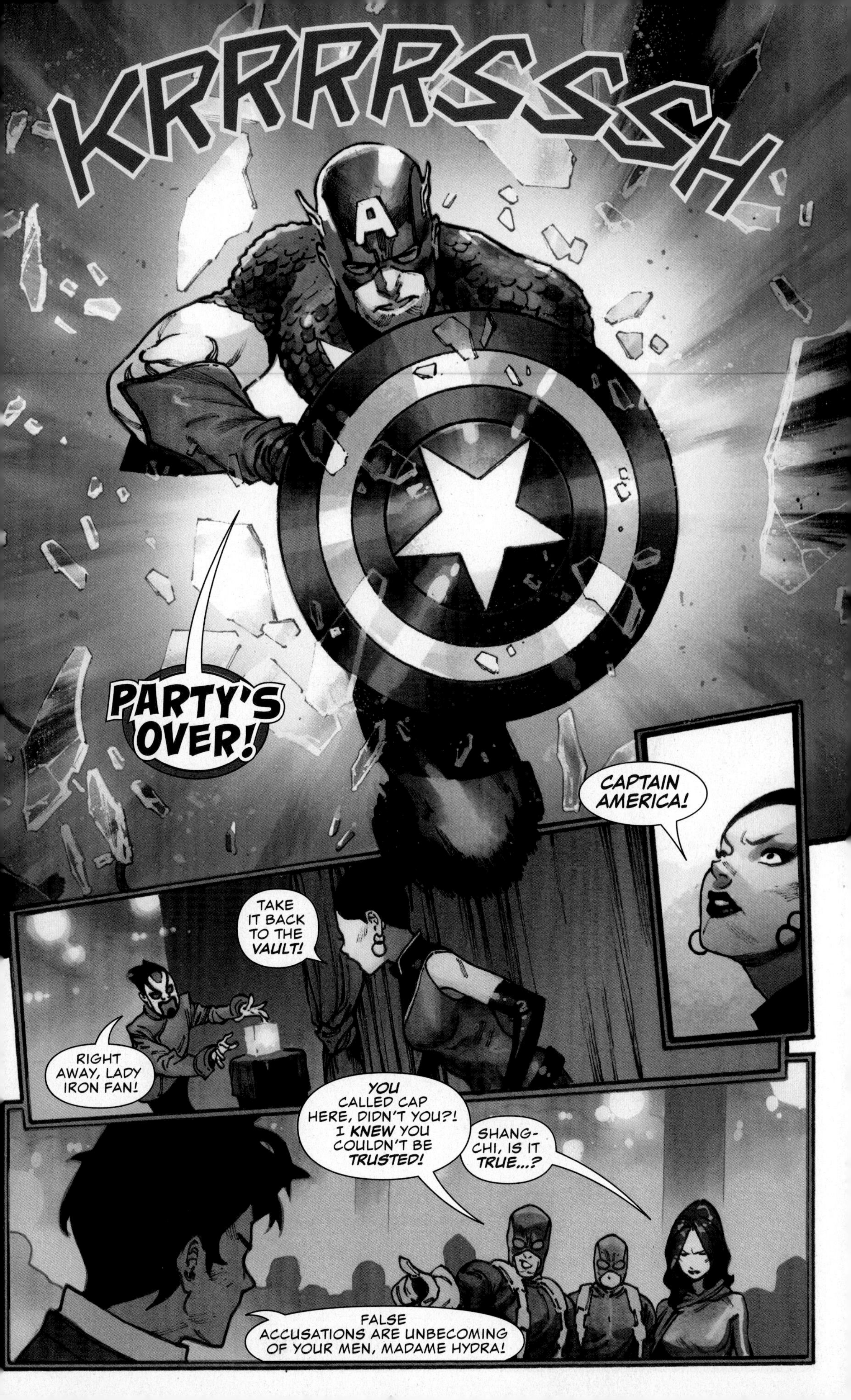
KRRRRSSSH
PARTY'S OVER!
CAPTAIN AMERICA!
TAKE IT BACK TO THE VAULT!
RIGHT AWAY, LADY IRON FAN!
YOU CALLED CAP HERE, DIDN'T YOU?! I KNEW YOU COULDN'T BE TRUSTED!
SHANG-CHI, IS IT TRUE...?
FALSE ACCUSATIONS ARE UNBECOMING OF YOUR MEN, MADAME HYDRA!

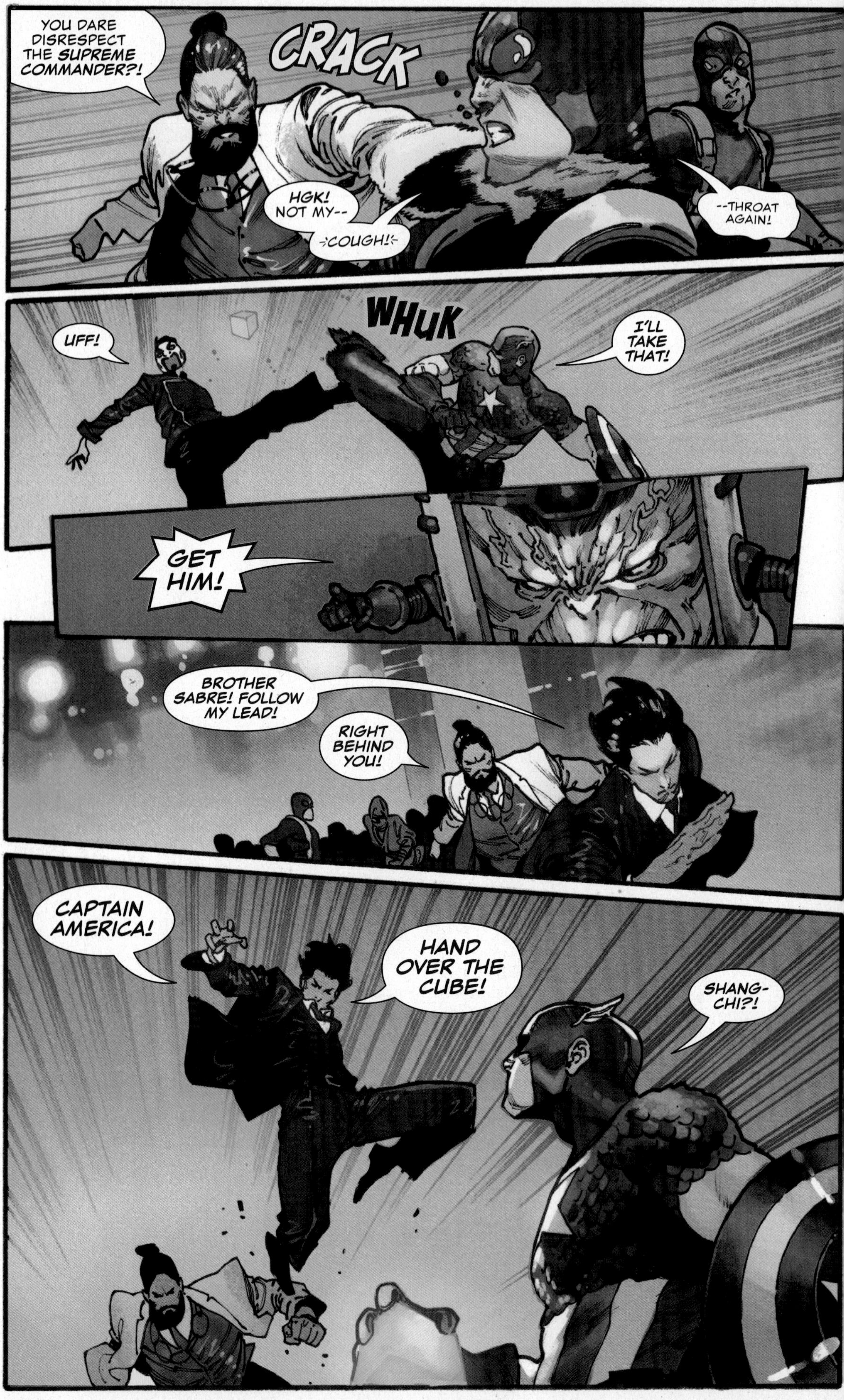
YOU DARE DISRESPECT THE SUPREME COMMANDER?!
CRACK
HGK! NOT MY--
COUGH!
--THROAT AGAIN!
UFF!
WHUK
I'LL TAKE THAT!
GET HIM!
BROTHER SABRE! FOLLOW MY LEAD!
RIGHT BEHIND YOU!
CAPTAIN AMERICA!
HAND OVER THE CUBE!
SHANG-CHI?!

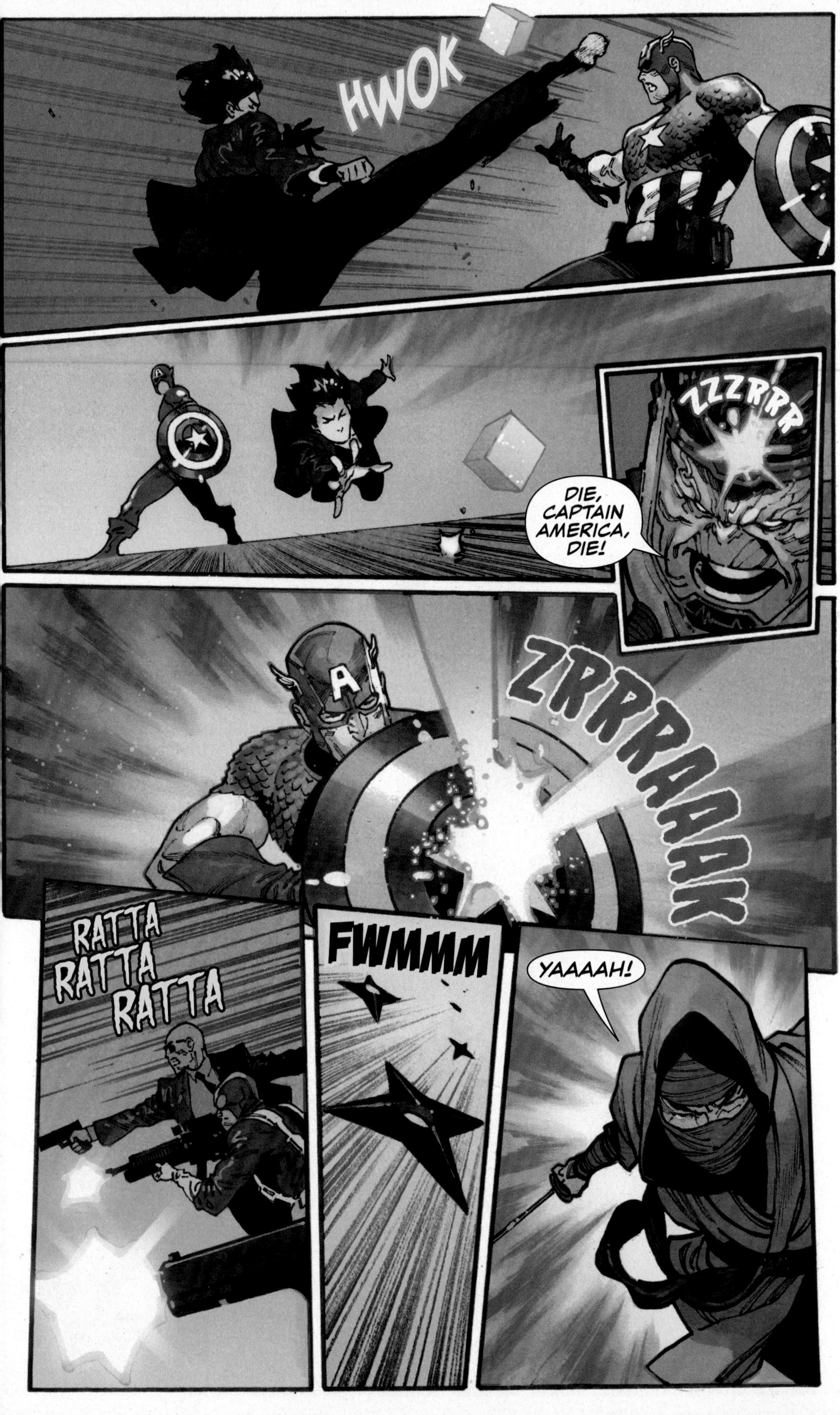
HWOK
ZZZRRR
DIE, CAPTAIN AMERICA, DIE!
ZRRRRAAAK
RATTA RATTA RATTA
FWMMM
YAAAAH!

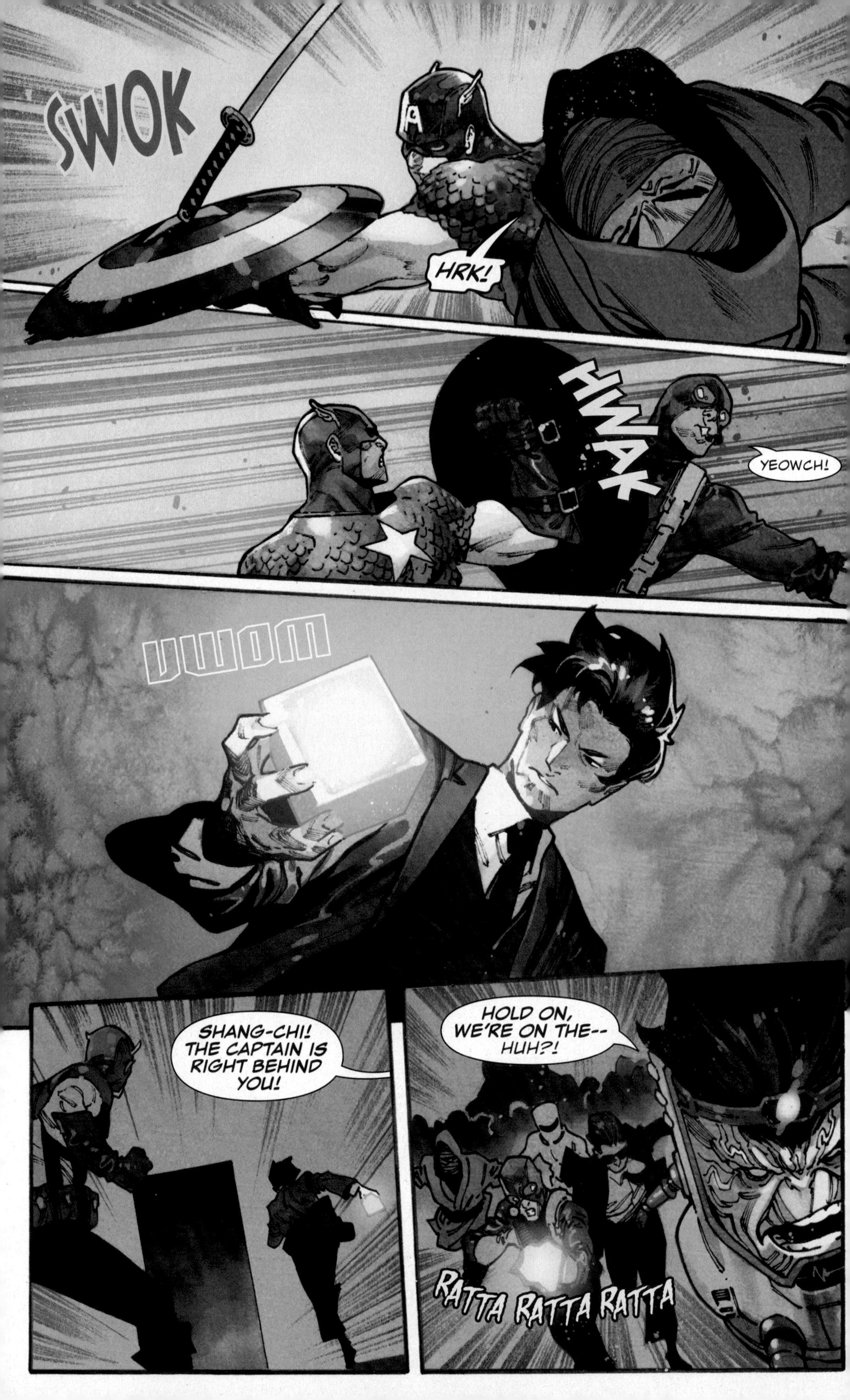
SWOK
HRK!
HWAK
YEOWCH!
VWOM
SHANG-CHI! THE CAPTAIN IS RIGHT BEHIND YOU!
HOLD ON, WE'RE ON THE-- HUH?!
RATTA RATTA RATTA

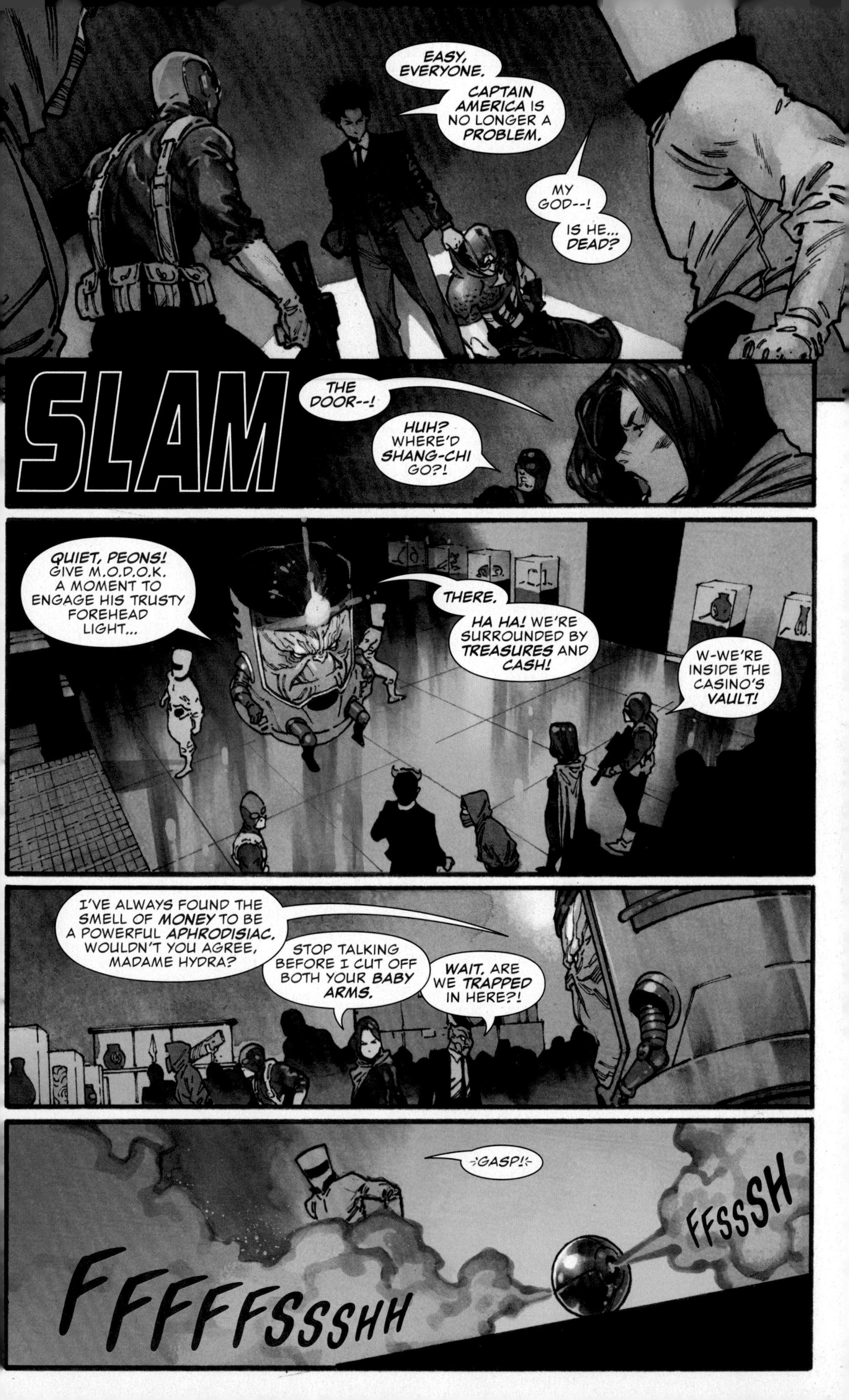
EASY, EVERYONE.
CAPTAIN AMERICA IS NO LONGER A PROBLEM.
MY GOD--!
IS HE... DEAD?
SLAM
THE DOOR--!
HUH? WHERE'D SHANG-CHI GO?!
QUIET, PEONS! GIVE M.O.D.O.K. A MOMENT TO ENGAGE HIS TRUSTY FOREHEAD LIGHT...
THERE.
HA HA! WE'RE SURROUNDED BY TREASURES AND CASH!
W-WE'RE INSIDE THE CASINO'S VAULT!
I'VE ALWAYS FOUND THE SMELL OF MONEY TO BE A POWERFUL APHRODISIAC. WOULDN'T YOU AGREE, MADAME HYDRA?
STOP TALKING BEFORE I CUT OFF BOTH YOUR BABY ARMS.
WAIT. ARE WE TRAPPED IN HERE?!
GASP!
FFSSSH
FFFFFSSSHH

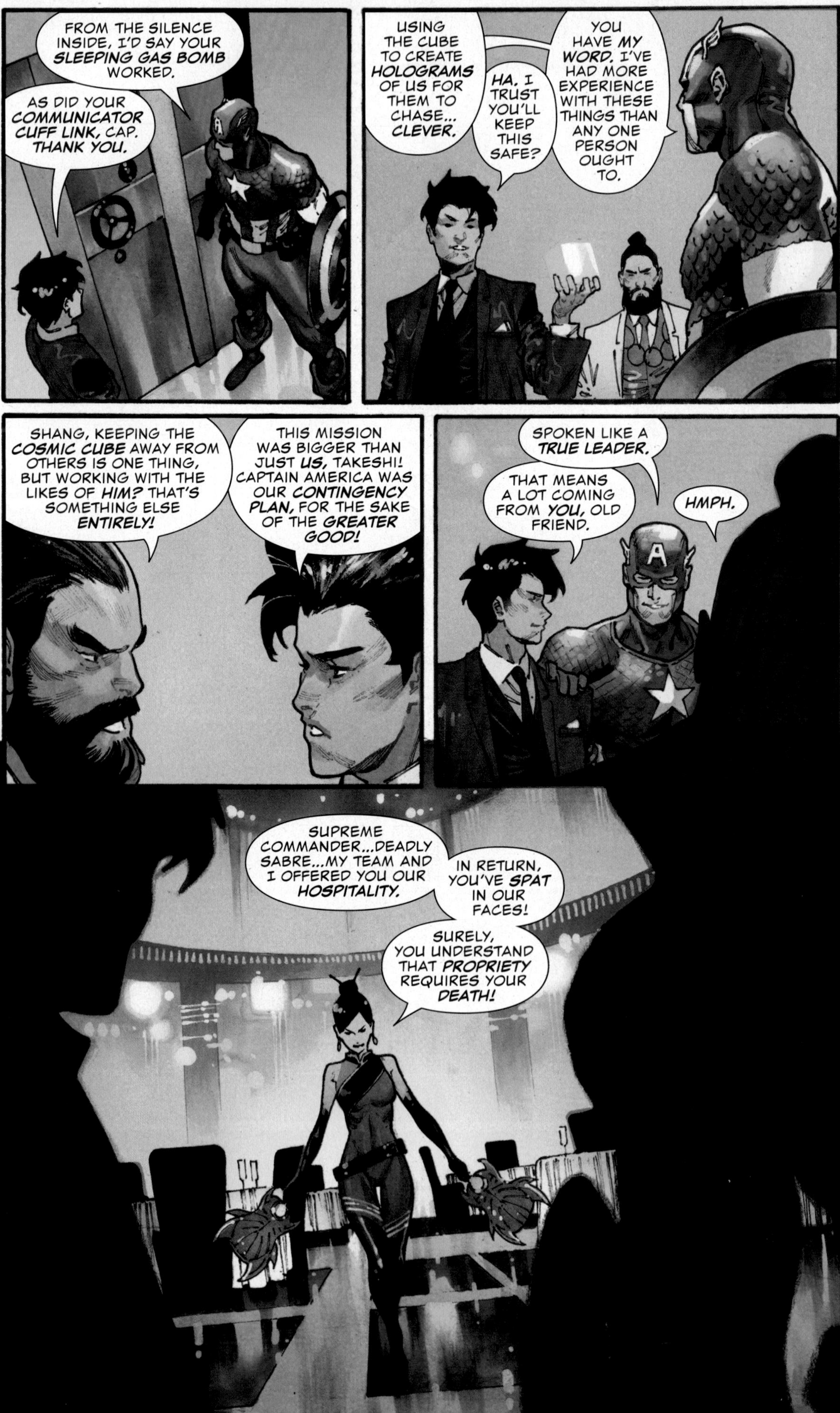
FROM THE SILENCE INSIDE, I'D SAY YOUR SLEEPING GAS BOMB WORKED.
AS DID YOUR COMMUNICATOR CUFF LINK, CAP. THANK YOU.
USING THE CUBE TO CREATE HOLOGRAMS OF US FOR THEM TO CHASE... CLEVER.
HA. I TRUST YOU'LL KEEP THIS SAFE?
YOU HAVE MY WORD. I'VE HAD MORE EXPERIENCE WITH THESE THINGS THAN ANY ONE PERSON OUGHT TO.
SHANG, KEEPING THE COSMIC CUBE AWAY FROM OTHERS IS ONE THING, BUT WORKING WITH THE LIKES OF HIM? THAT'S SOMETHING ELSE ENTIRELY!
THIS MISSION WAS BIGGER THAN JUST US, TAKESHI! CAPTAIN AMERICA WAS OUR CONTINGENCY PLAN, FOR THE SAKE OF THE GREATER GOOD!
SPOKEN LIKE A TRUE LEADER.
THAT MEANS A LOT COMING FROM YOU, OLD FRIEND.
HMPH.
SUPREME COMMANDER...DEADLY SABRE...MY TEAM AND I OFFERED YOU OUR HOSPITALITY.
IN RETURN, YOU'VE SPAT IN OUR FACES!
SURELY, YOU UNDERSTAND THAT PROPRIETY REQUIRES YOUR DEATH!

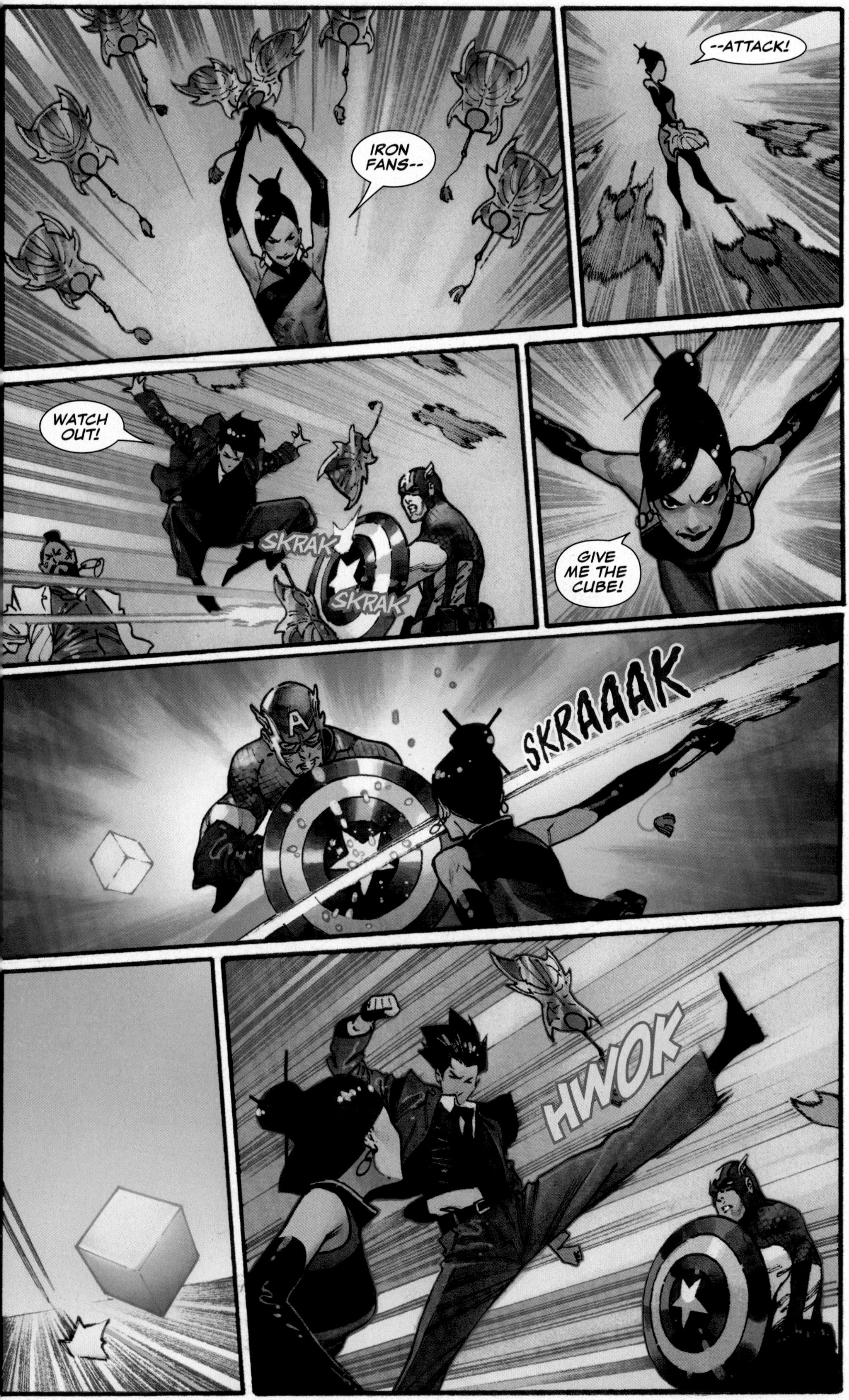
IRON FANS--
--ATTACK!
WATCH OUT!
SKRAK
SKRAK
GIVE ME THE CUBE!
SKRAAAK
HWOK

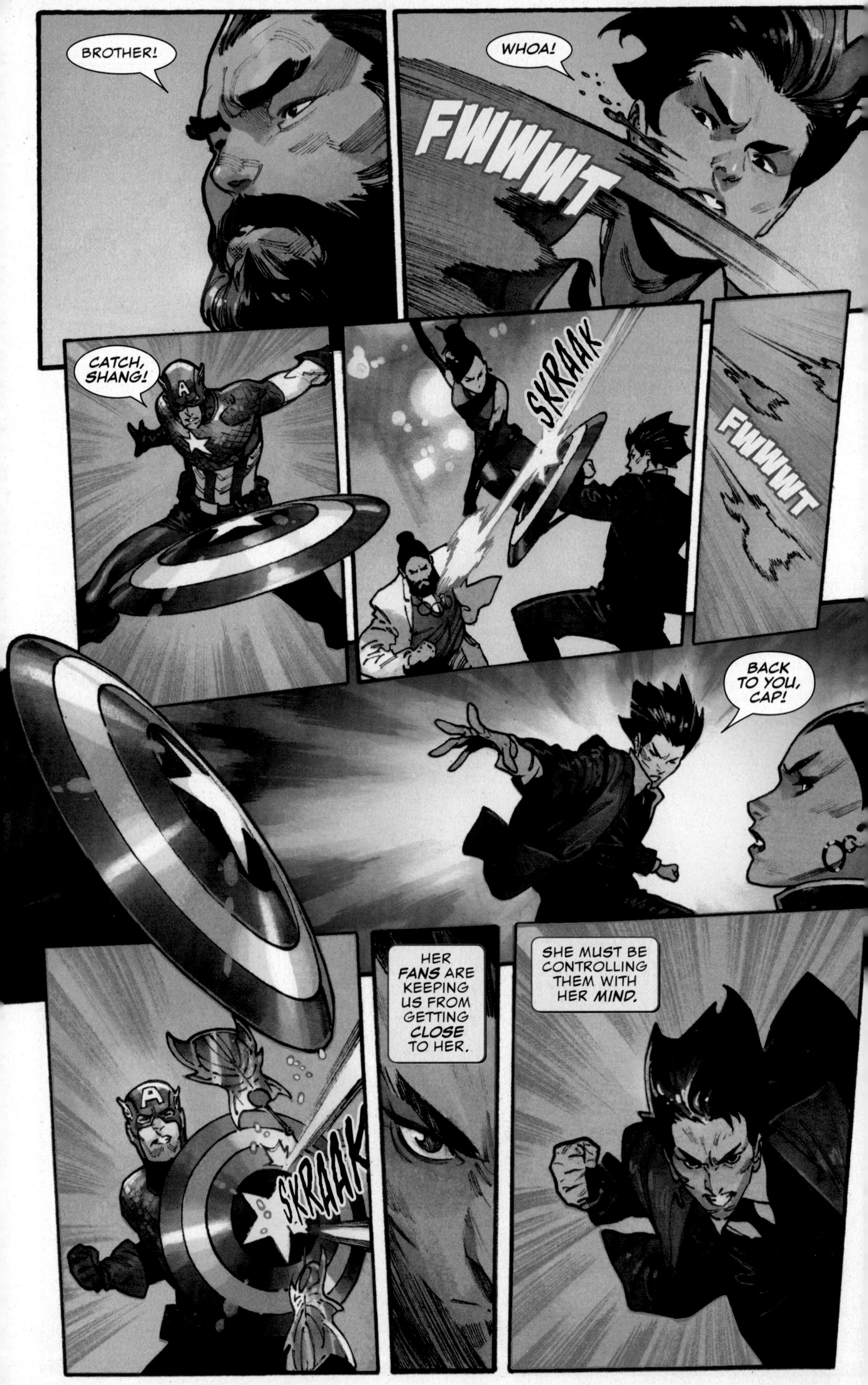
BROTHER!
WHOA!
FWWWT
CATCH, SHANG!
SKRAAK
FWWWT
BACK TO YOU, CAP!
SKRAAK
HER FANS ARE KEEPING US FROM GETTING CLOSE TO HER.
SHE MUST BE CONTROLLING THEM WITH HER MIND.

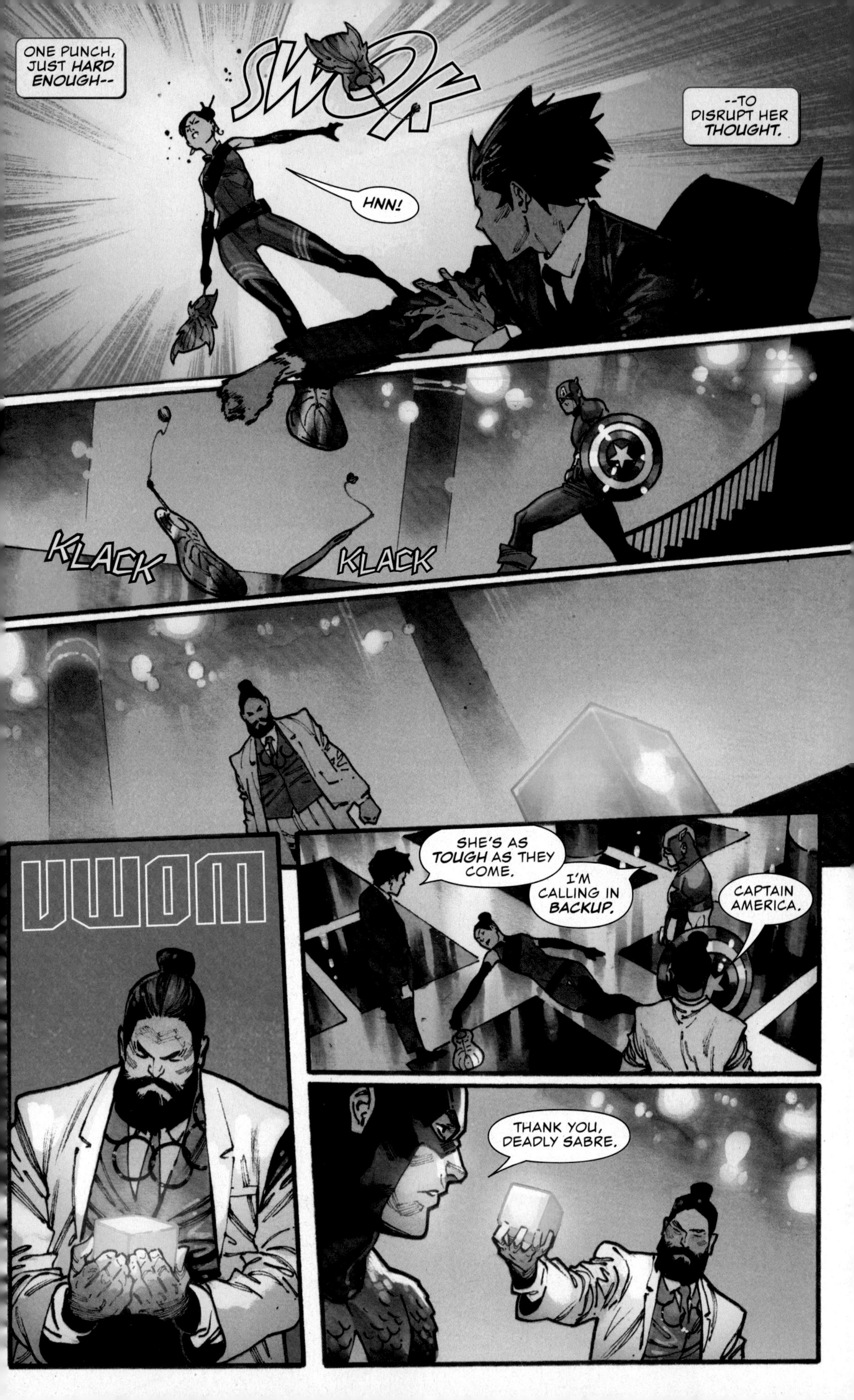
ONE PUNCH, JUST HARD ENOUGH--
SWOK
--TO DISRUPT HER THOUGHT.
HNN!
KLACK
KLACK
VWOM
SHE'S AS TOUGH AS THEY COME.
I'M CALLING IN BACKUP.
CAPTAIN AMERICA.
THANK YOU, DEADLY SABRE.

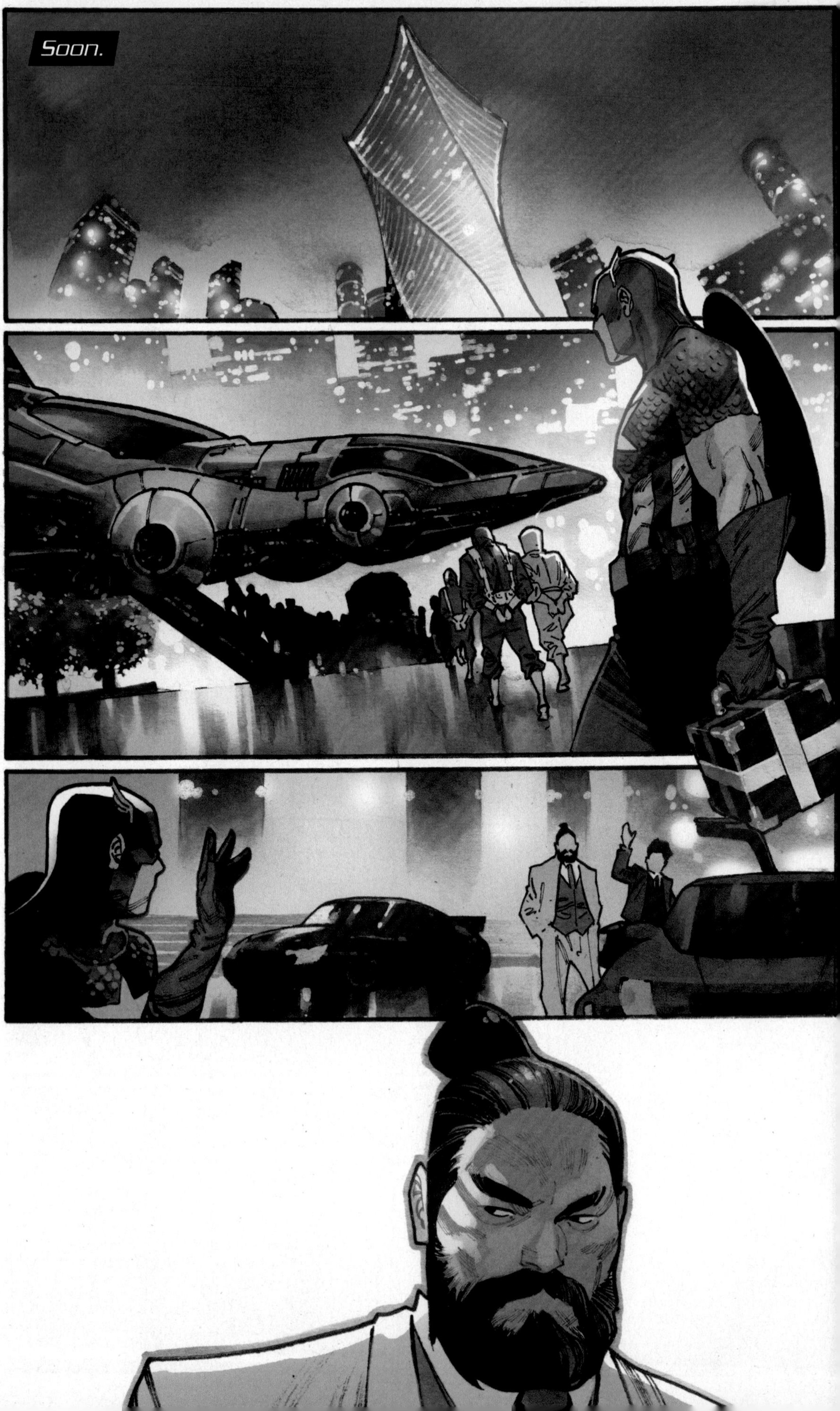
Soon.

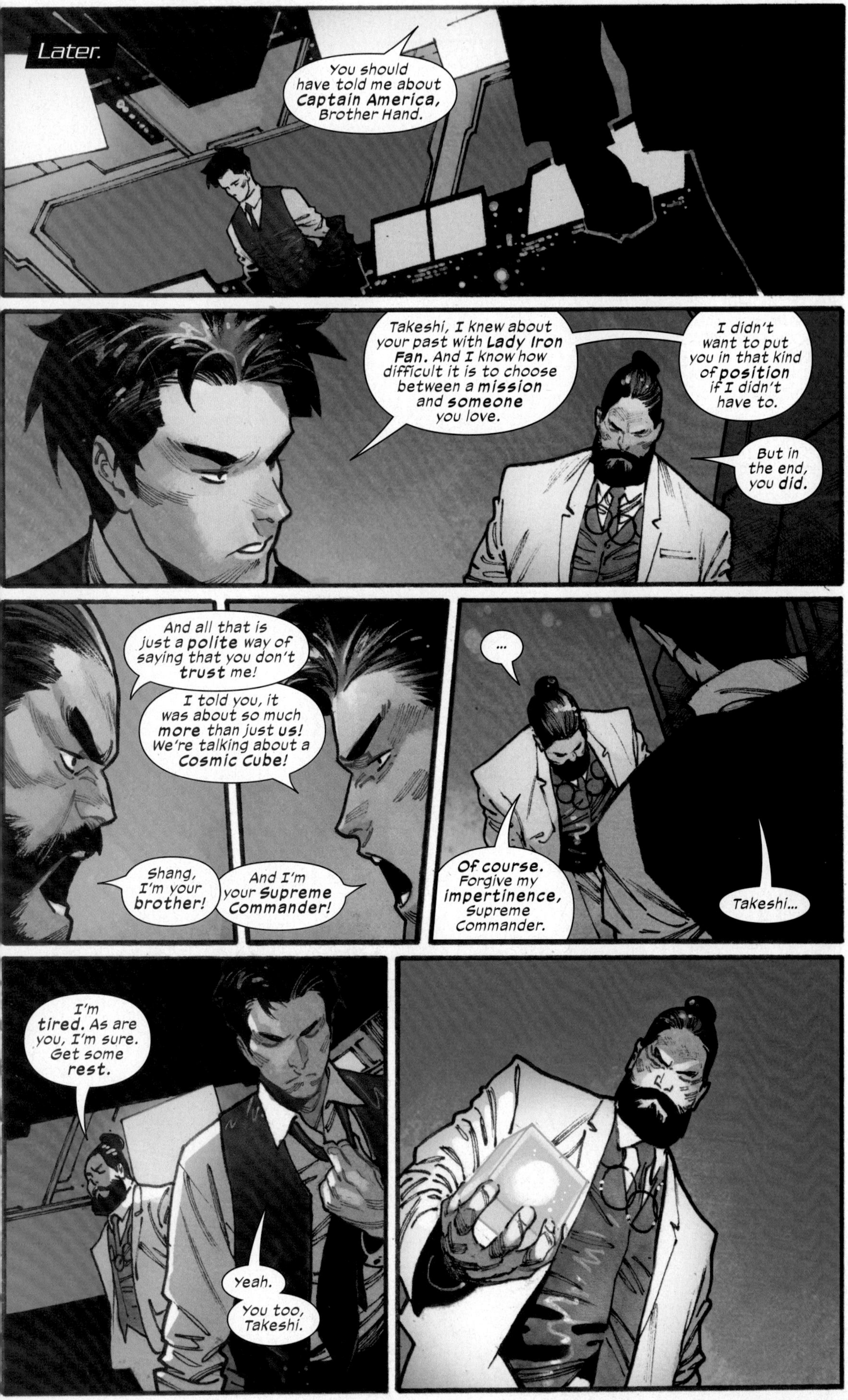
Later.
You should have told me about Captain America, Brother Hand.
Takeshi, I knew about your past with Lady Iron Fan. And I know how difficult it is to choose between a mission and someone you love.
I didn't want to put you in that kind of position if I didn't have to.
But in the end, you did.
And all that is just a polite way of saying that you don't trust me!
I told you, it was about so much more than just us! We're talking about a Cosmic Cube!
Shang, I'm your brother!
And I'm your Supreme Commander!
...
Of course. Forgive my impertinence, Supreme Commander.
Takeshi...
I'm tired. As are you, I'm sure. Get some rest.
Yeah.
You too, Takeshi.

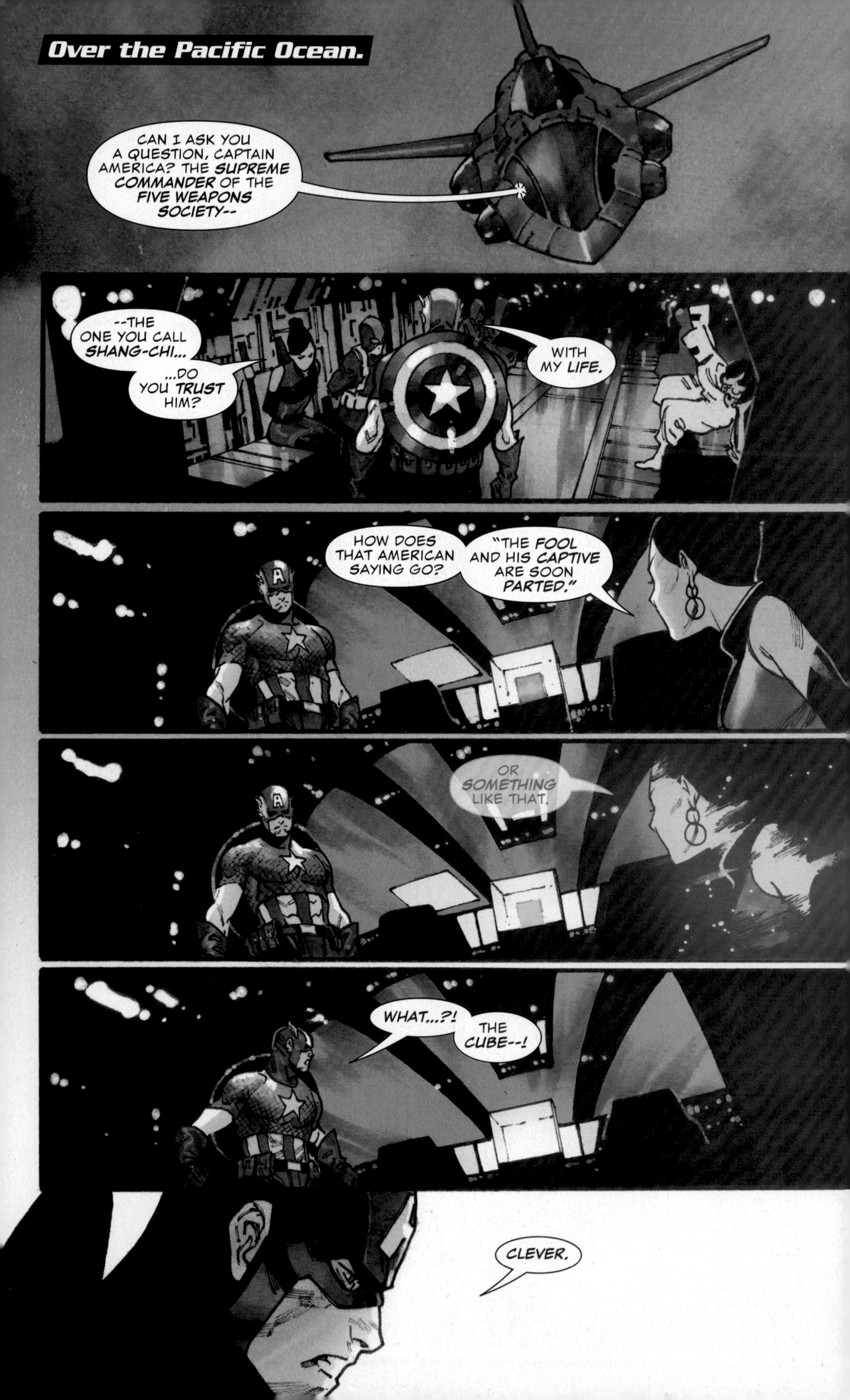
Over the Pacific Ocean.
CAN I ASK YOU A QUESTION, CAPTAIN AMERICA? THE SUPREME COMMANDER OF THE FIVE WEAPONS SOCIETY--
--THE ONE YOU CALL SHANG-CHI...
...DO YOU TRUST HIM?
WITH MY LIFE.
HOW DOES THAT AMERICAN SAYING GO?
"THE FOOL AND HIS CAPTIVE ARE SOON PARTED."
OR SOMETHING LIKE THAT.
WHAT...?!
THE CUBE--!
CLEVER.

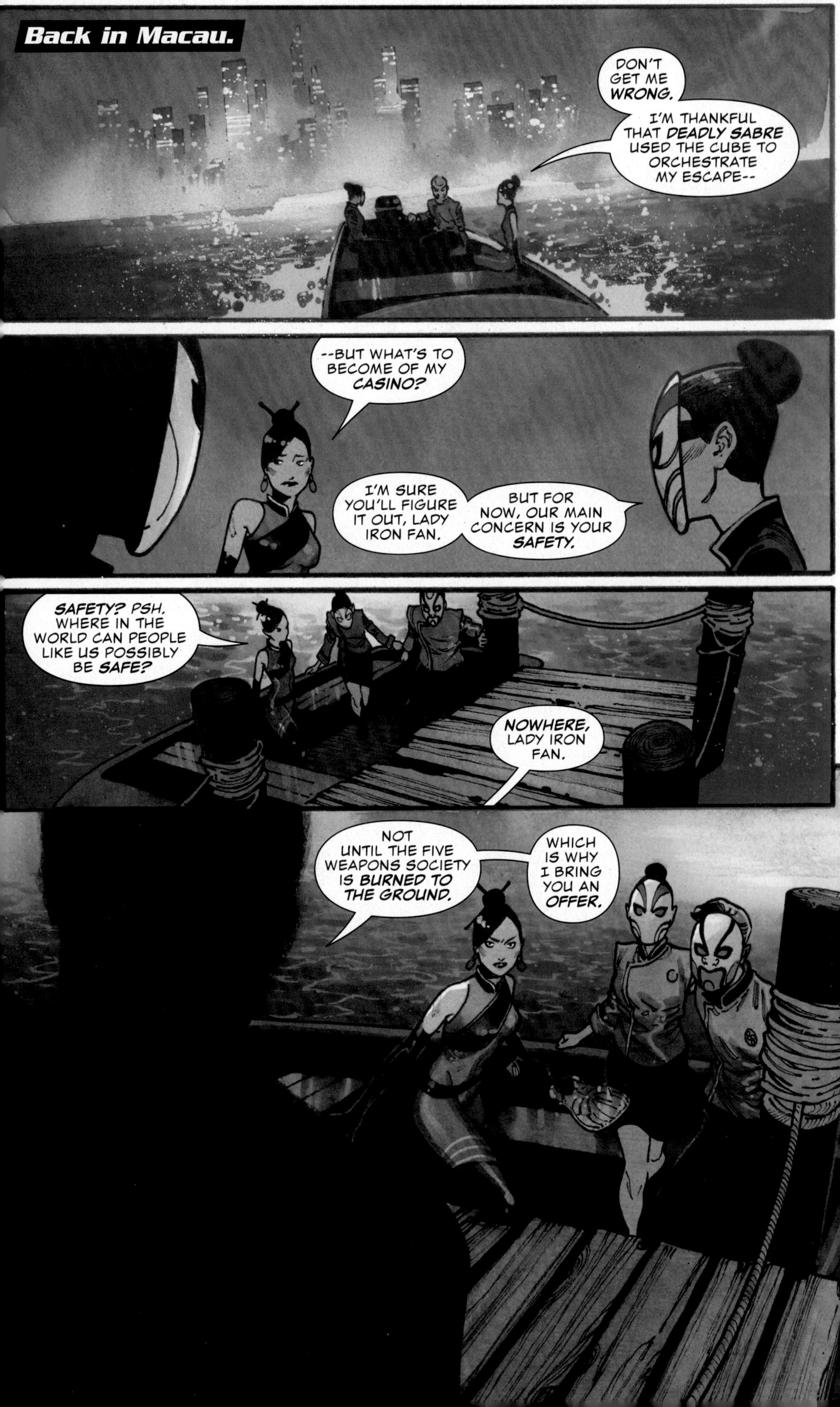
Back in Macau.
DON'T GET ME WRONG.
I'M THANKFUL THAT DEADLY SABRE USED THE CUBE TO ORCHESTRATE MY ESCAPE--
--BUT WHAT'S TO BECOME OF MY CASINO?
I'M SURE YOU'LL FIGURE IT OUT, LADY IRON FAN.
BUT FOR NOW, OUR MAIN CONCERN IS YOUR SAFETY.
SAFETY? PSH. WHERE IN THE WORLD CAN PEOPLE LIKE US POSSIBLY BE SAFE?
NOWHERE, LADY IRON FAN.
NOT UNTIL THE FIVE WEAPONS SOCIETY IS BURNED TO THE GROUND.
WHICH IS WHY I BRING YOU AN OFFER.

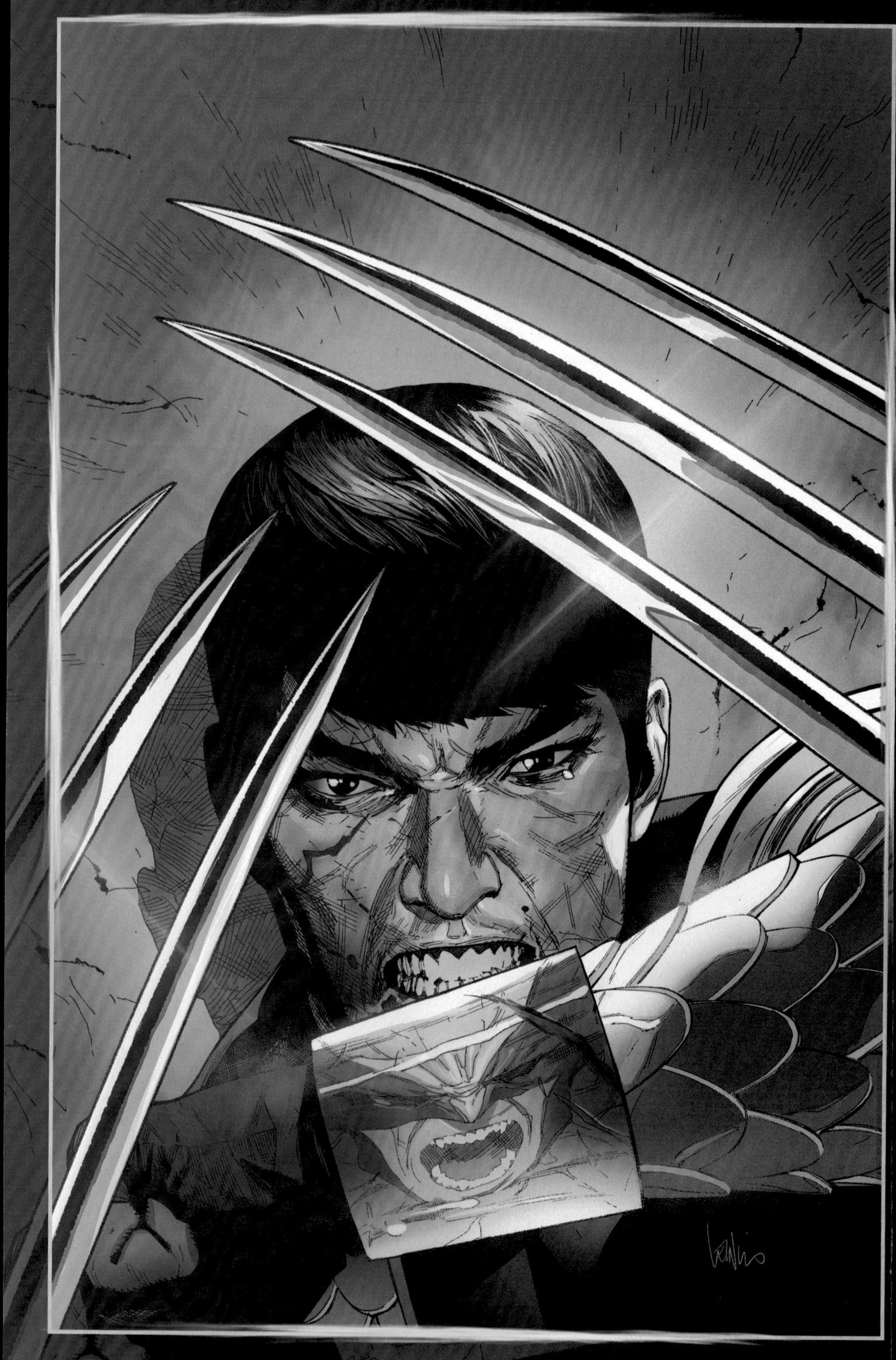

THREE

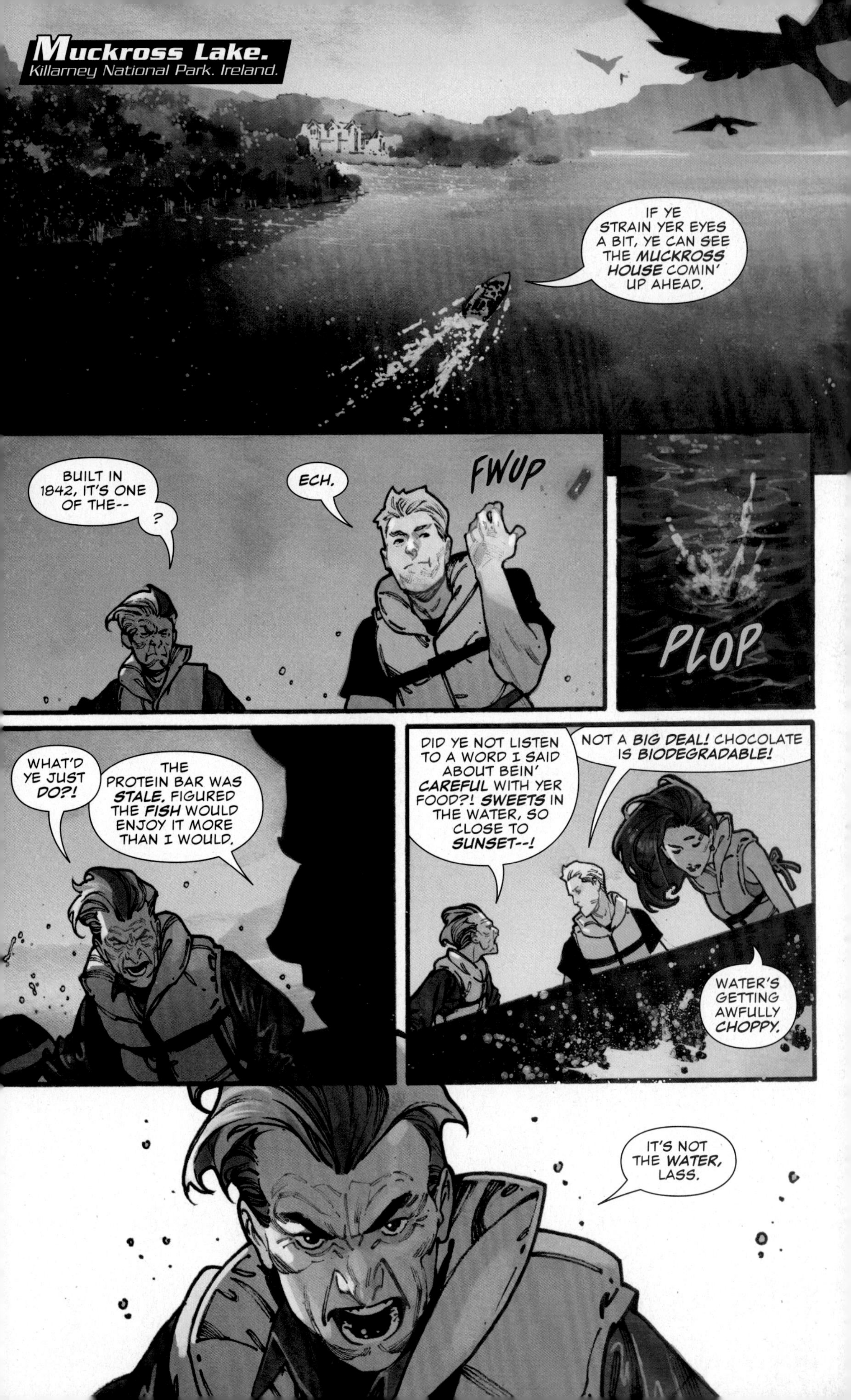
Muckross Lake.
Killarney National Park. Ireland.
IF YE STRAIN YER EYES A BIT, YE CAN SEE THE MUCKROSS HOUSE COMIN' UP AHEAD.
BUILT IN 1842, IT'S ONE OF THE--
?
ECH.
FWUP
PLOP
WHAT'D YE JUST DO?!
THE PROTEIN BAR WAS STALE. FIGURED THE FISH WOULD ENJOY IT MORE THAN I WOULD.
DID YE NOT LISTEN TO A WORD I SAID ABOUT BEIN' CAREFUL WITH YER FOOD?! SWEETS IN THE WATER, SO CLOSE TO SUNSET--!
NOT A BIG DEAL! CHOCOLATE IS BIODEGRADABLE!
WATER'S GETTING AWFULLY CHOPPY.
IT'S NOT THE WATER, LASS.

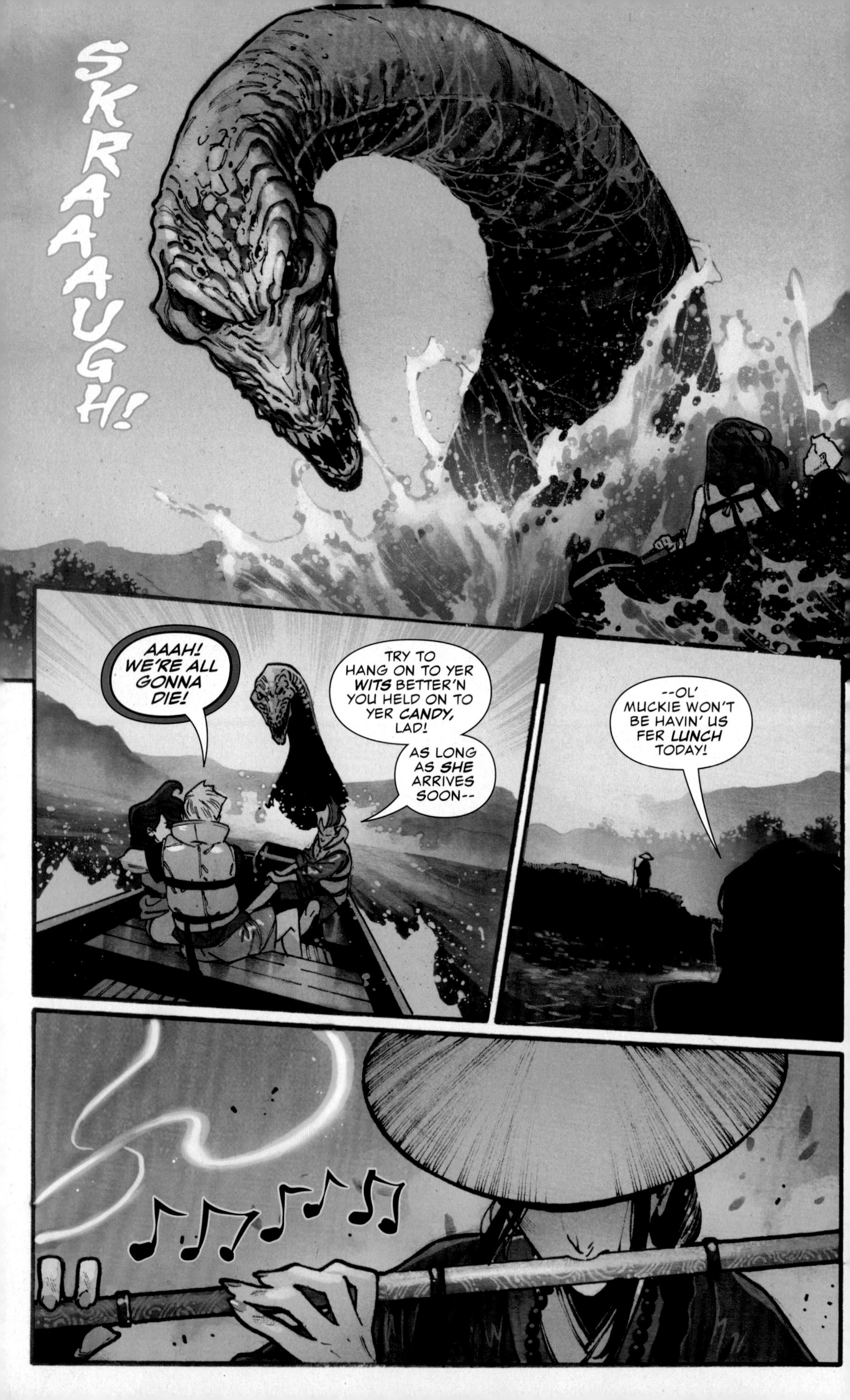
SKRAAAUGH!
AAAH! WE'RE ALL GONNA DIE!
TRY TO HANG ON TO YER WITS BETTER'N YOU HELD ON TO YER CANDY, LAD!
AS LONG AS SHE ARRIVES SOON--
--OL' MUCKIE WON'T BE HAVIN' US FER LUNCH TODAY!

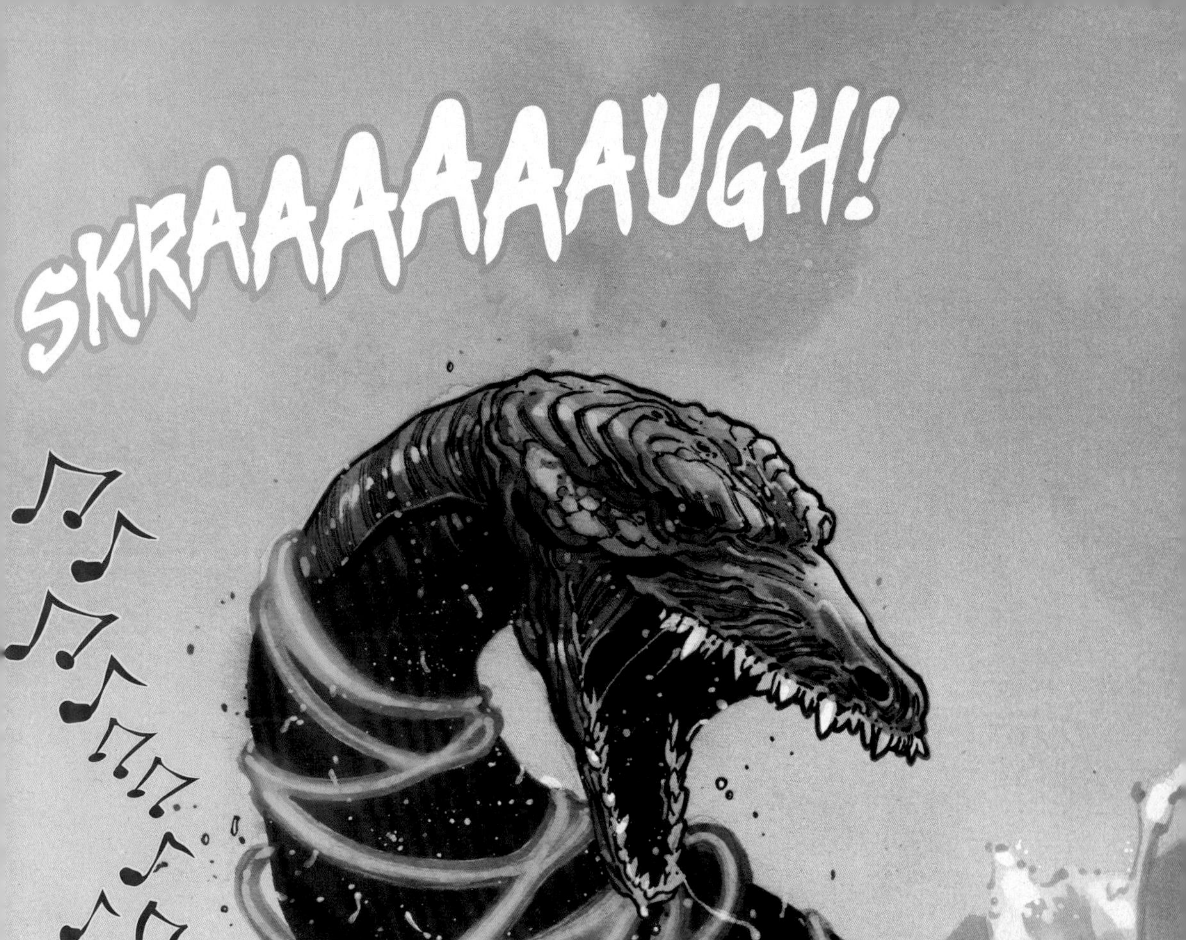
SKRAAAAAAAUGH!
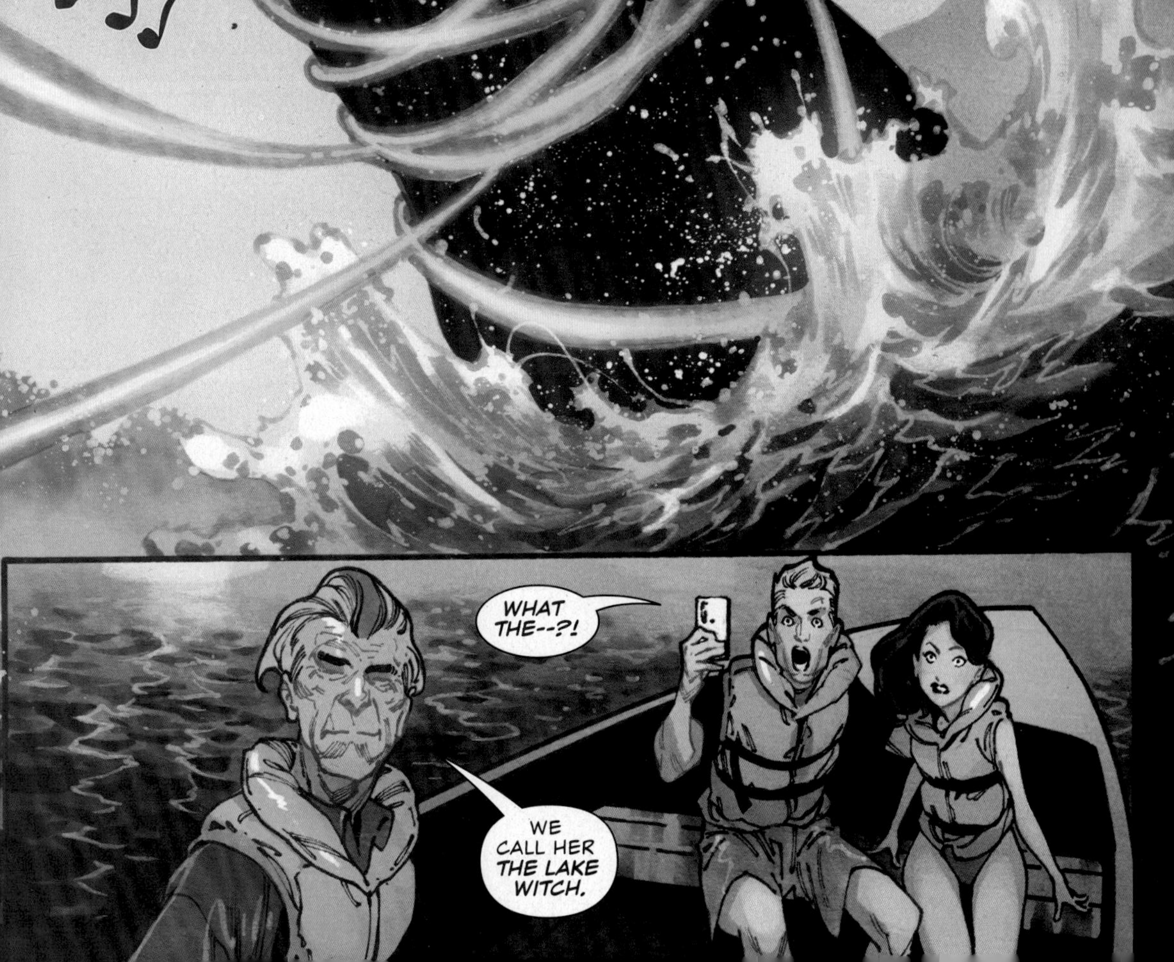
WHAT THE--?!
WE CALL HER THE LAKE WITCH.

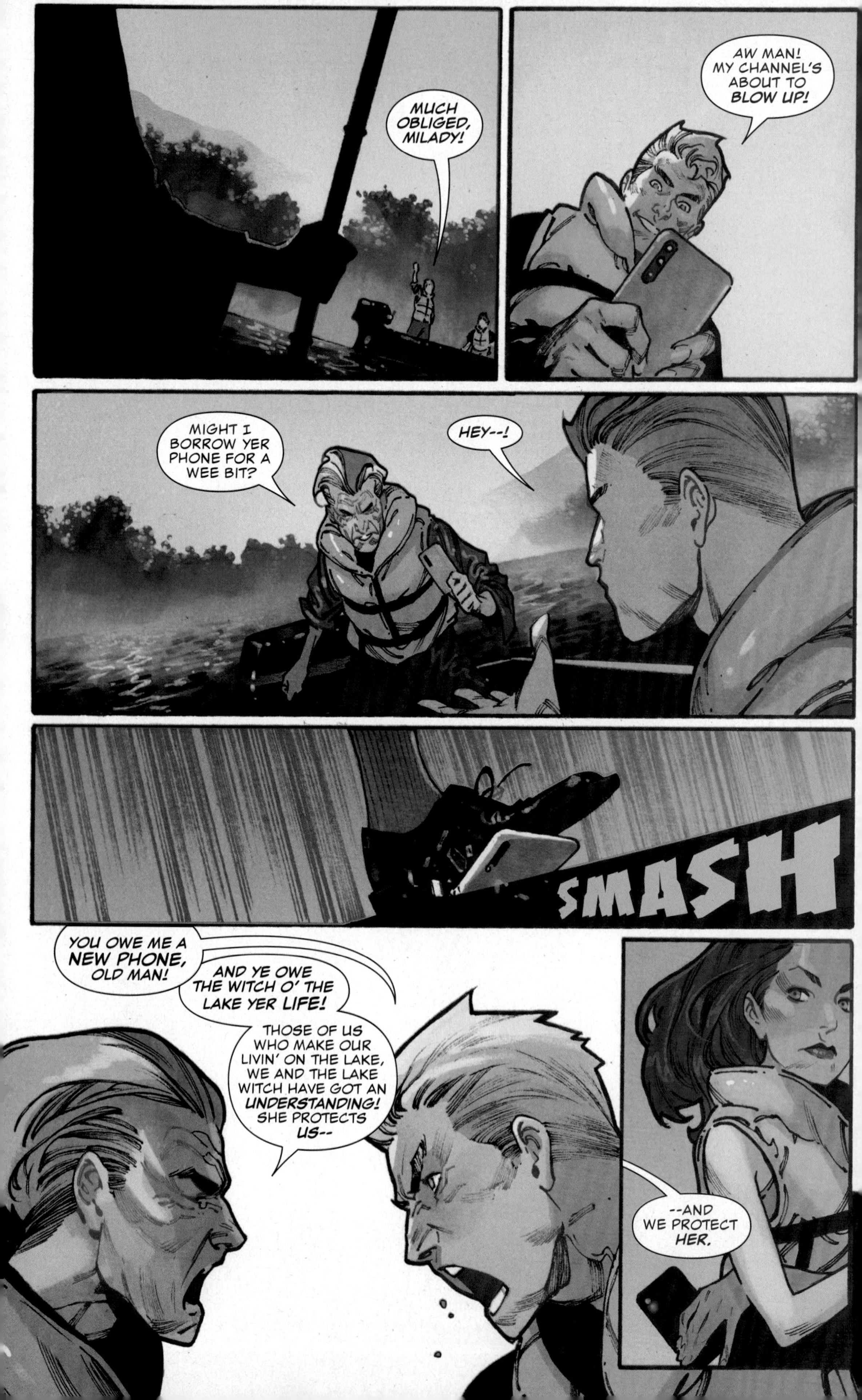
MUCH OBLIGED, MILADY!
AW MAN! MY CHANNEL'S ABOUT TO BLOW UP!
MIGHT I BORROW YER PHONE FOR A WEE BIT?
HEY--!
SMASH
YOU OWE ME A NEW PHONE, OLD MAN!
AND YE OWE THE WITCH O' THE LAKE YER LIFE!
THOSE OF US WHO MAKE OUR LIVIN' ON THE LAKE, WE AND THE LAKE WITCH HAVE GOT AN UNDERSTANDING! SHE PROTECTS US--
--AND WE PROTECT HER.

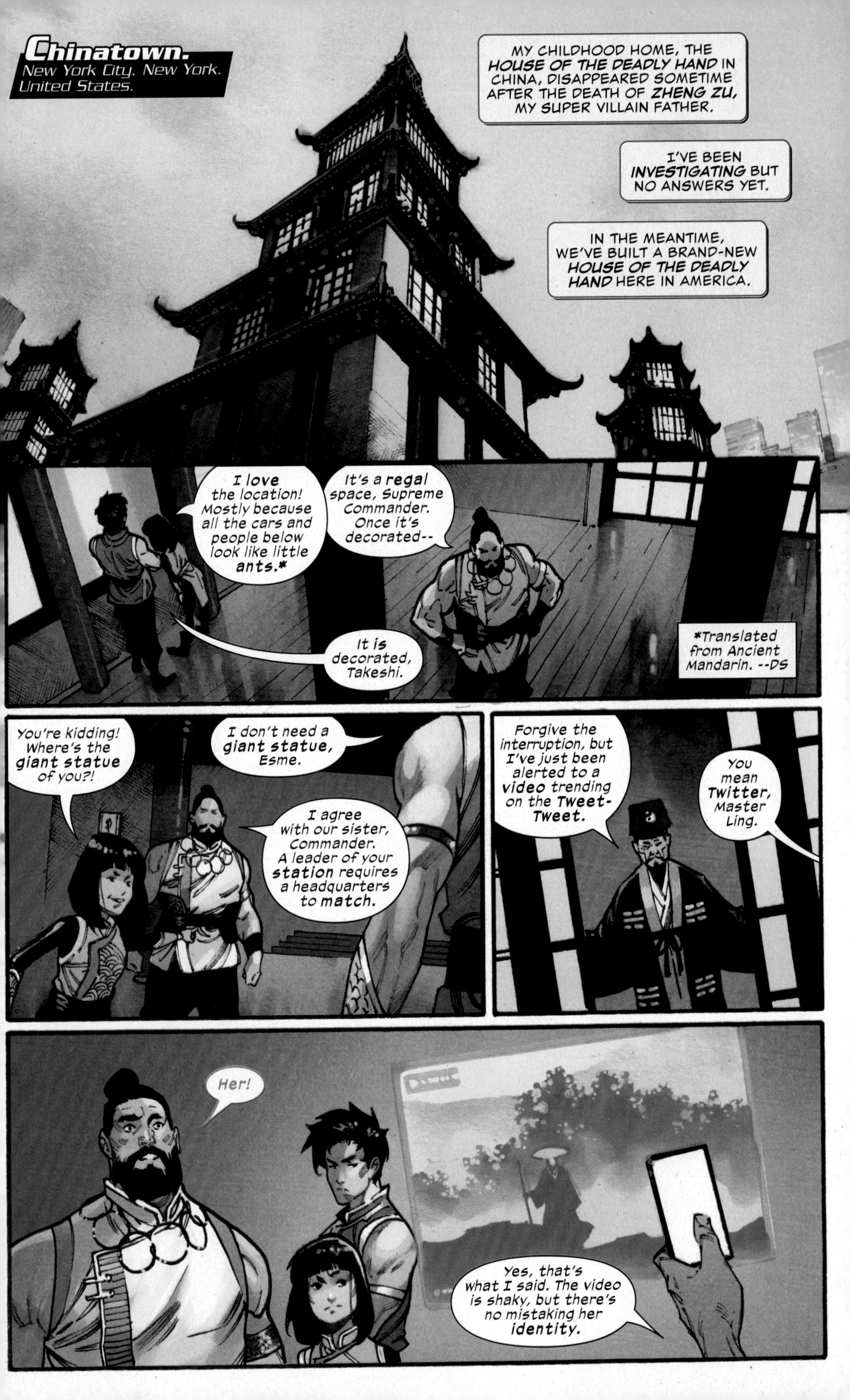
Chinatown.
New York City. New York. United States.
MY CHILDHOOD HOME, THE HOUSE OF THE DEADLY HAND IN CHINA, DISAPPEARED SOMETIME AFTER THE DEATH OF ZHENG ZU, MY SUPER VILLAIN FATHER.
I'VE BEEN INVESTIGATING BUT NO ANSWERS YET.
IN THE MEANTIME, WE'VE BUILT A BRAND-NEW HOUSE OF THE DEADLY HAND HERE IN AMERICA.
I love the location! Mostly because all the cars and people below look like little ants.*
It's a regal space, Supreme Commander. Once it's decorated--
It is decorated, Takeshi.
*Translated from Ancient Mandarin. --DS
You're kidding! Where's the giant statue of you?!
I don't need a giant statue, Esme.
I agree with our sister, Commander. A leader of your station requires a headquarters to match.
Forgive the interruption, but I've just been alerted to a video trending on the Tweet-Tweet.
You mean Twitter, Master Ling.
Her!
Yes, that's what I said. The video is shaky, but there's no mistaking her identity.

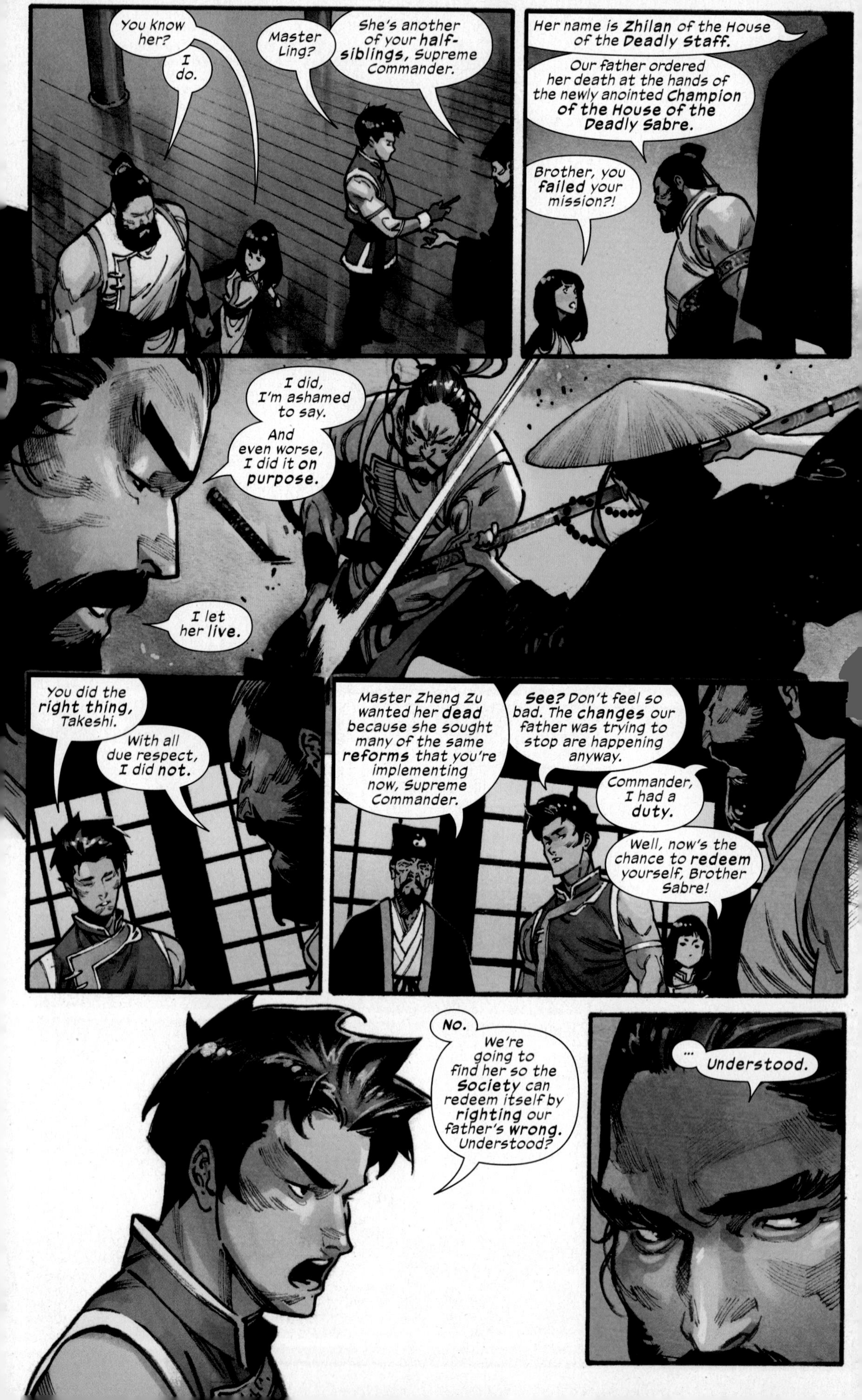
You know her?
I do.
Master Ling?
She's another of your half-siblings, Supreme Commander.
Her name is Zhilan of the House of the Deadly Staff.
Our father ordered her death at the hands of the newly anointed Champion of the House of the Deadly Sabre.
Brother, you failed your mission?!
I did, I'm ashamed to say.
And even worse, I did it on purpose.
I let her live.
You did the right thing, Takeshi.
With all due respect, I did not.
Master Zheng Zu wanted her dead because she sought many of the same reforms that you're implementing now, Supreme Commander.
See? Don't feel so bad. The changes our father was trying to stop are happening anyway.
Commander, I had a duty.
Well, now's the chance to redeem yourself, Brother Sabre!
No.
We're going to find her so the Society can redeem itself by righting our father's wrong. Understood?
... Understood.

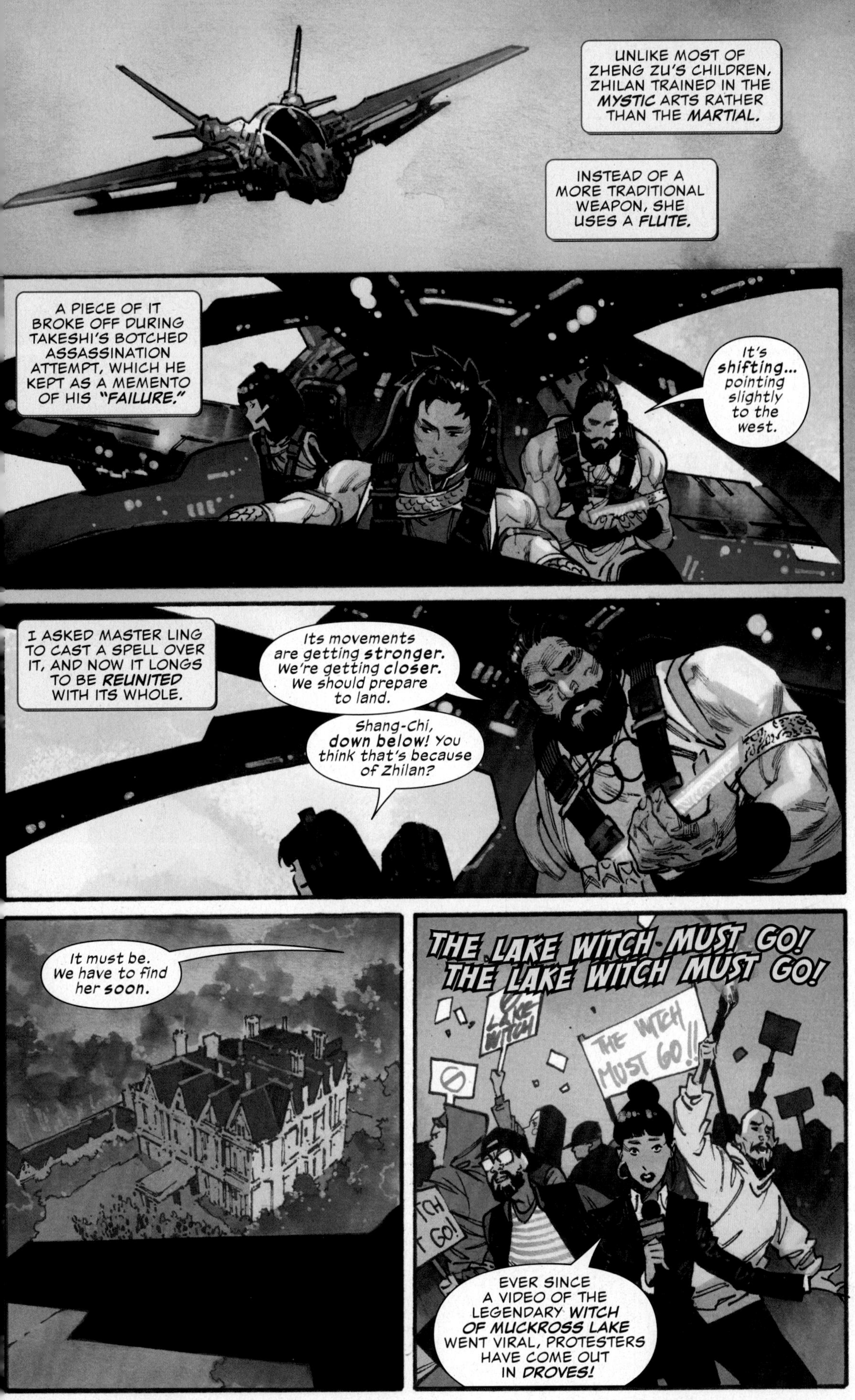

UNLIKE MOST OF ZHENG ZU'S CHILDREN, ZHILAN TRAINED IN THE MYSTIC ARTS RATHER THAN THE MARTIAL.
INSTEAD OF A MORE TRADITIONAL WEAPON, SHE USES A FLUTE.
A PIECE OF IT BROKE OFF DURING TAKESHI'S BOTCHED ASSASSINATION ATTEMPT, WHICH HE KEPT AS A MEMENTO OF HIS "FAILURE."
It's shifting... pointing slightly to the west.
I ASKED MASTER LING TO CAST A SPELL OVER IT, AND NOW IT LONGS TO BE REUNITED WITH ITS WHOLE.
Its movements are getting stronger. We're getting closer. We should prepare to land.
Shang-Chi, down below! You think that's because of Zhilan?
It must be. We have to find her soon.
THE LAKE WITCH MUST GO! THE LAKE WITCH MUST GO!
THE WITCH MUST GO!!
EVER SINCE A VIDEO OF THE LEGENDARY WITCH OF MUCKROSS LAKE WENT VIRAL, PROTESTERS HAVE COME OUT IN DROVES!

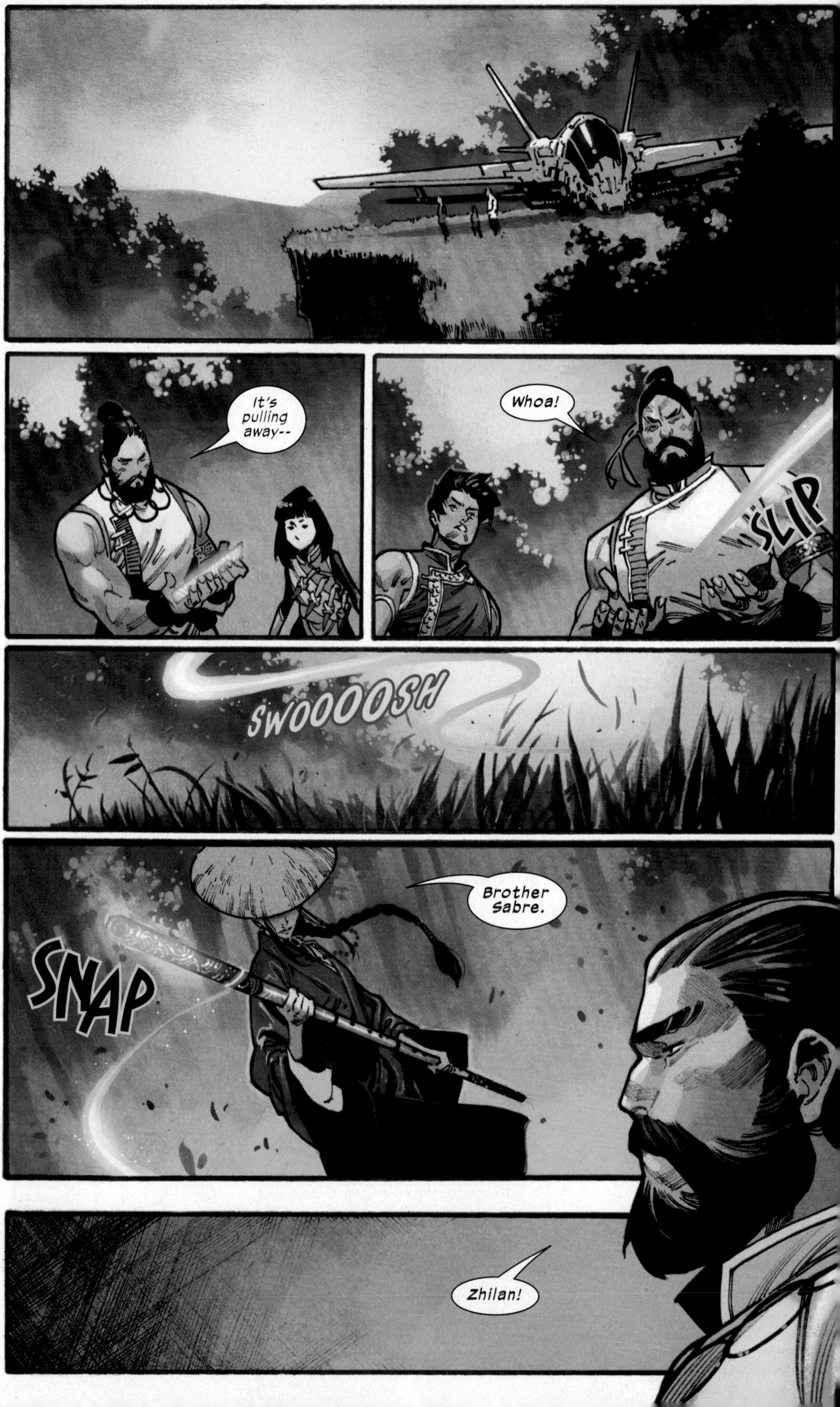
It's pulling away--
Whoa!
SLIP
SWOOOOSH
SNAP
Brother Sabre.
Zhilan!

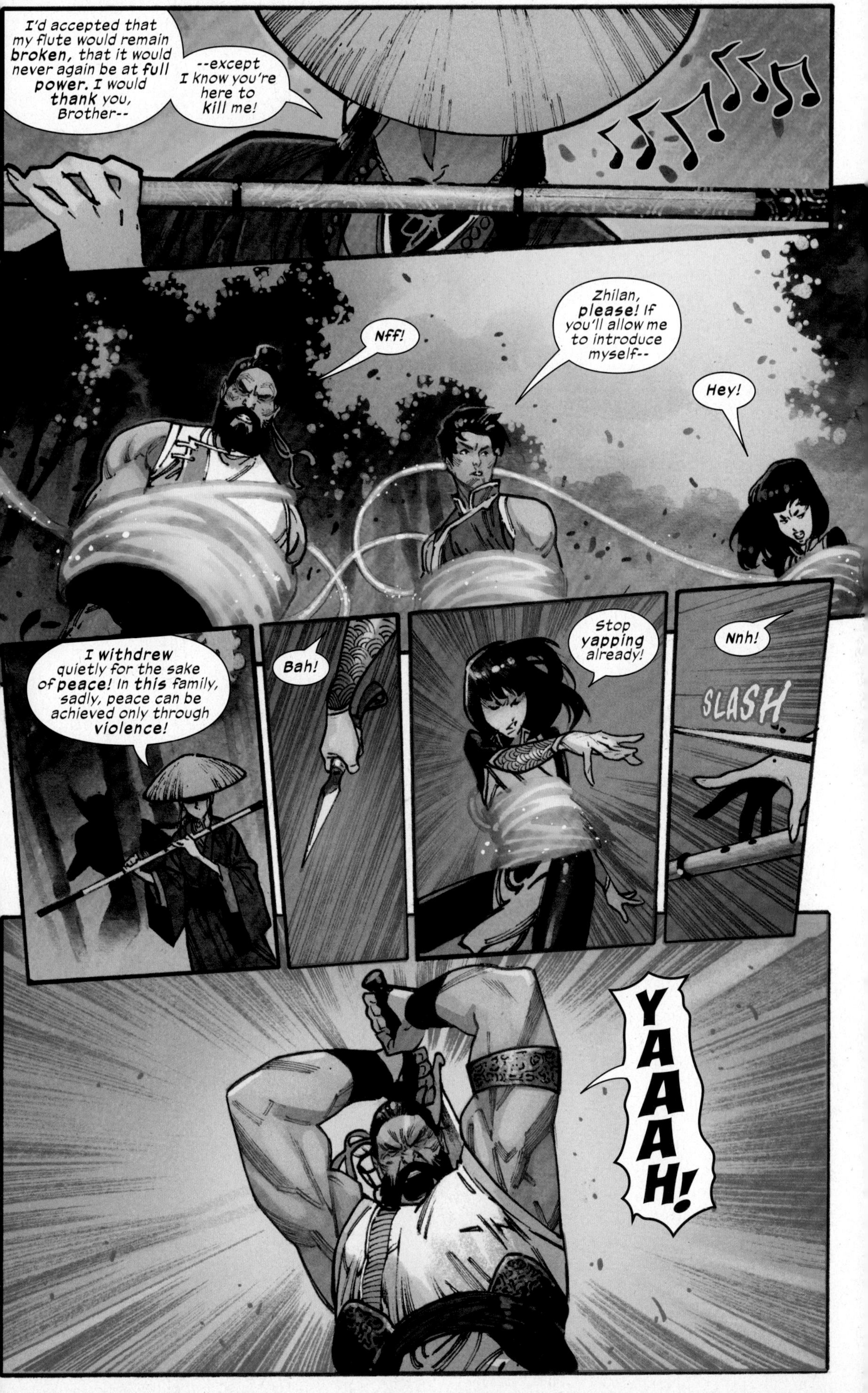
I'd accepted that my flute would remain broken, that it would never again be at full power. I would thank you, Brother--
--except I know you're here to kill me!
Nff!
Zhilan, please! If you'll allow me to introduce myself--
Hey!
I withdrew quietly for the sake of peace! In this family, sadly, peace can be achieved only through violence!
Bah!
Stop yapping already!
Nnh!
SLASH
YAAAH!

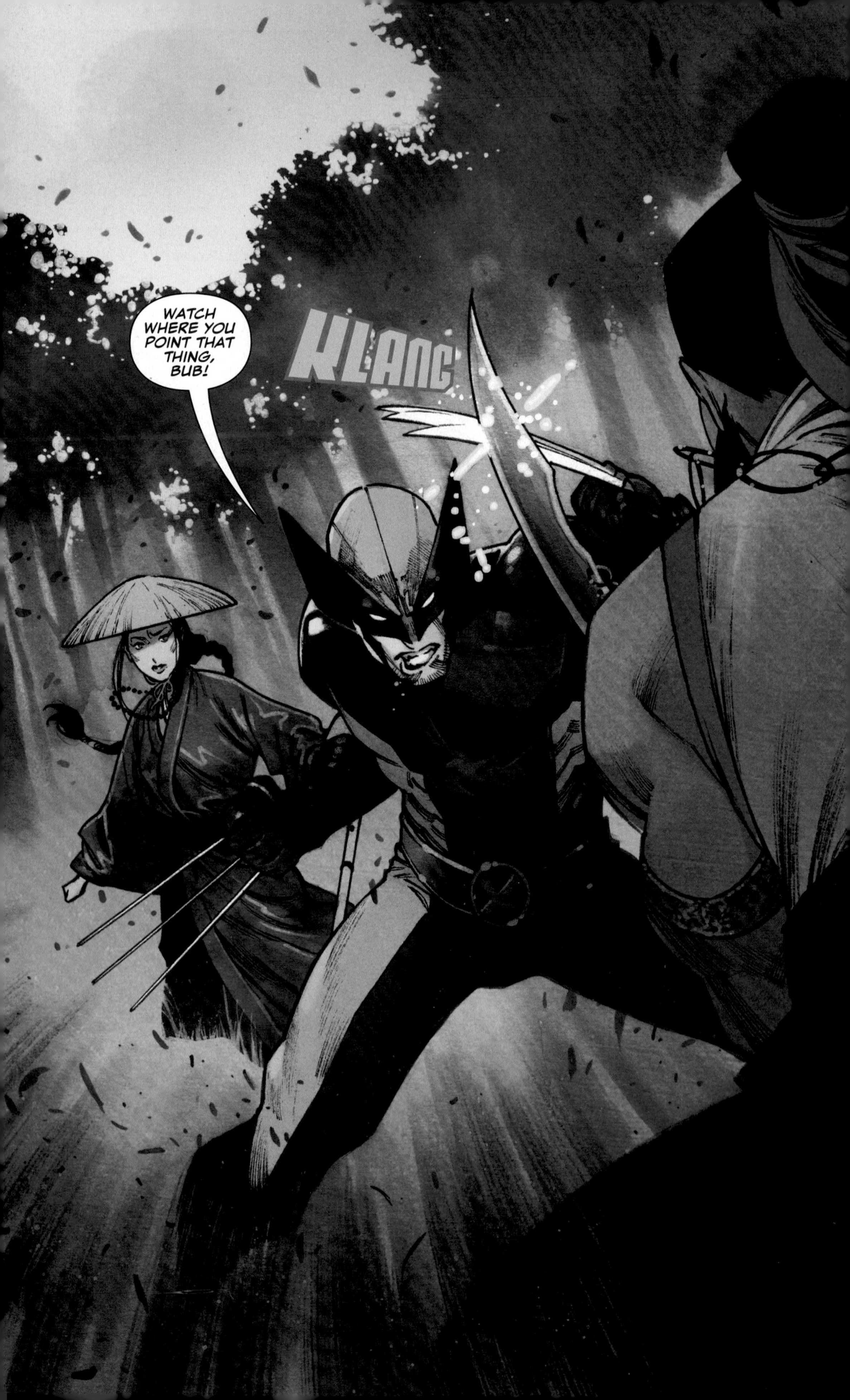
WATCH WHERE YOU POINT THAT THING, BUB!
KLANG

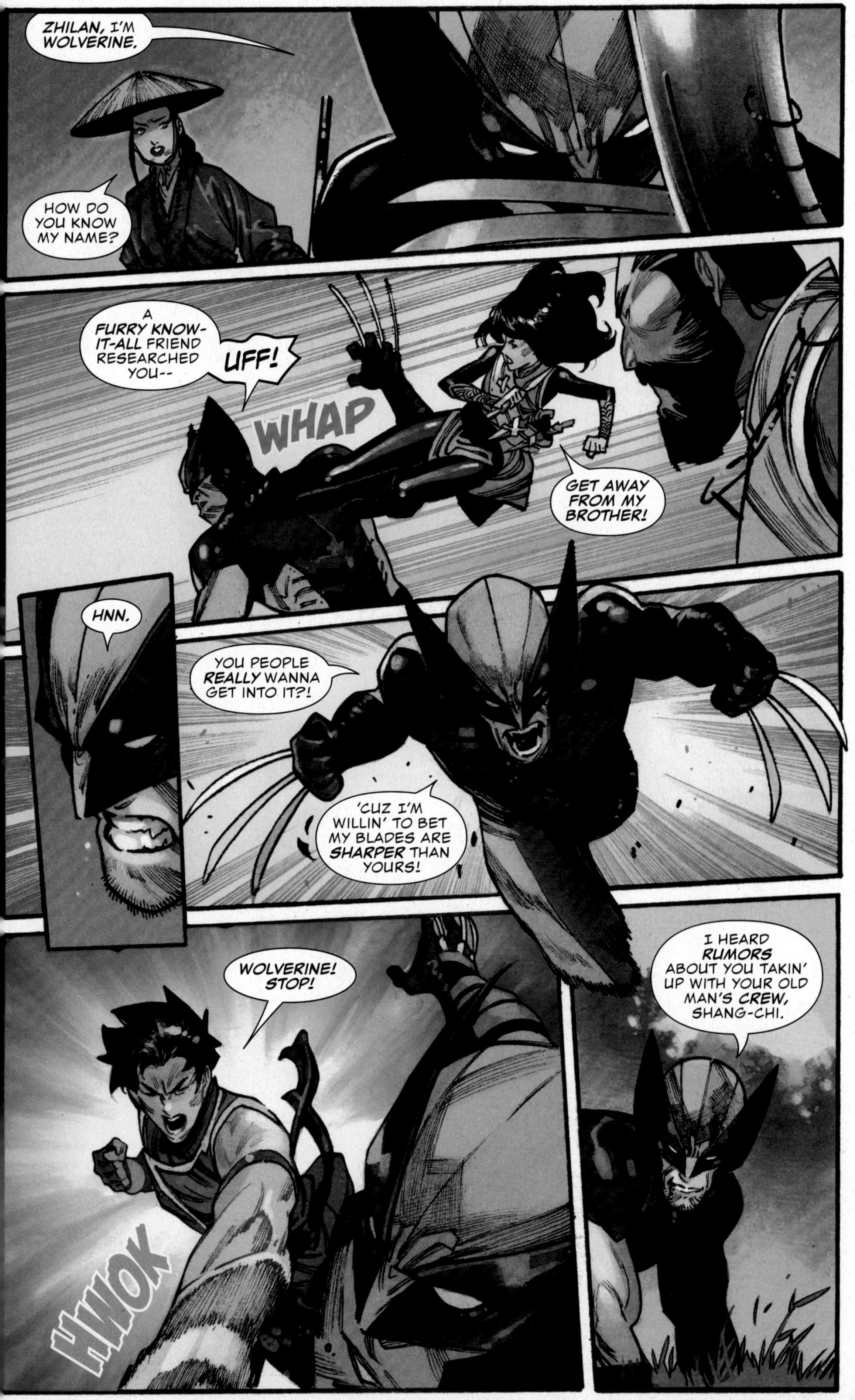
ZHILAN, I'M WOLVERINE.
HOW DO YOU KNOW MY NAME?
A FURRY KNOW-IT-ALL FRIEND RESEARCHED YOU--
UFF!
WHAP
GET AWAY FROM MY BROTHER!
HNN.
YOU PEOPLE REALLY WANNA GET INTO IT?!
'CUZ I'M WILLIN' TO BET MY BLADES ARE SHARPER THAN YOURS!
WOLVERINE! STOP!
HWOK
I HEARD RUMORS ABOUT YOU TAKIN' UP WITH YOUR OLD MAN'S CREW, SHANG-CHI.

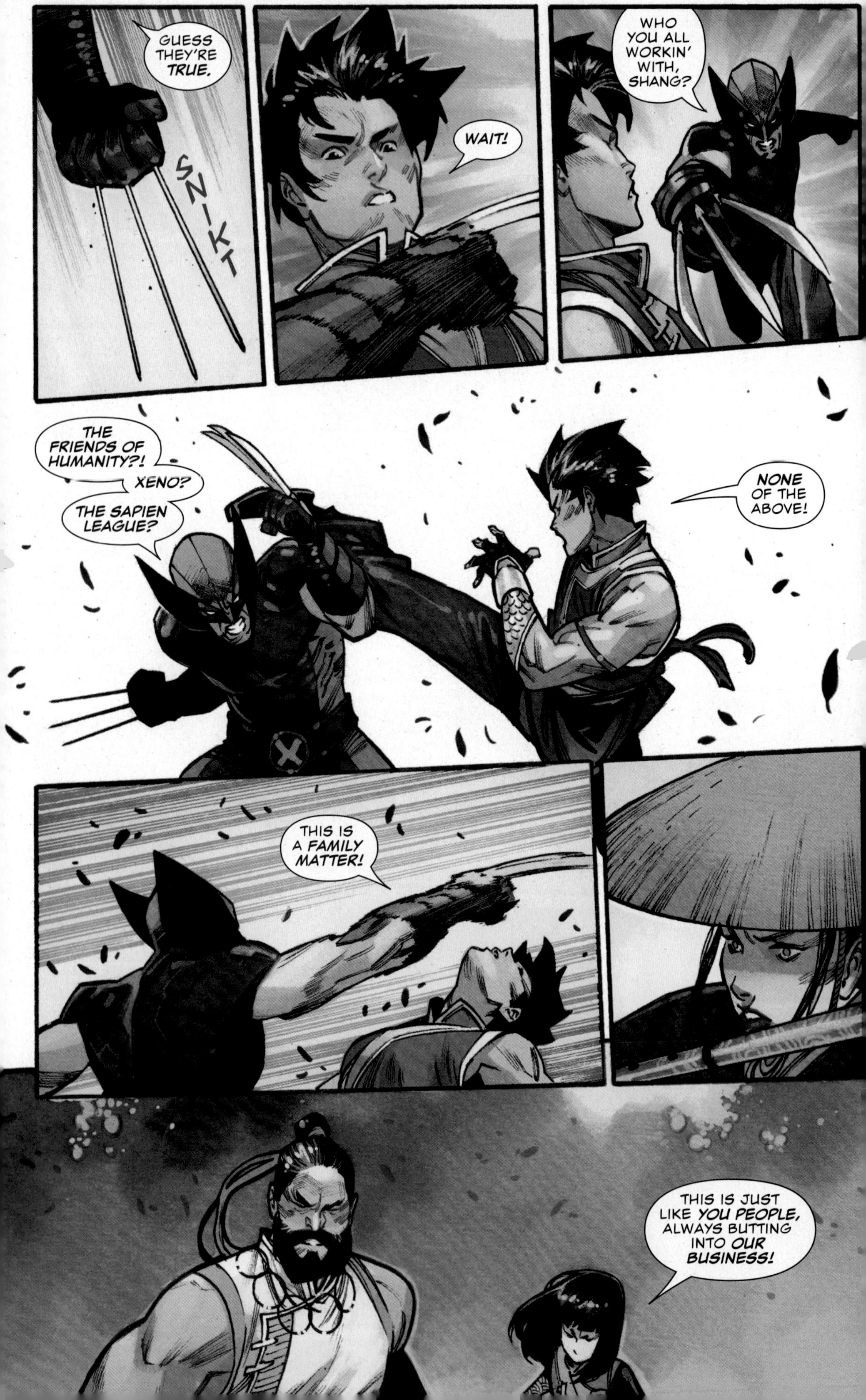
GUESS THEY'RE TRUE.
SNIKT
WAIT!
WHO YOU ALL WORKIN' WITH, SHANG?
THE FRIENDS OF HUMANITY?!
XENO?
THE SAPIEN LEAGUE?
NONE OF THE ABOVE!
THIS IS A FAMILY MATTER!
THIS IS JUST LIKE YOU PEOPLE, ALWAYS BUTTING INTO OUR BUSINESS!

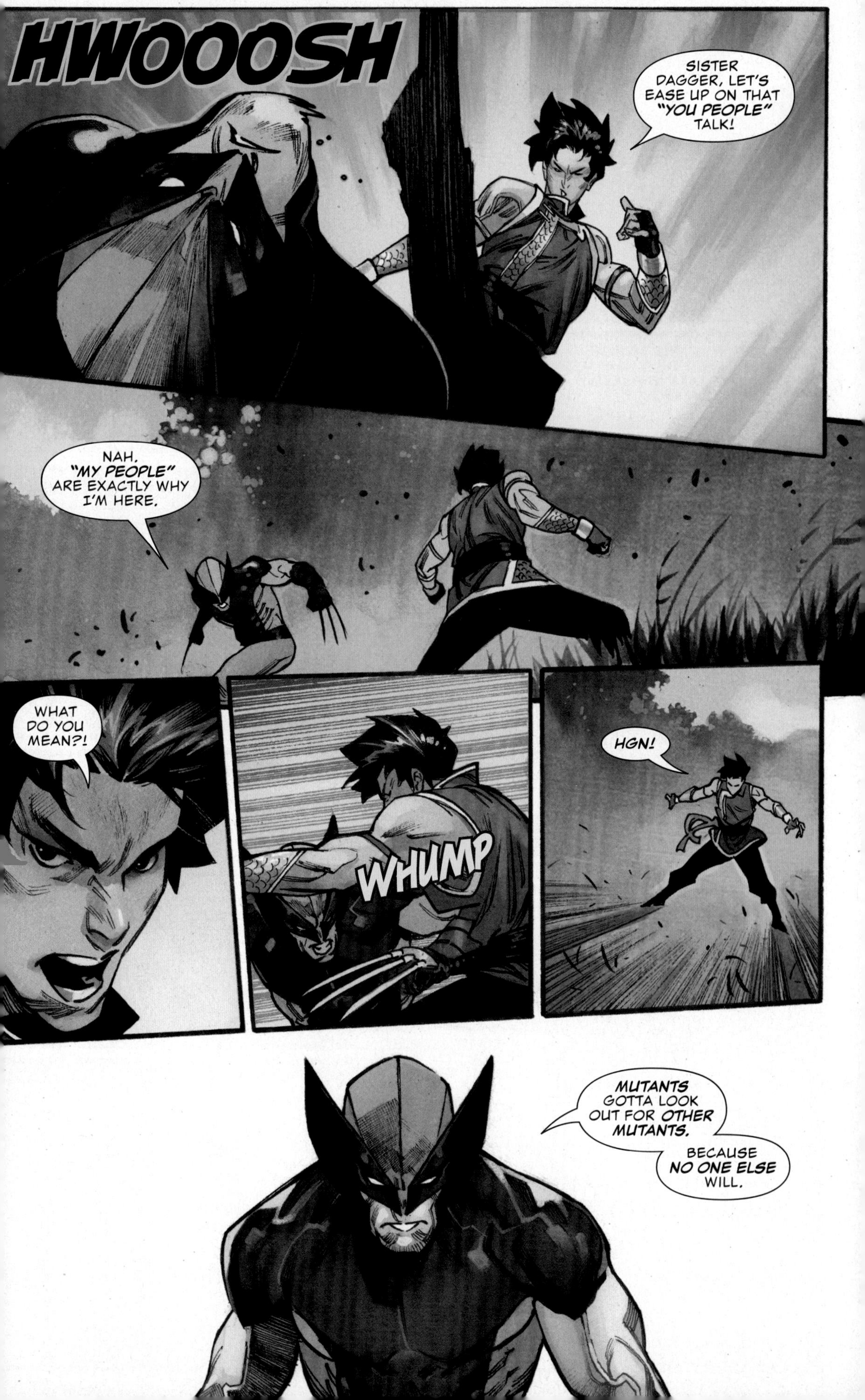
HWOOOSH
SISTER DAGGER, LET'S EASE UP ON THAT "YOU PEOPLE" TALK!
NAH. "MY PEOPLE" ARE EXACTLY WHY I'M HERE.
WHAT DO YOU MEAN?!
WHUMP
HGN!
MUTANTS GOTTA LOOK OUT FOR OTHER MUTANTS.
BECAUSE NO ONE ELSE WILL.

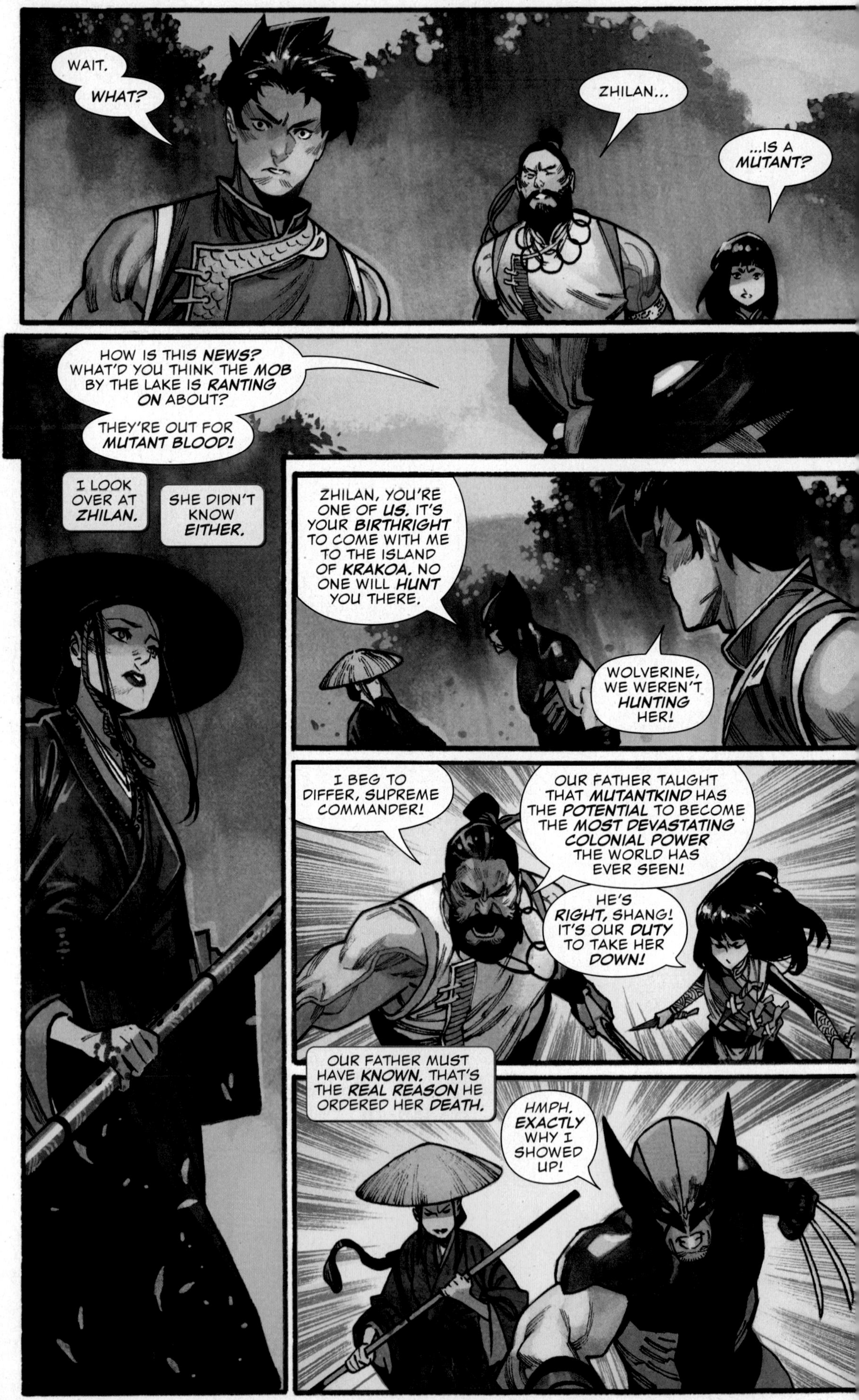
WAIT. WHAT?
ZHILAN...
...IS A MUTANT?
HOW IS THIS NEWS? WHAT'D YOU THINK THE MOB BY THE LAKE IS RANTING ON ABOUT?
THEY'RE OUT FOR MUTANT BLOOD!
I LOOK OVER AT ZHILAN.
SHE DIDN'T KNOW EITHER.
ZHILAN, YOU'RE ONE OF US. IT'S YOUR BIRTHRIGHT TO COME WITH ME TO THE ISLAND OF KRAKOA. NO ONE WILL HUNT YOU THERE.
WOLVERINE, WE WEREN'T HUNTING HER!
I BEG TO DIFFER, SUPREME COMMANDER!
OUR FATHER TAUGHT THAT MUTANTKIND HAS THE POTENTIAL TO BECOME THE MOST DEVASTATING COLONIAL POWER THE WORLD HAS EVER SEEN!
HE'S RIGHT, SHANG! IT'S OUR DUTY TO TAKE HER DOWN!
OUR FATHER MUST HAVE KNOWN. THAT'S THE REAL REASON HE ORDERED HER DEATH.
HMPH. EXACTLY WHY I SHOWED UP!

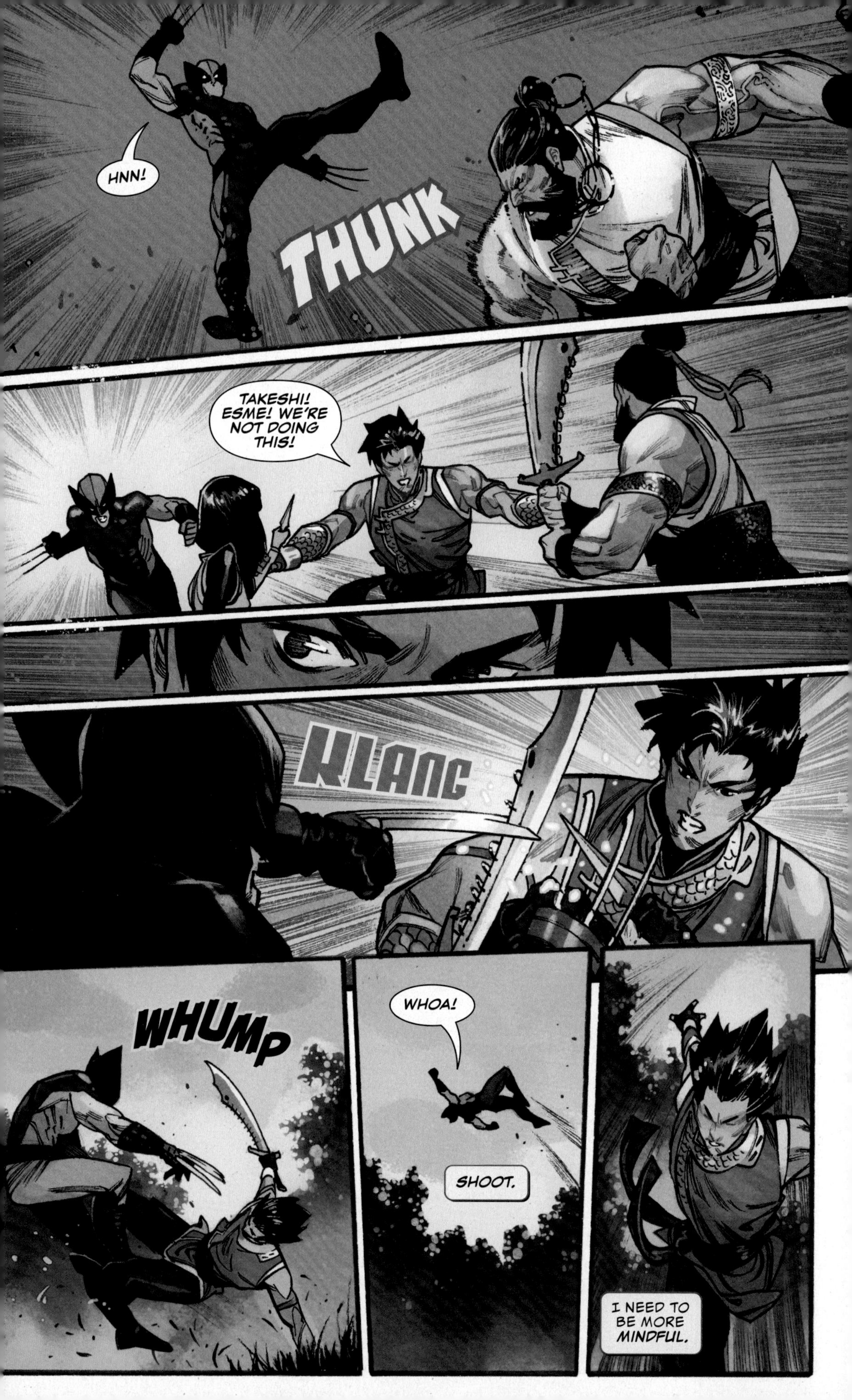
HNN!
THUNK
TAKESHI! ESME! WE'RE NOT DOING THIS!
KLANG
WHUMP
WHOA!
SHOOT.
I NEED TO BE MORE MINDFUL.

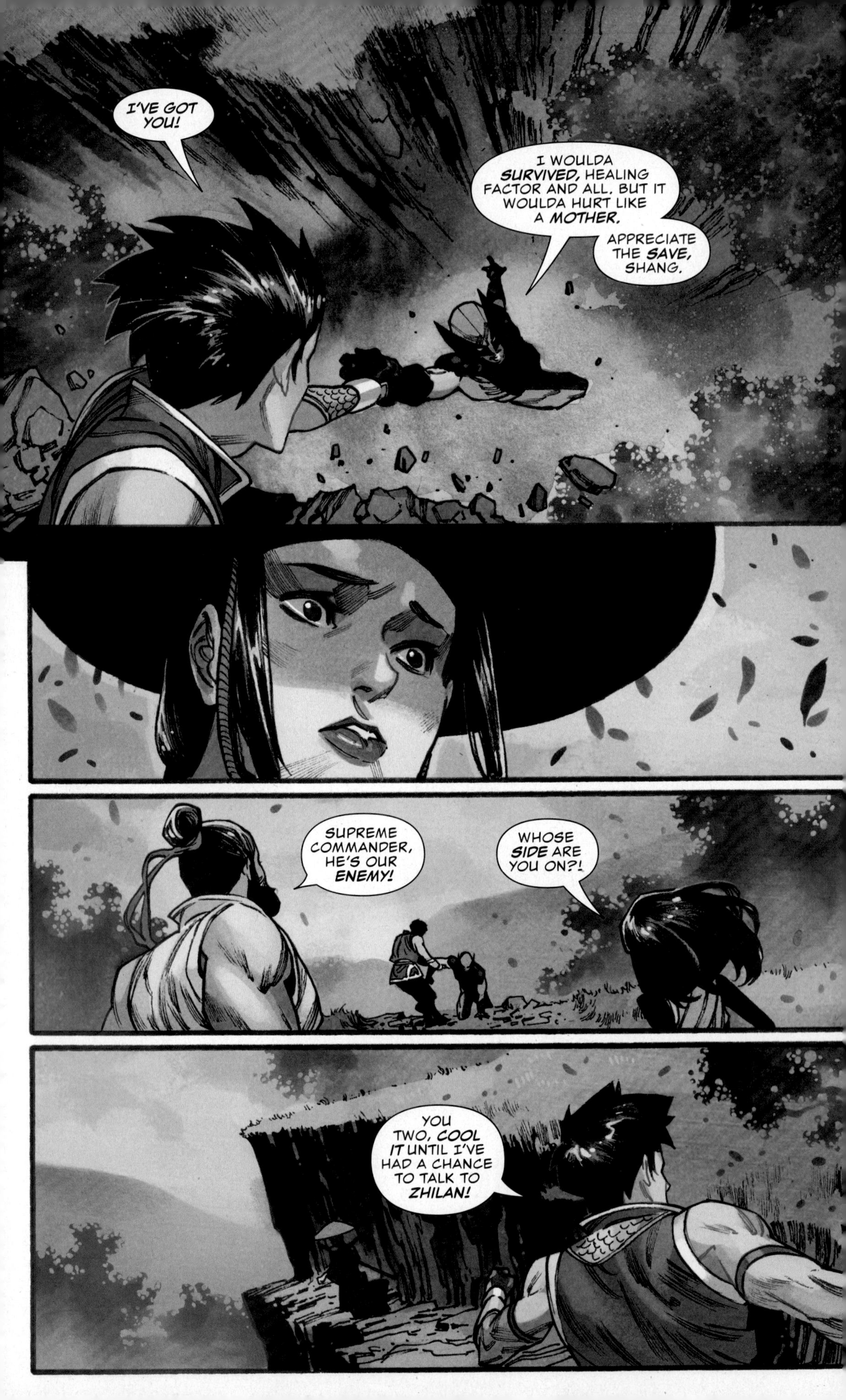
I'VE GOT YOU!
I WOULDA SURVIVED, HEALING FACTOR AND ALL. BUT IT WOULDA HURT LIKE A MOTHER.
APPRECIATE THE SAVE, SHANG.
SUPREME COMMANDER, HE'S OUR ENEMY!
WHOSE SIDE ARE YOU ON?!
YOU TWO, COOL IT UNTIL I'VE HAD A CHANCE TO TALK TO ZHILAN!

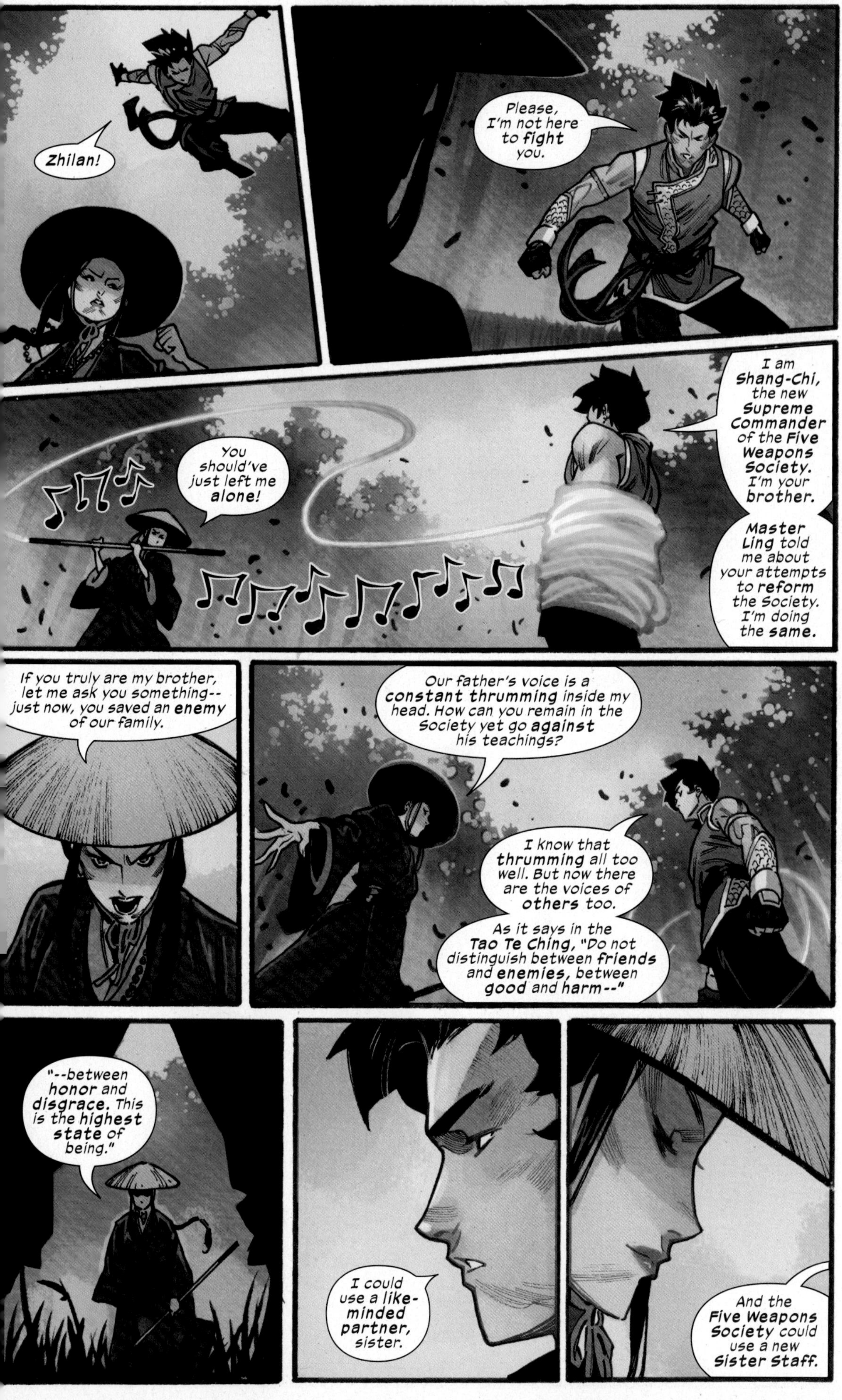
Zhilan!
Please, I'm not here to fight you.
I am Shang-Chi, the new Supreme Commander of the Five Weapons Society. I'm your brother.
Master Ling told me about your attempts to reform the Society. I'm doing the same.
You should've just left me alone!
If you truly are my brother, let me ask you something-- just now, you saved an enemy of our family.
Our father's voice is a constant thrumming inside my head. How can you remain in the Society yet go against his teachings?
I know that thrumming all too well. But now there are the voices of others too.
As it says in the Tao Te Ching, "Do not distinguish between friends and enemies, between good and harm--"
"--between honor and disgrace. This is the highest state of being."
I could use a like-minded partner, sister.
And the Five Weapons Society could use a new Sister Staff.

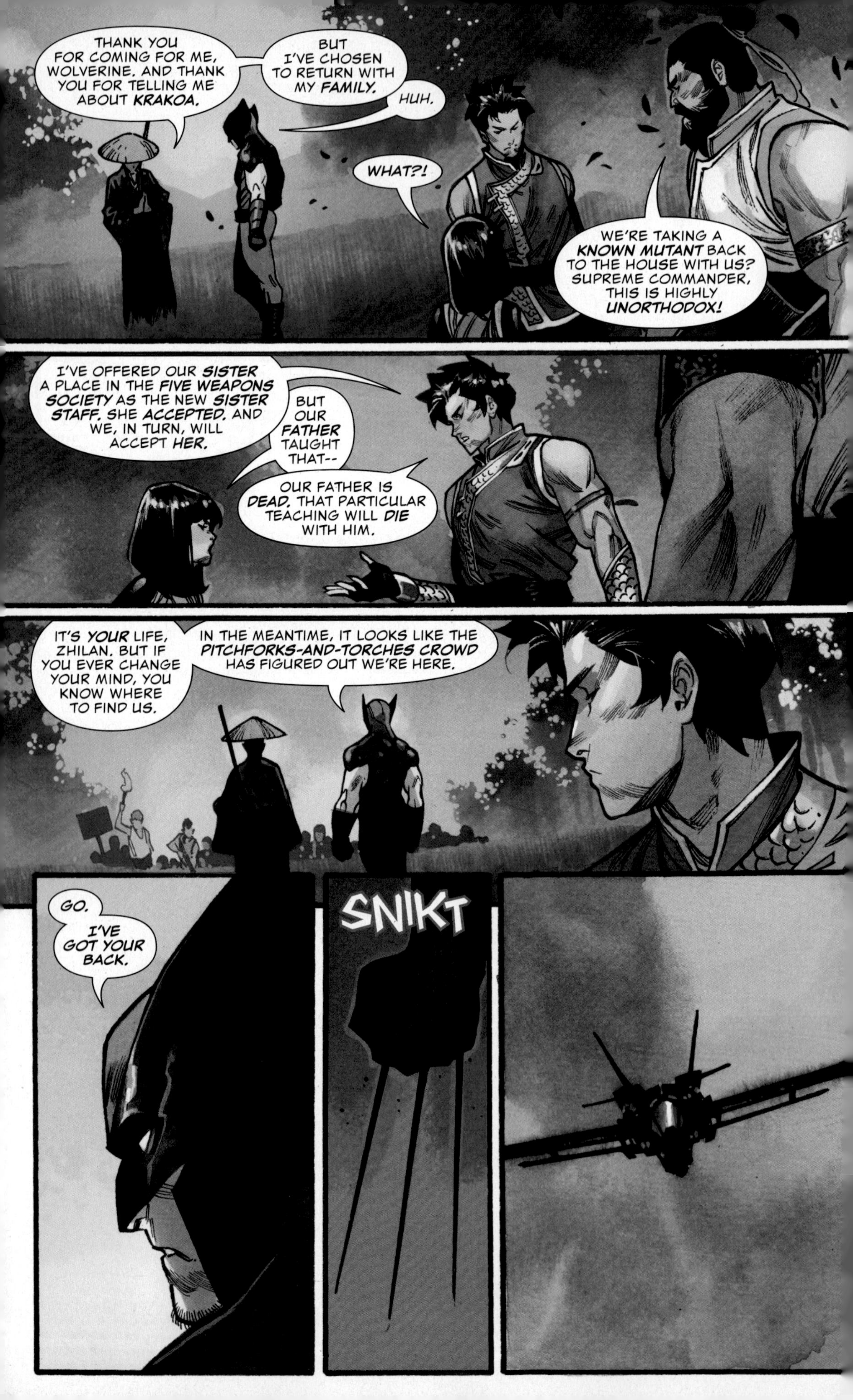

THANK YOU FOR COMING FOR ME, WOLVERINE. AND THANK YOU FOR TELLING ME ABOUT KRAKOA.
BUT I'VE CHOSEN TO RETURN WITH MY FAMILY.
HUH.
WHAT?!
WE'RE TAKING A KNOWN MUTANT BACK TO THE HOUSE WITH US? SUPREME COMMANDER, THIS IS HIGHLY UNORTHODOX!
I'VE OFFERED OUR SISTER A PLACE IN THE FIVE WEAPONS SOCIETY AS THE NEW SISTER STAFF. SHE ACCEPTED. AND WE, IN TURN, WILL ACCEPT HER.
BUT OUR FATHER TAUGHT THAT--
OUR FATHER IS DEAD. THAT PARTICULAR TEACHING WILL DIE WITH HIM.
IT'S YOUR LIFE, ZHILAN. BUT IF YOU EVER CHANGE YOUR MIND, YOU KNOW WHERE TO FIND US.
IN THE MEANTIME, IT LOOKS LIKE THE PITCHFORKS-AND-TORCHES CROWD HAS FIGURED OUT WE'RE HERE.
GO.
I'VE GOT YOUR BACK.
SNIKT

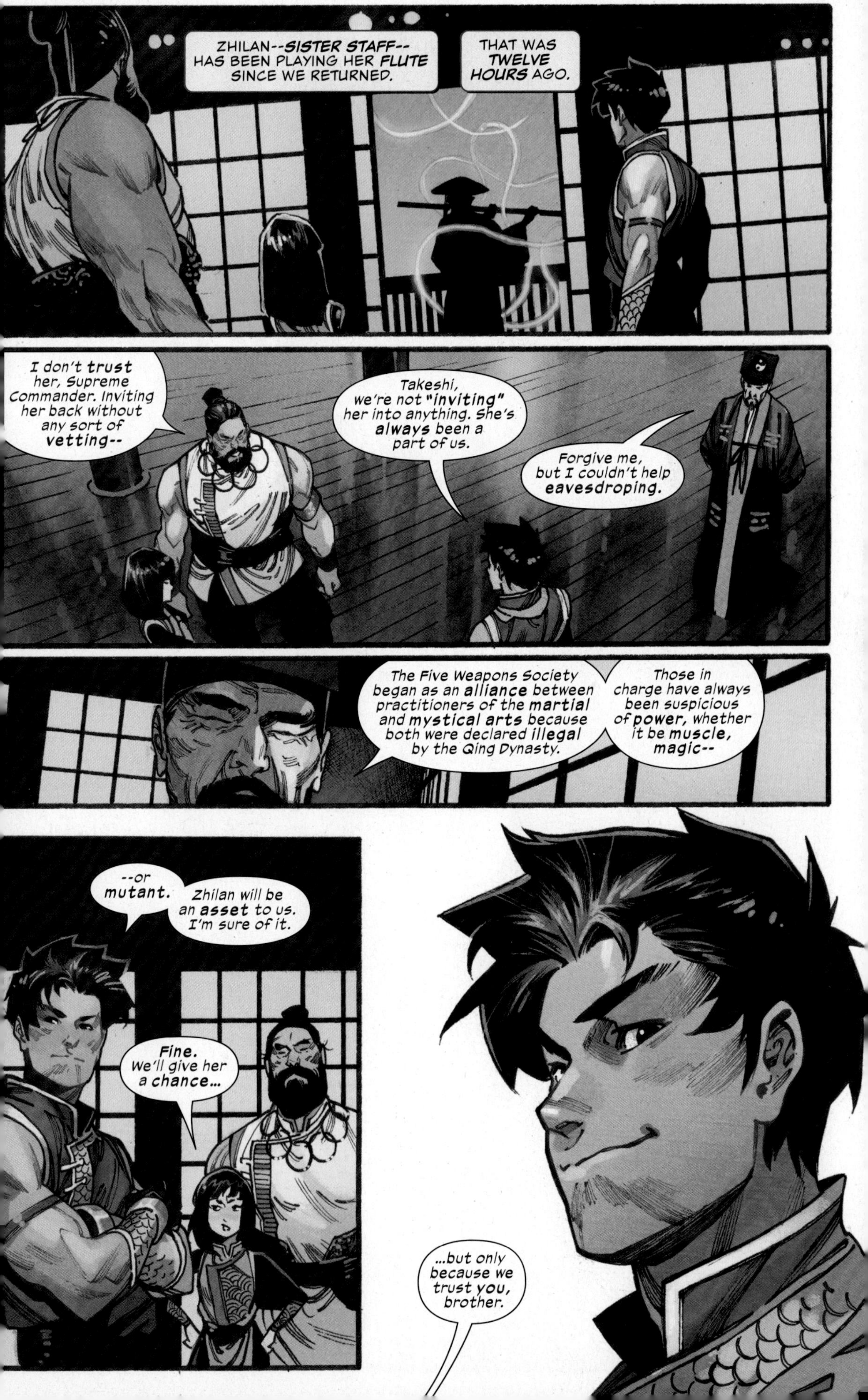
ZHILAN--SISTER STAFF--HAS BEEN PLAYING HER FLUTE SINCE WE RETURNED.
THAT WAS TWELVE HOURS AGO.
I don't trust her, Supreme Commander. Inviting her back without any sort of vetting--
Takeshi, we're not "inviting" her into anything. She's always been a part of us.
Forgive me, but I couldn't help eavesdroping.
The Five Weapons Society began as an alliance between practitioners of the martial and mystical arts because both were declared illegal by the Qing Dynasty.
Those in charge have always been suspicious of power, whether it be muscle, magic--
--or mutant.
Zhilan will be an asset to us. I'm sure of it.
Fine. We'll give her a chance...
...but only because we trust you, brother.

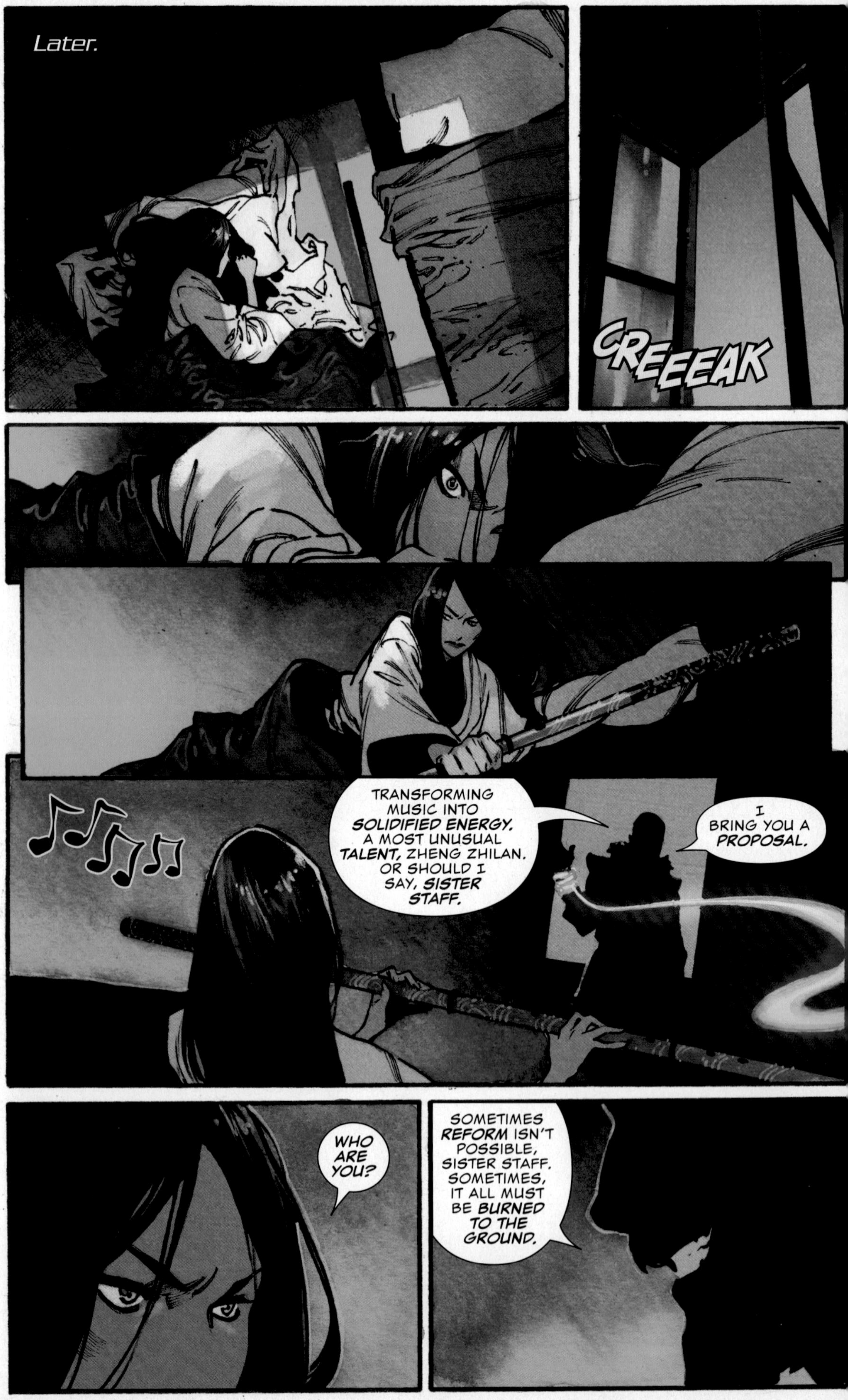
Later.
CREEEAK
TRANSFORMING MUSIC INTO SOLIDIFIED ENERGY. A MOST UNUSUAL TALENT, ZHENG ZHILAN. OR SHOULD I SAY, SISTER STAFF.
I BRING YOU A PROPOSAL.
WHO ARE YOU?
SOMETIMES REFORM ISN'T POSSIBLE, SISTER STAFF. SOMETIMES, IT ALL MUST BE BURNED TO THE GROUND.

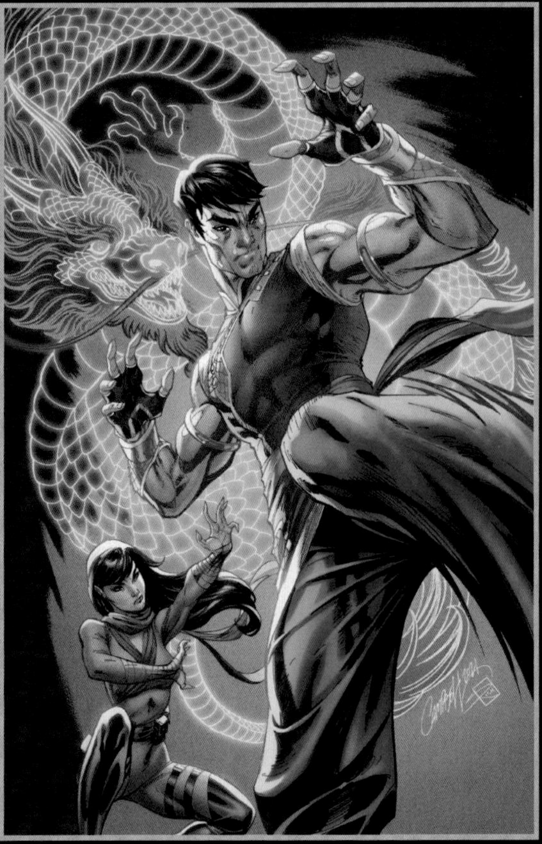

#1 VARIANT BY
J. SCOTT CAMPBELL & SABINE RICH

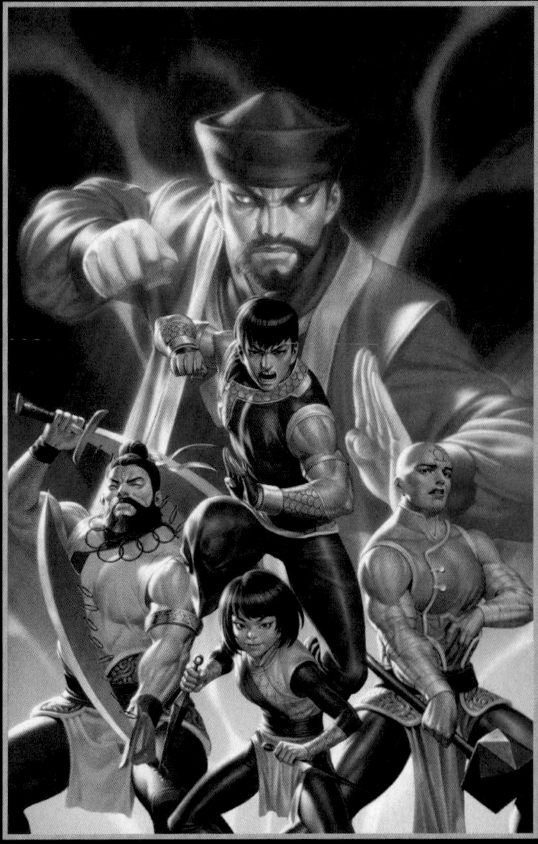

#1 VARIANT BY
JUNGGEUN YOON

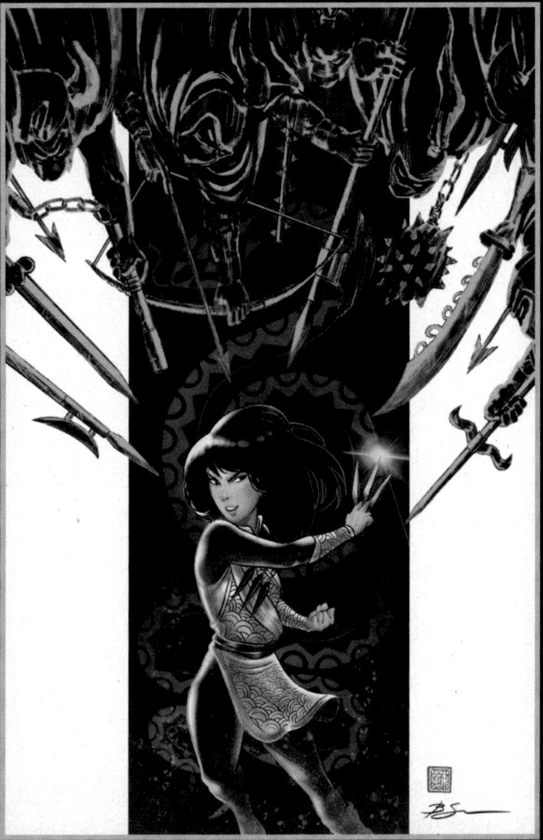

#1 VARIANT BY
BENJAMIN SU

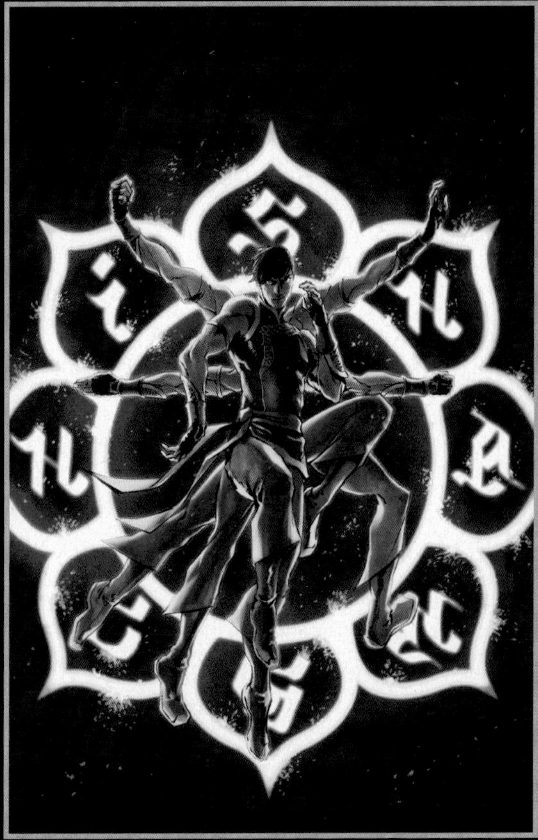

#1 VARIANT BY
SUPERLOG

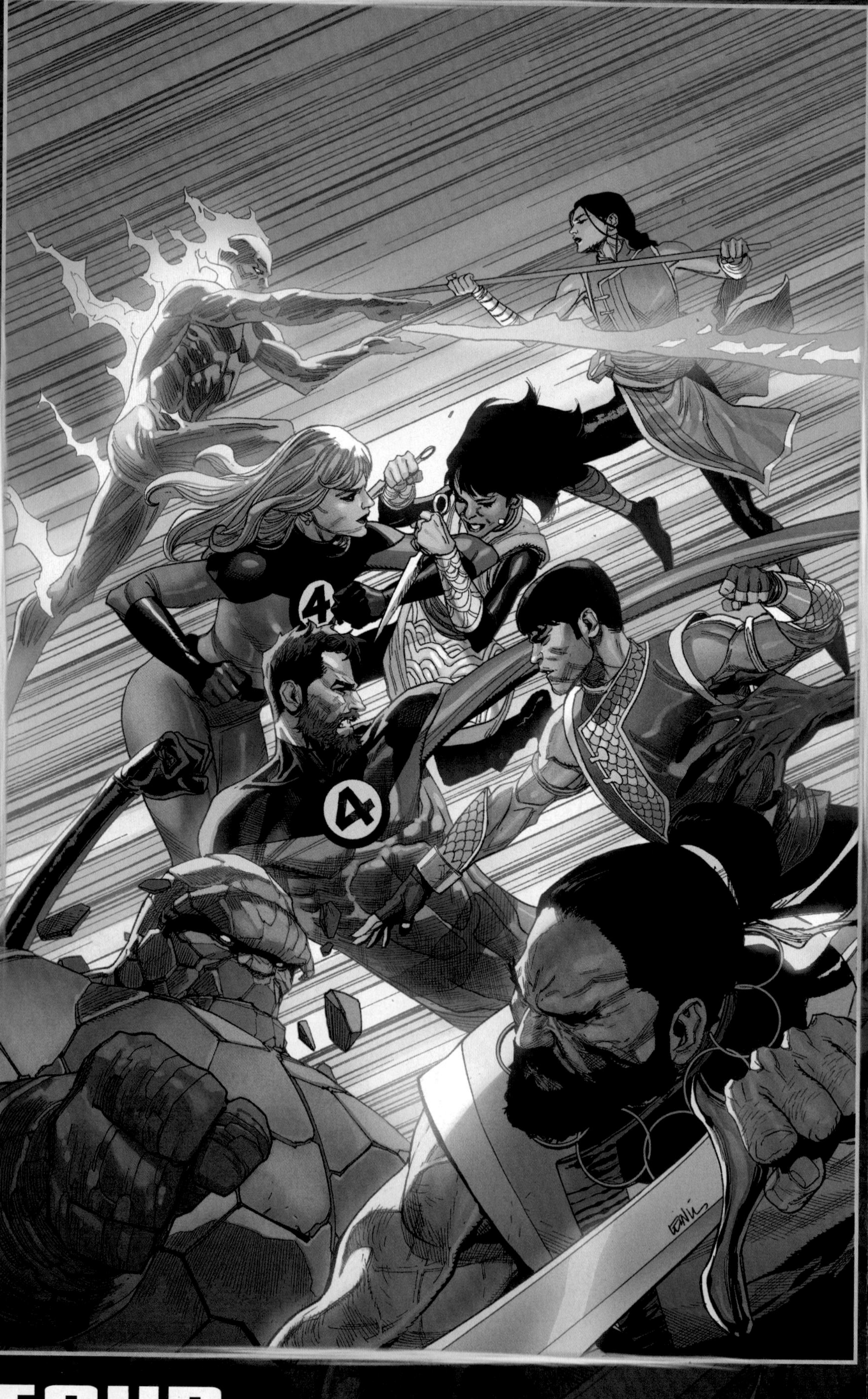

FOUR

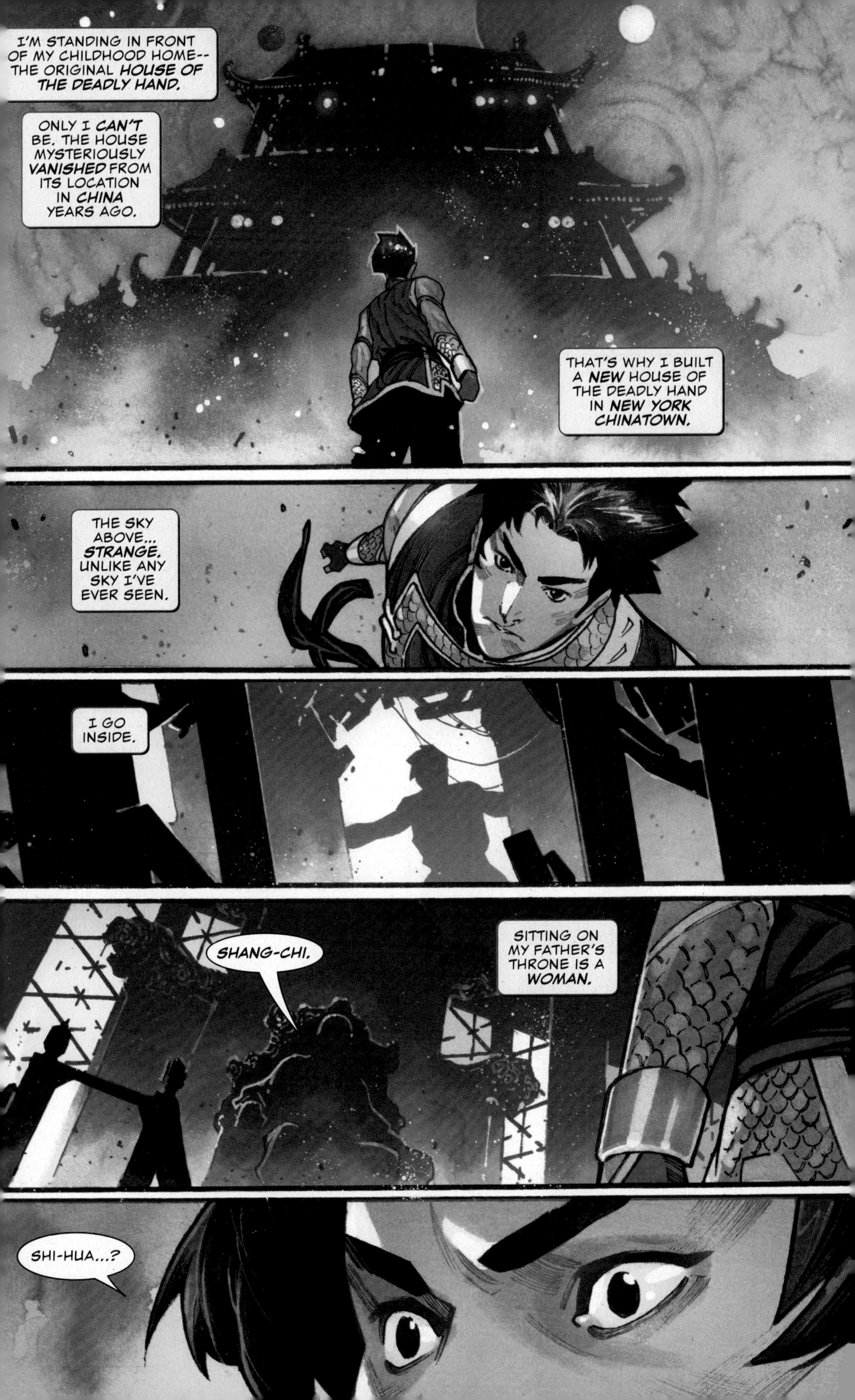
I'M STANDING IN FRONT OF MY CHILDHOOD HOME-- THE ORIGINAL HOUSE OF THE DEADLY HAND.
ONLY I CAN'T BE. THE HOUSE MYSTERIOUSLY VANISHED FROM ITS LOCATION IN CHINA YEARS AGO.
THAT'S WHY I BUILT A NEW HOUSE OF THE DEADLY HAND IN NEW YORK CHINATOWN.
THE SKY ABOVE... STRANGE. UNLIKE ANY SKY I'VE EVER SEEN.
I GO INSIDE.
SHANG-CHI.
SITTING ON MY FATHER'S THRONE IS A WOMAN.
SHI-HUA...?

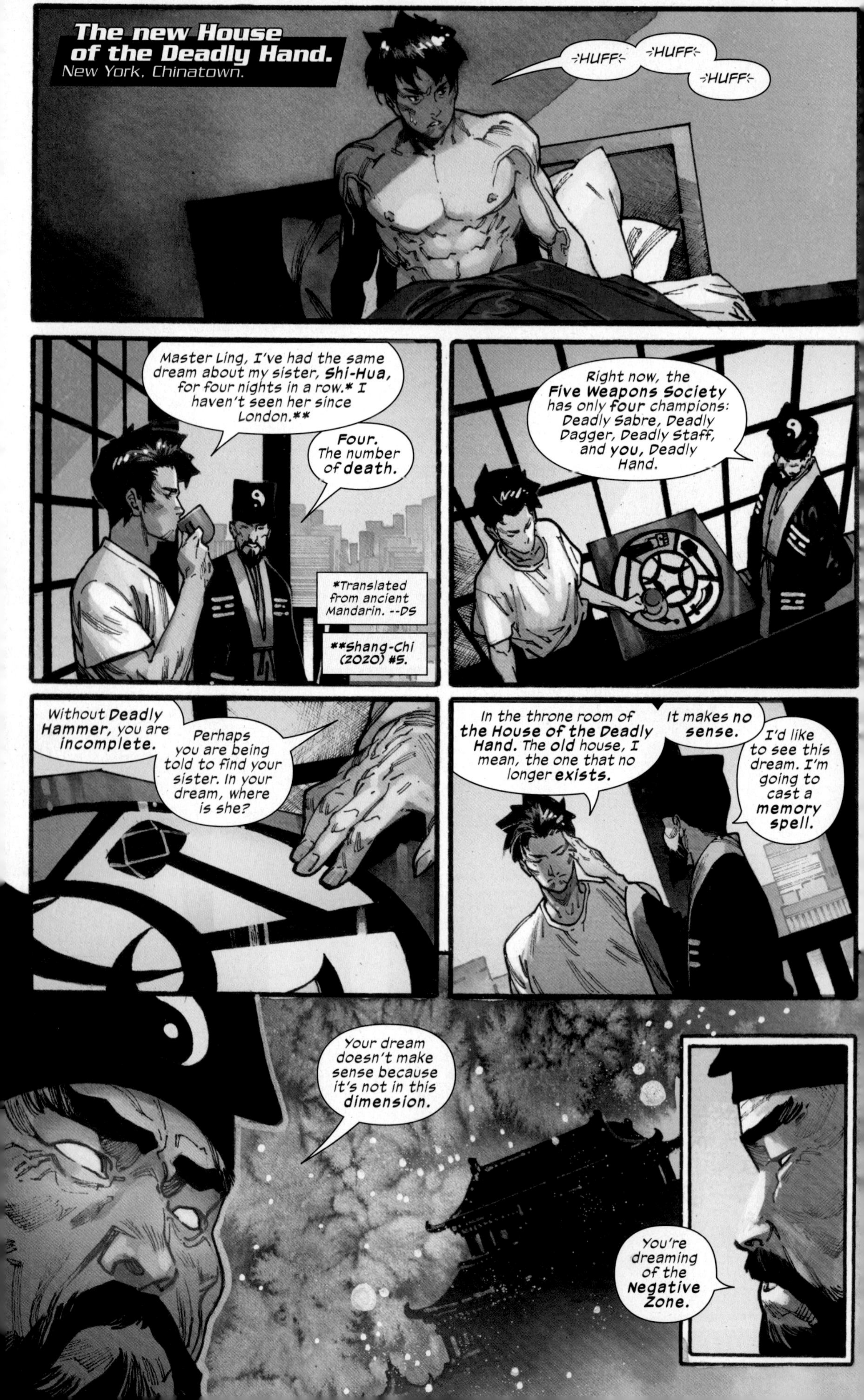
The new House of the Deadly Hand.
New York, Chinatown.
HUFF
HUFF
HUFF
Master Ling, I've had the same dream about my sister, Shi-Hua, for four nights in a row.* I haven't seen her since London.**
Four. The number of death.
*Translated from ancient Mandarin. --DS
**Shang-Chi (2020) #5.
Right now, the Five Weapons Society has only four champions: Deadly Sabre, Deadly Dagger, Deadly Staff, and you, Deadly Hand.
Without Deadly Hammer, you are incomplete.
Perhaps you are being told to find your sister. In your dream, where is she?
In the throne room of the House of the Deadly Hand. The old house, I mean, the one that no longer exists.
It makes no sense.
I'd like to see this dream. I'm going to cast a memory spell.
Your dream doesn't make sense because it's not in this dimension.
You're dreaming of the Negative Zone.

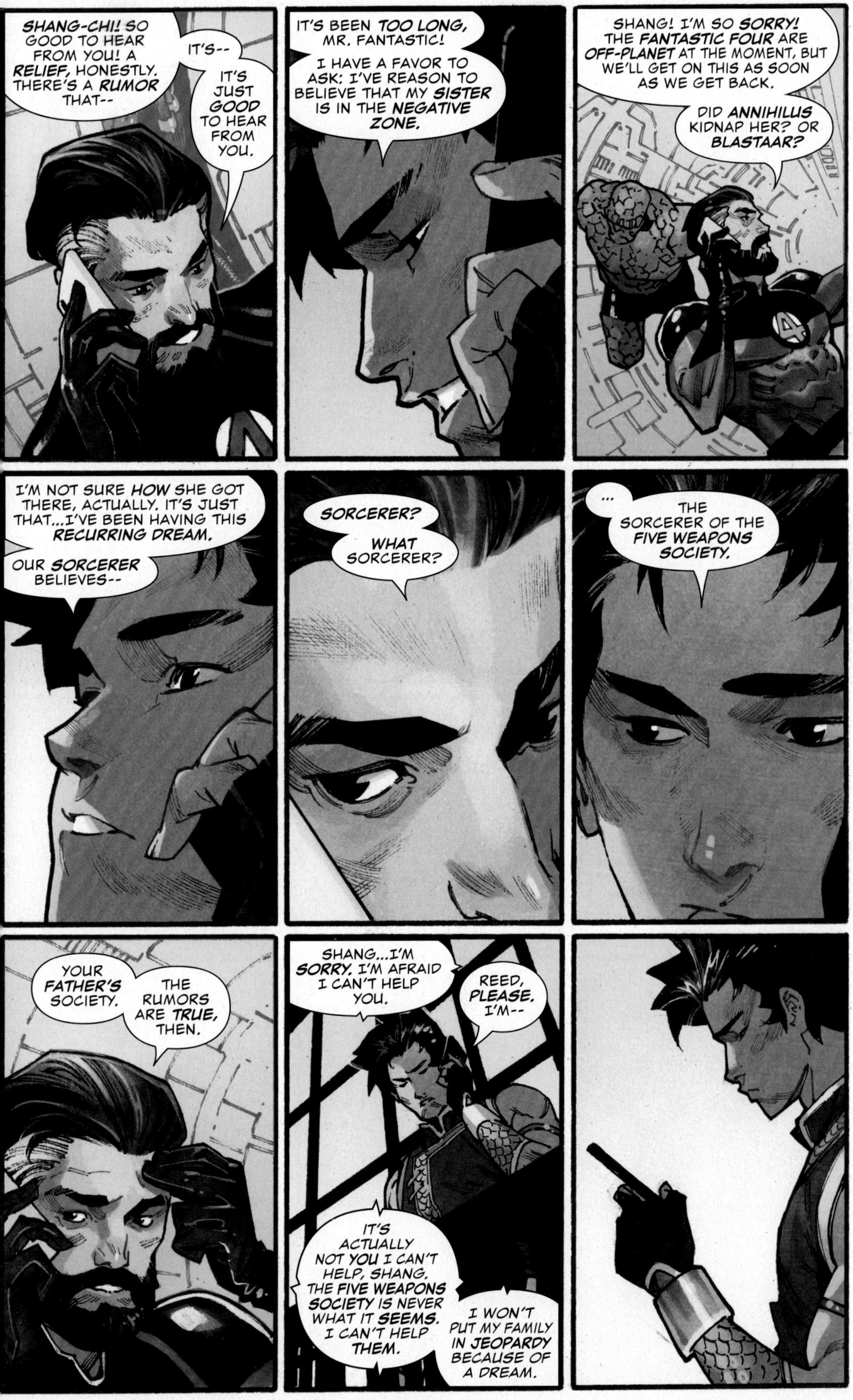
SHANG-CHI! SO GOOD TO HEAR FROM YOU! A RELIEF, HONESTLY. THERE'S A RUMOR THAT--
IT'S--
IT'S JUST GOOD TO HEAR FROM YOU.
IT'S BEEN TOO LONG, MR. FANTASTIC!
I HAVE A FAVOR TO ASK: I'VE REASON TO BELIEVE THAT MY SISTER IS IN THE NEGATIVE ZONE.
SHANG! I'M SO SORRY! THE FANTASTIC FOUR ARE OFF-PLANET AT THE MOMENT, BUT WE'LL GET ON THIS AS SOON AS WE GET BACK.
DID ANNIHILUS KIDNAP HER? OR BLASTAAR?
I'M NOT SURE HOW SHE GOT THERE, ACTUALLY. IT'S JUST THAT...I'VE BEEN HAVING THIS RECURRING DREAM.
OUR SORCERER BELIEVES--
SORCERER?
WHAT SORCERER?
...
THE SORCERER OF THE FIVE WEAPONS SOCIETY.
YOUR FATHER'S SOCIETY.
THE RUMORS ARE TRUE, THEN.
SHANG...I'M SORRY. I'M AFRAID I CAN'T HELP YOU.
REED, PLEASE. I'M--
IT'S ACTUALLY NOT YOU I CAN'T HELP, SHANG. THE FIVE WEAPONS SOCIETY IS NEVER WHAT IT SEEMS. I CAN'T HELP THEM.
I WON'T PUT MY FAMILY IN JEOPARDY BECAUSE OF A DREAM.

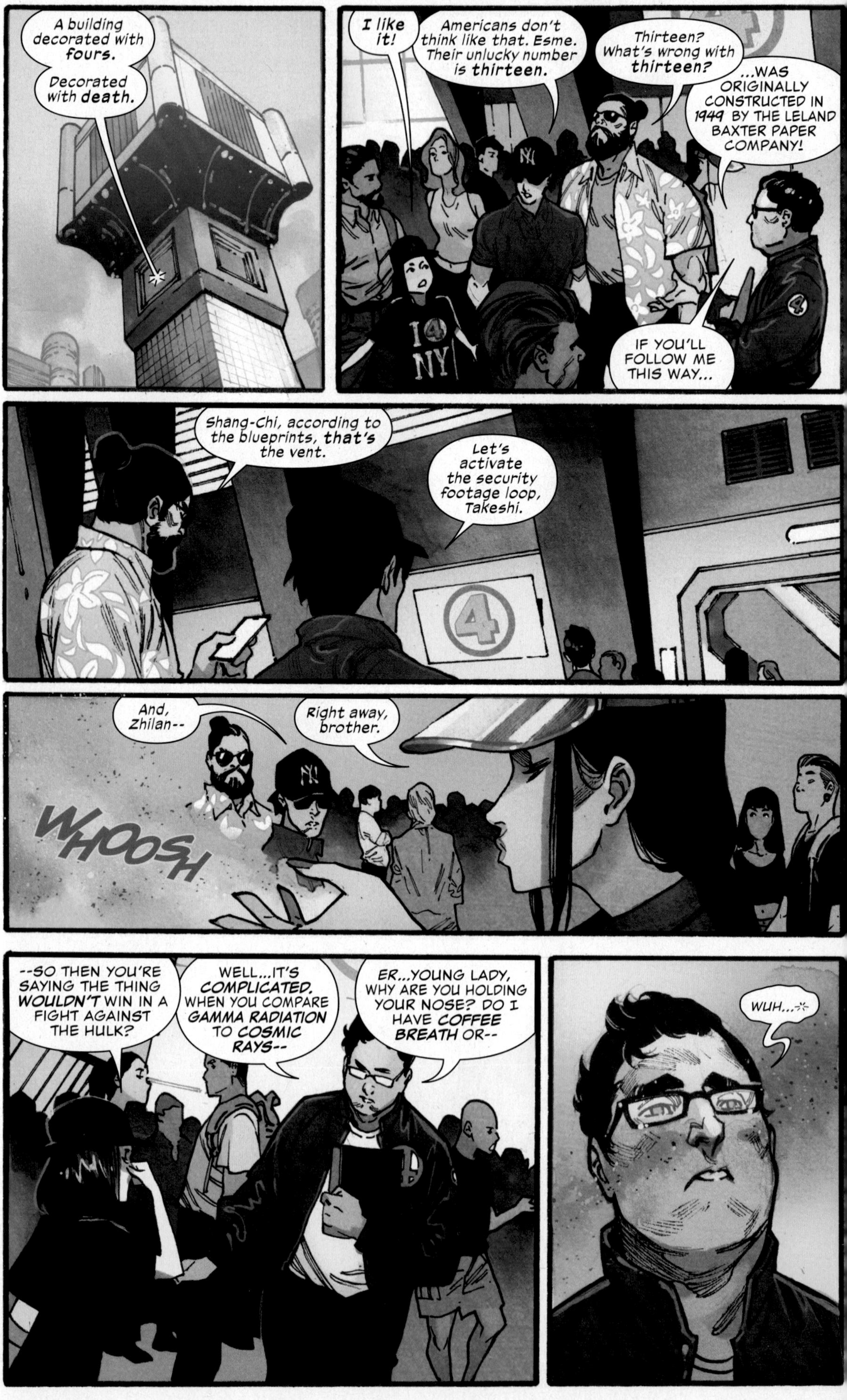
A building decorated with fours.
Decorated with death.
I like it!
Americans don't think like that. Esme. Their unlucky number is thirteen.
Thirteen? What's wrong with thirteen?
...WAS ORIGINALLY CONSTRUCTED IN 1949 BY THE LELAND BAXTER PAPER COMPANY!
IF YOU'LL FOLLOW ME THIS WAY...
Shang-Chi, according to the blueprints, that's the vent.
Let's activate the security footage loop, Takeshi.
And, Zhilan--
Right away, brother.
WHOOSH
--SO THEN YOU'RE SAYING THE THING WOULDN'T WIN IN A FIGHT AGAINST THE HULK?
WELL...IT'S COMPLICATED. WHEN YOU COMPARE GAMMA RADIATION TO COSMIC RAYS--
ER...YOUNG LADY, WHY ARE YOU HOLDING YOUR NOSE? DO I HAVE COFFEE BREATH OR--
WUH...

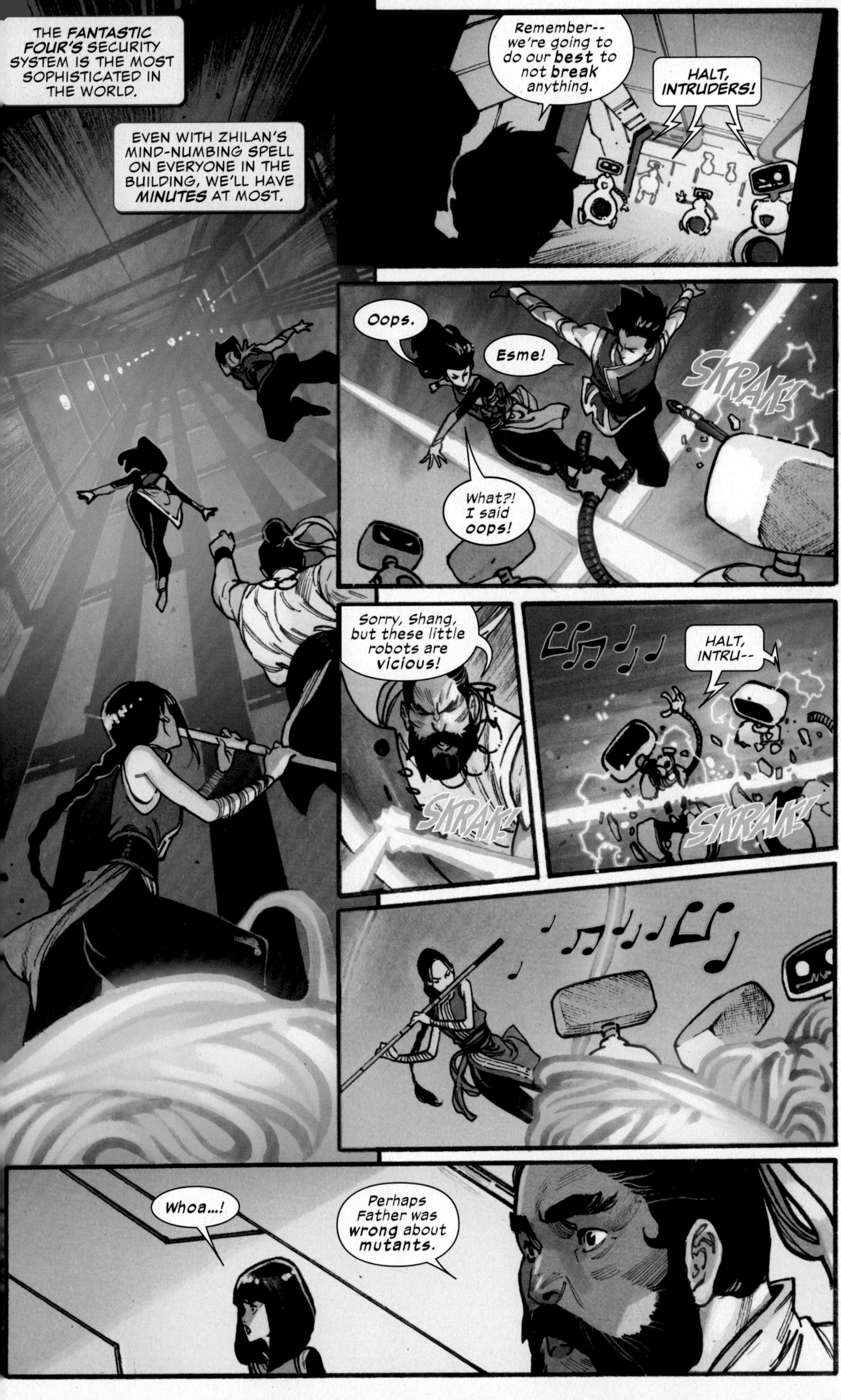
THE FANTASTIC FOUR'S SECURITY SYSTEM IS THE MOST SOPHISTICATED IN THE WORLD.
EVEN WITH ZHILAN'S MIND-NUMBING SPELL ON EVERYONE IN THE BUILDING, WE'LL HAVE MINUTES AT MOST.
Remember-- we're going to do our best to not break anything.
HALT, INTRUDERS!
Oops.
Esme!
SKRAK!
What?! I said oops!
Sorry, Shang, but these little robots are vicious!
SKRAK!
HALT, INTRU--
SKRAK!
Whoa...!
Perhaps Father was wrong about mutants.

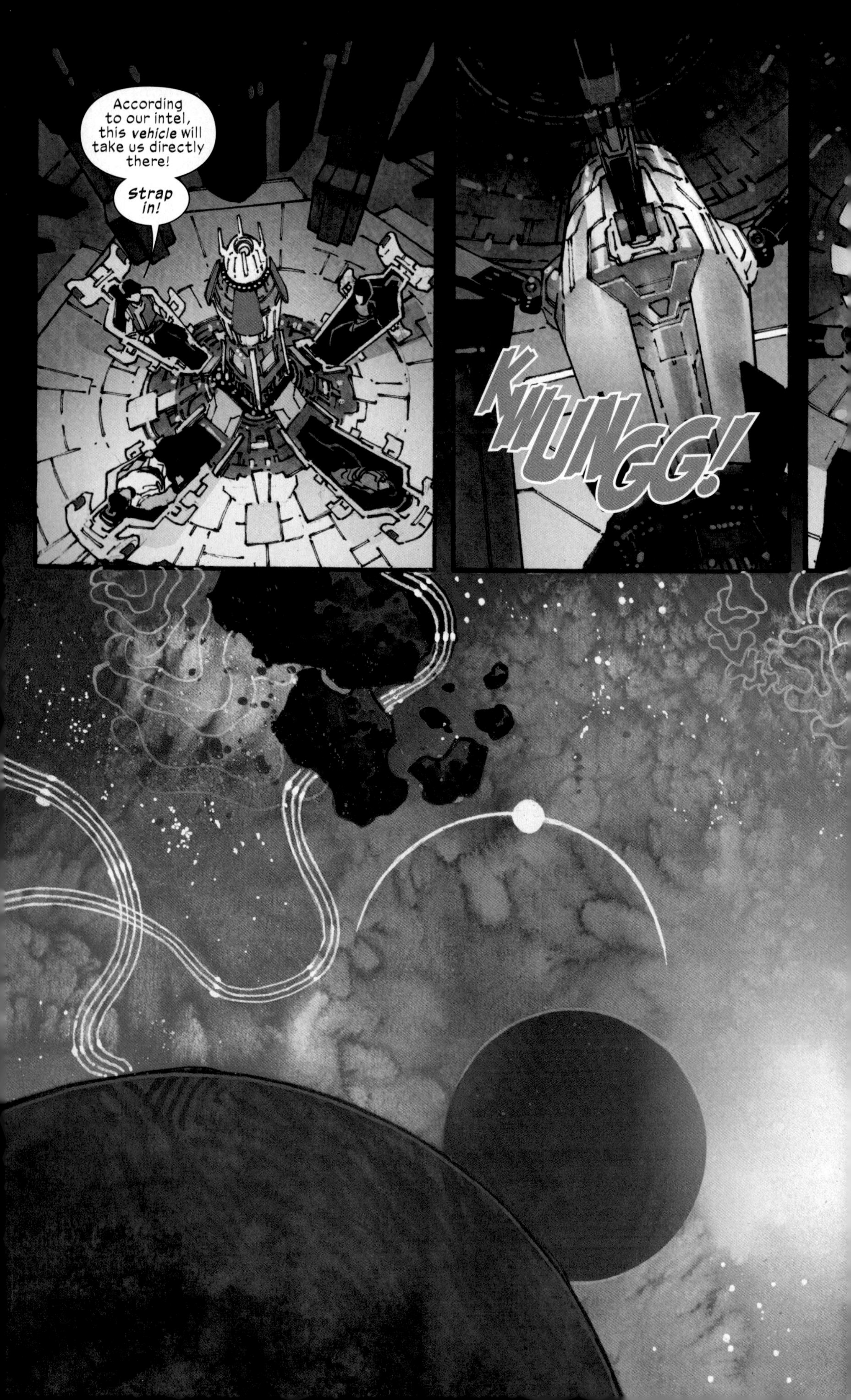
According to our intel, this *vehicle* will take us directly there!
Strap in!
KWUNGG!

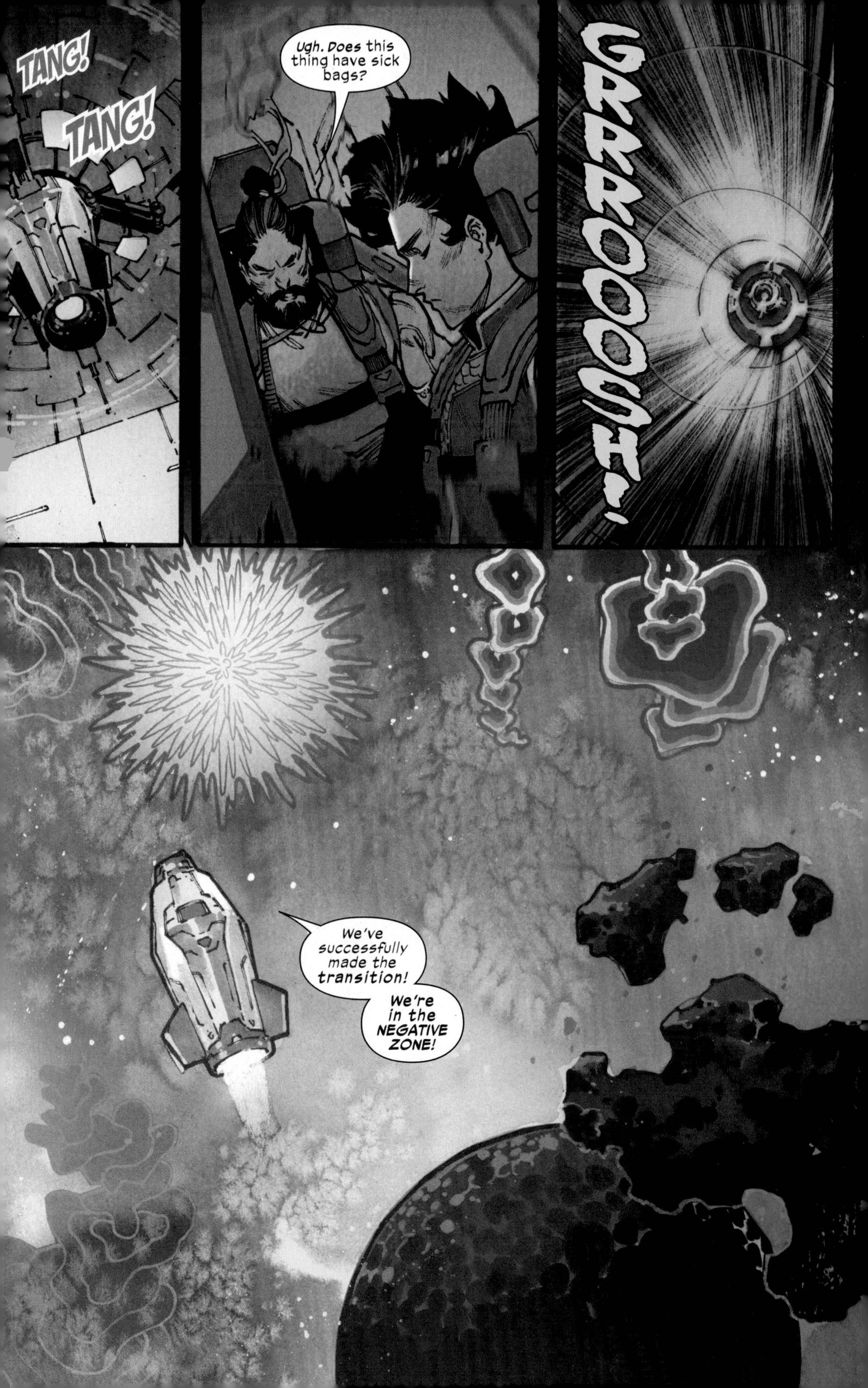
TANG!
TANG!
Ugh. Does this thing have sick bags?
GRRROOOSH!
We've successfully made the transition!
We're in the NEGATIVE ZONE!

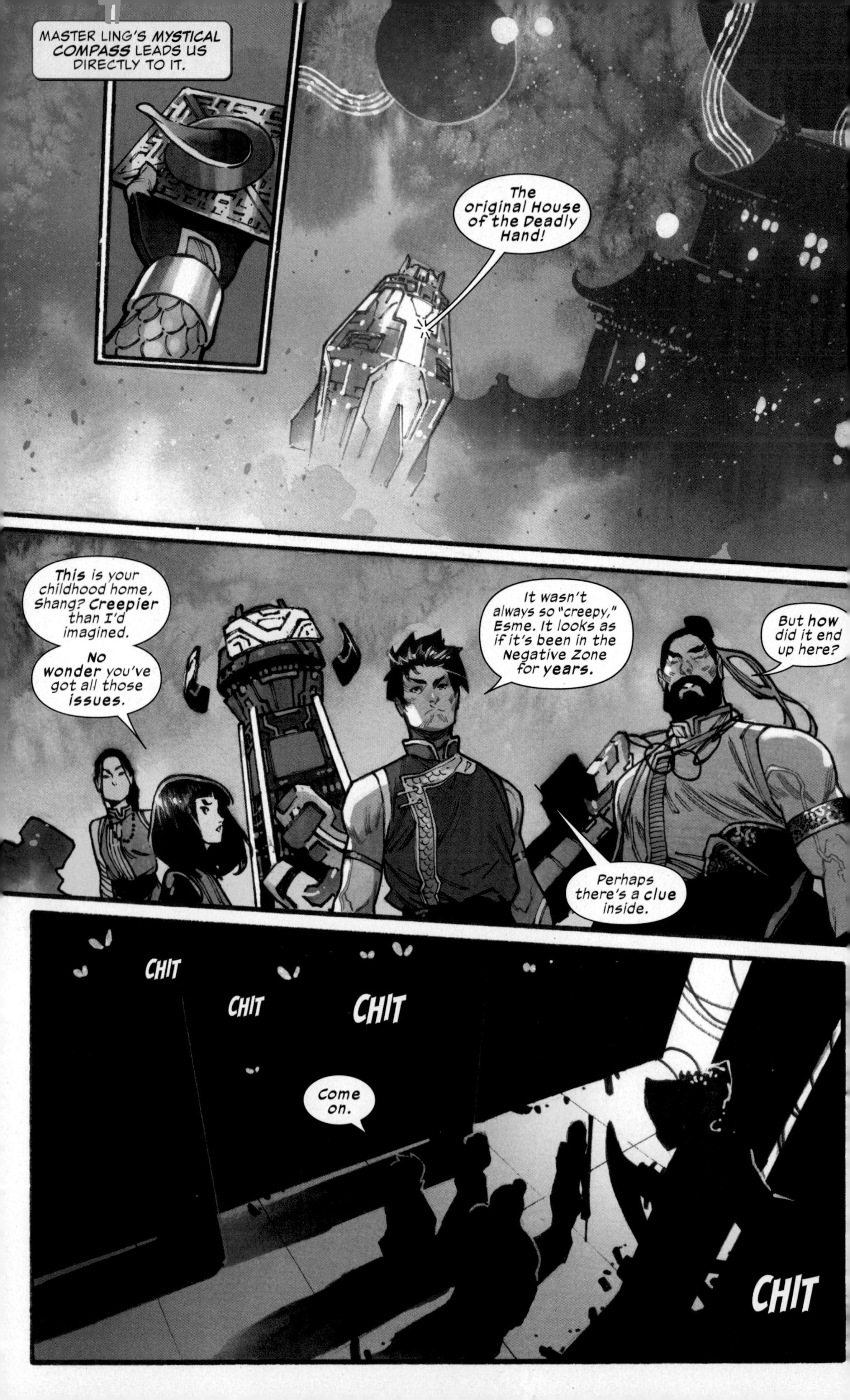
MASTER LING'S MYSTICAL COMPASS LEADS US DIRECTLY TO IT.
The original House of the Deadly Hand!
This is your childhood home, Shang? Creepier than I'd imagined.
No wonder you've got all those issues.
It wasn't always so "creepy," Esme. It looks as if it's been in the Negative Zone for years.
But how did it end up here?
Perhaps there's a clue inside.
CHIT
CHIT
CHIT
Come on.
CHIT

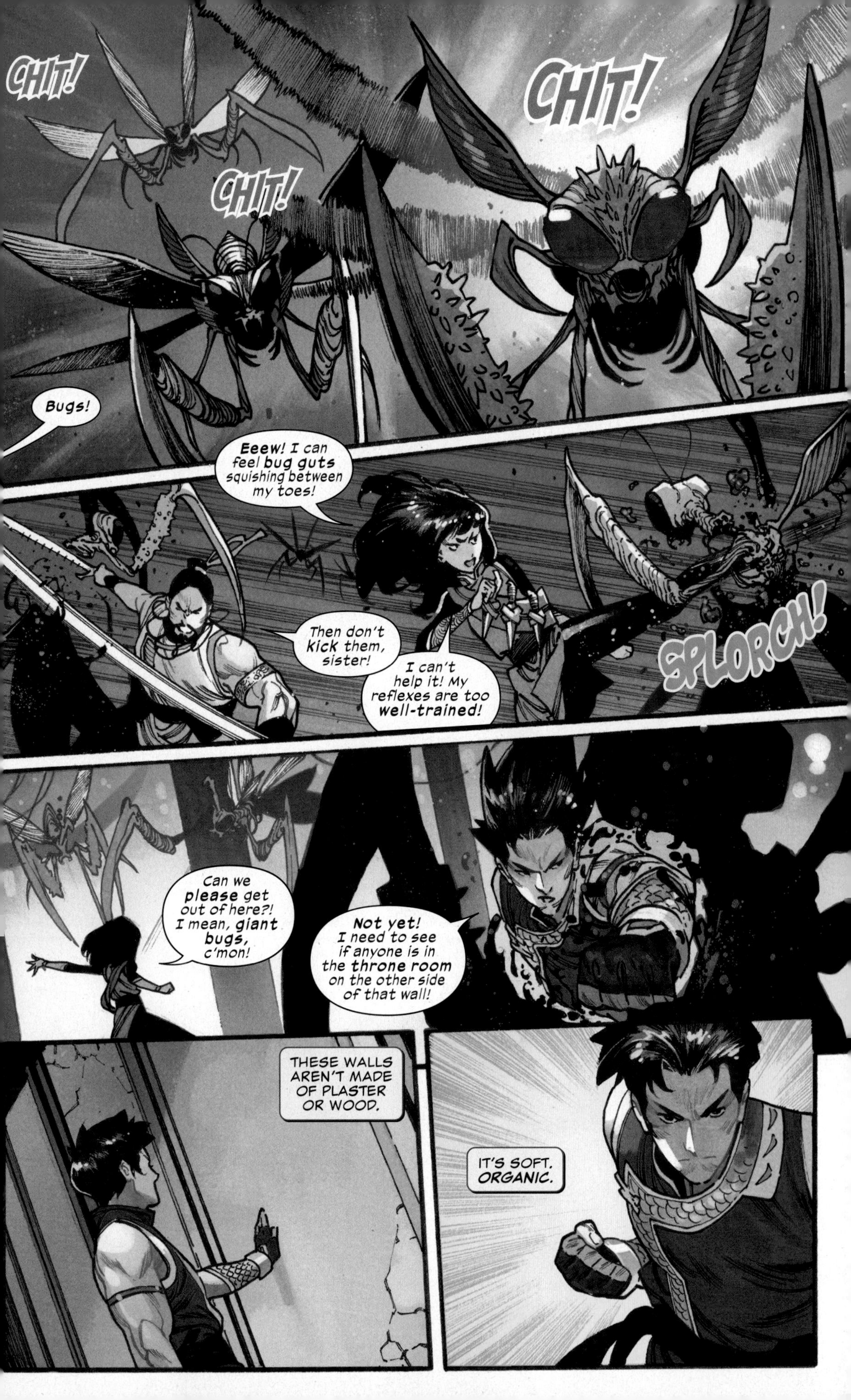
CHIT!
CHIT!
CHIT!
Bugs!
Eeew! I can feel bug guts squishing between my toes!
Then don't kick them, sister!
I can't help it! My reflexes are too well-trained!
SPLORCH!
Can we please get out of here?! I mean, giant bugs, c'mon!
Not yet! I need to see if anyone is in the throne room on the other side of that wall!
THESE WALLS AREN'T MADE OF PLASTER OR WOOD.
IT'S SOFT. ORGANIC.

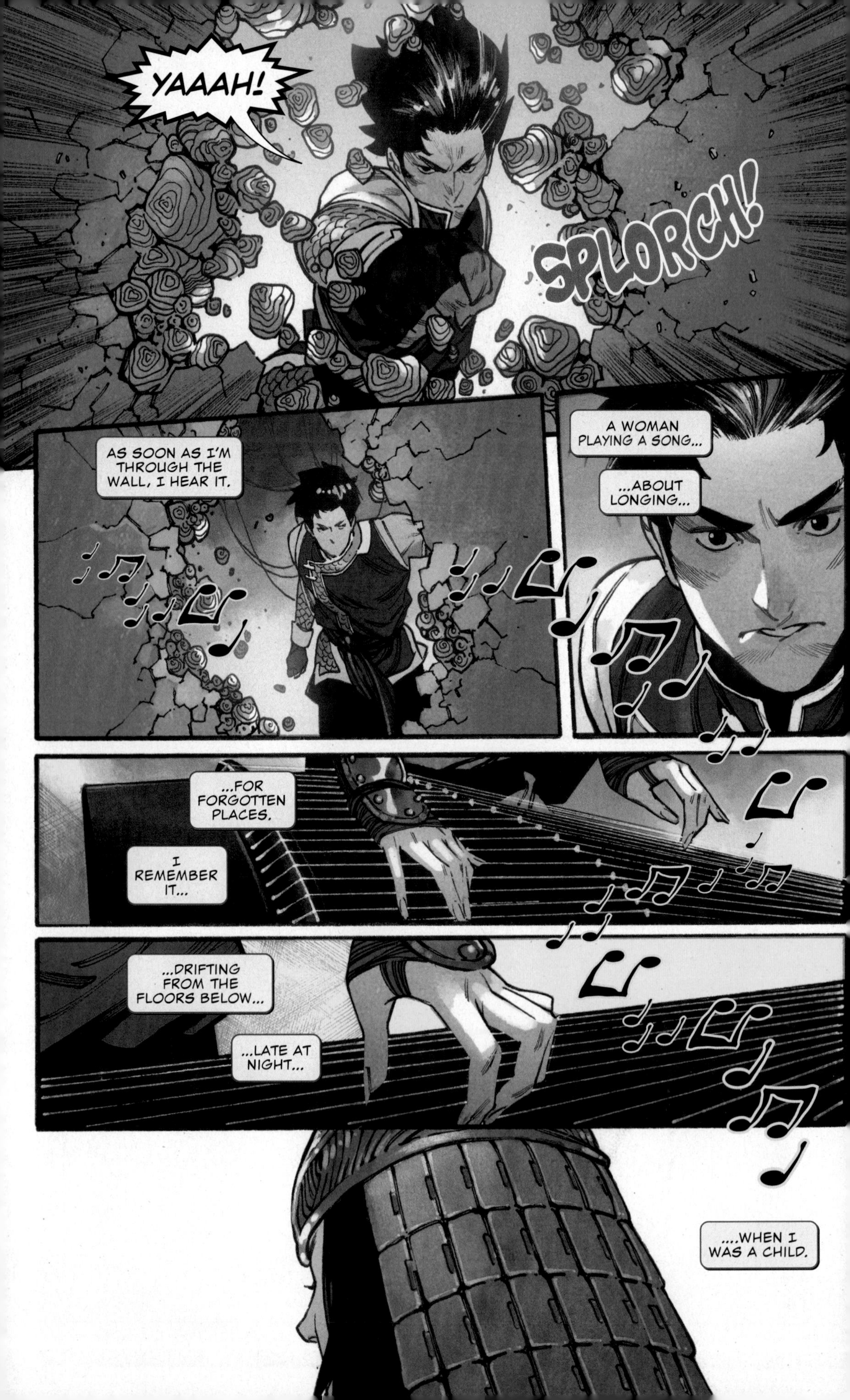
YAAAH!
SPLORCH!
AS SOON AS I'M THROUGH THE WALL, I HEAR IT.
A WOMAN PLAYING A SONG...
...ABOUT LONGING...
...FOR FORGOTTEN PLACES.
I REMEMBER IT...
...DRIFTING FROM THE FLOORS BELOW...
...LATE AT NIGHT...
....WHEN I WAS A CHILD.

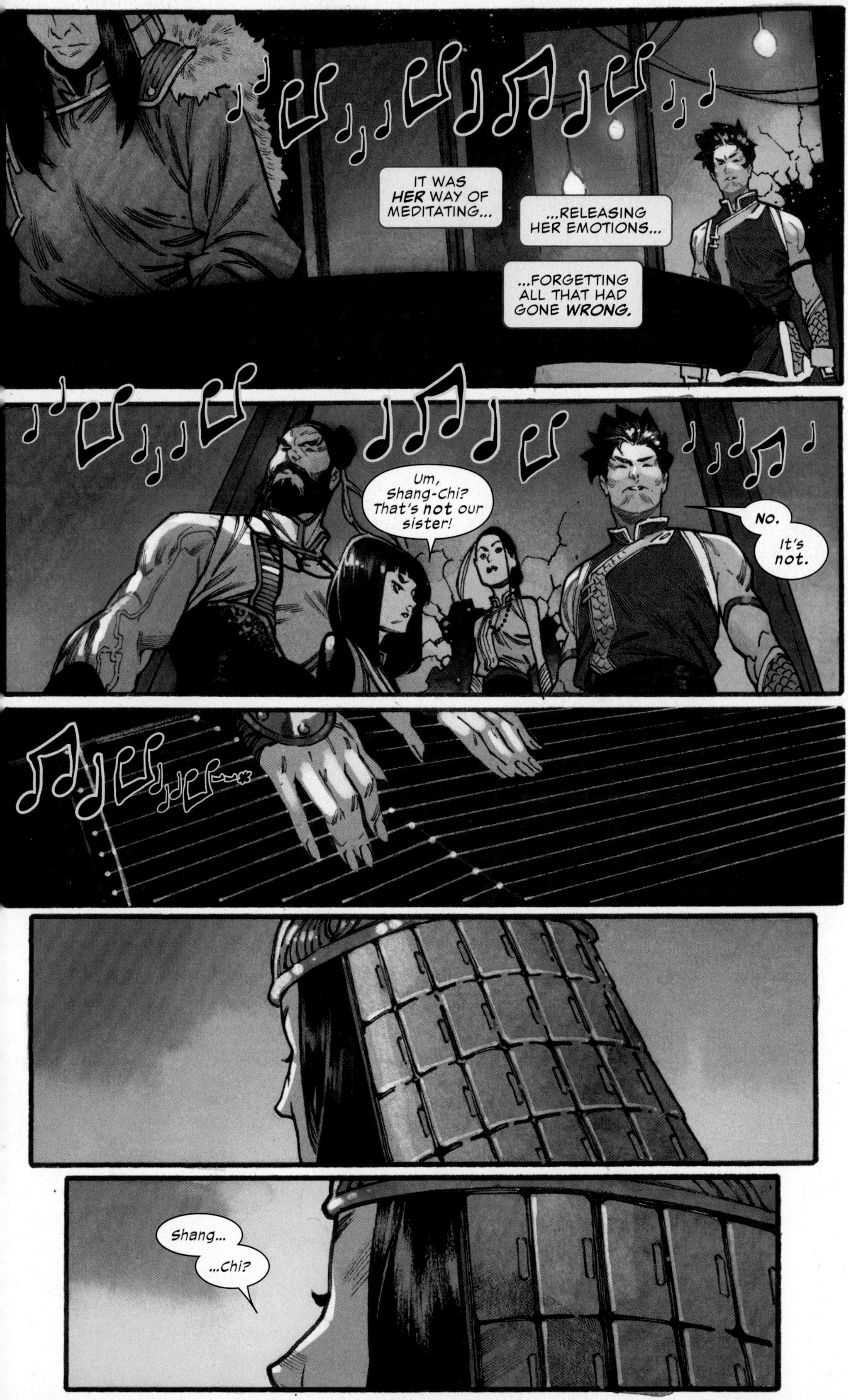
IT WAS HER WAY OF MEDITATING...
...RELEASING HER EMOTIONS...
...FORGETTING ALL THAT HAD GONE WRONG.
Um, Shang-Chi? That's not our sister!
No.
It's not.
Shang...
...Chi?

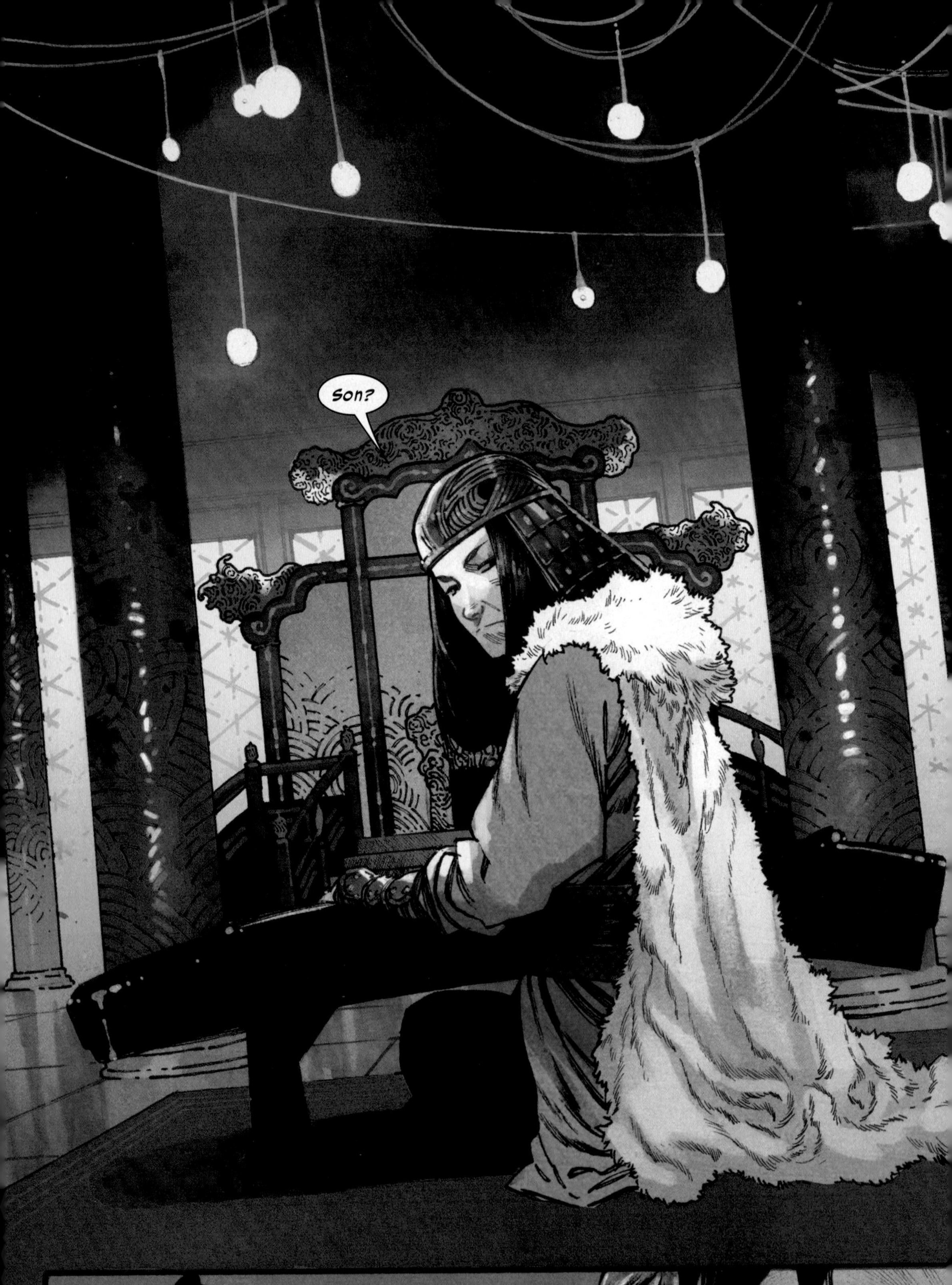
Son?

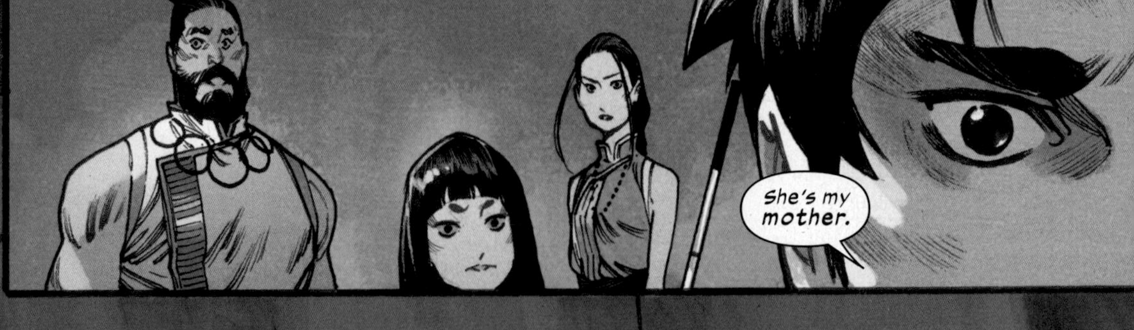
She's my mother.

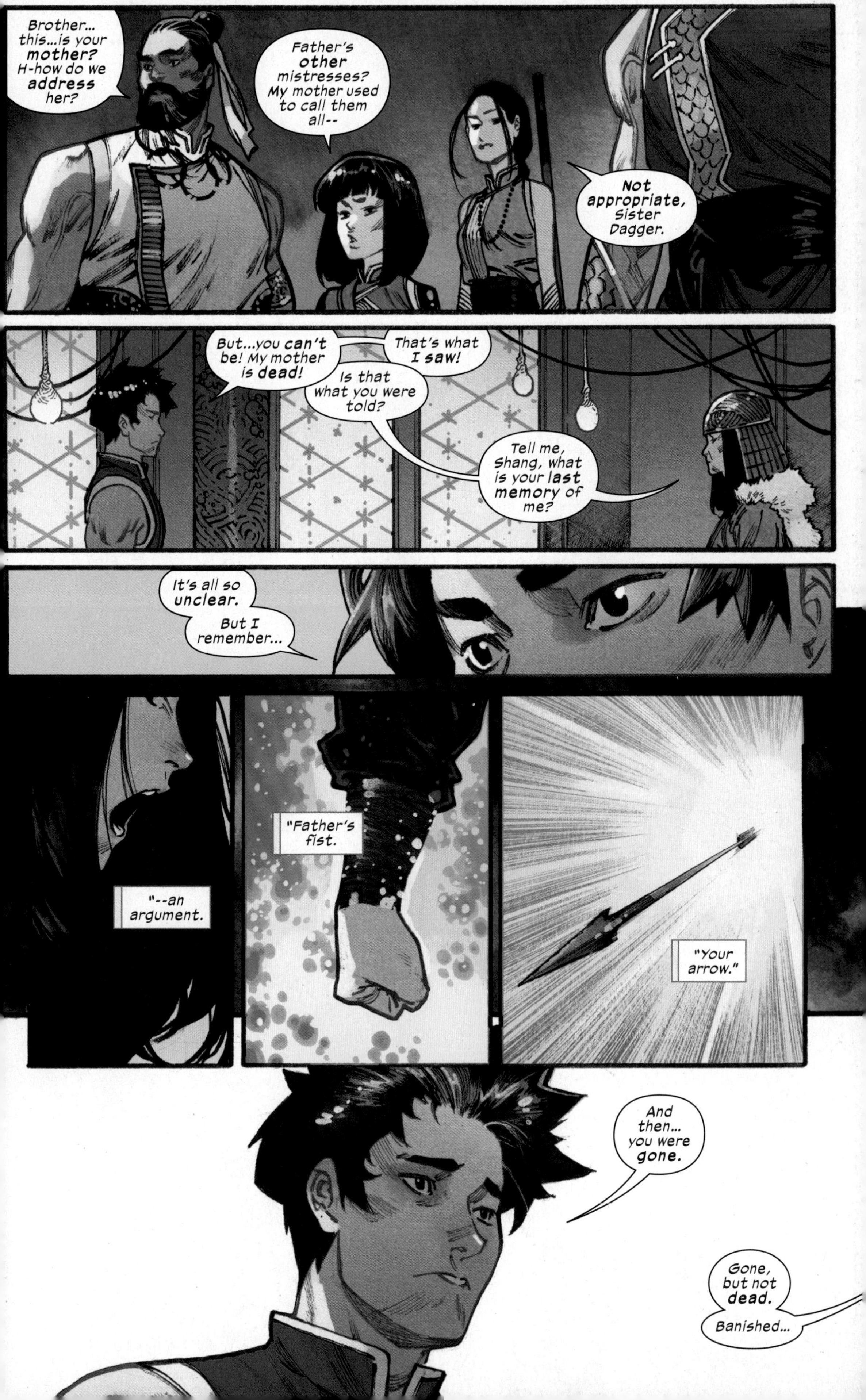
Brother... this...is your mother? H-how do we address her?
Father's other mistresses? My mother used to call them all--
Not appropriate, Sister Dagger.
But...you can't be! My mother is dead!
That's what I saw!
Is that what you were told?
Tell me, Shang, what is your last memory of me?
It's all so unclear.
But I remember...
"--an argument.
"Father's fist.
"Your arrow."
And then... you were gone.
Gone, but not dead.
Banished...

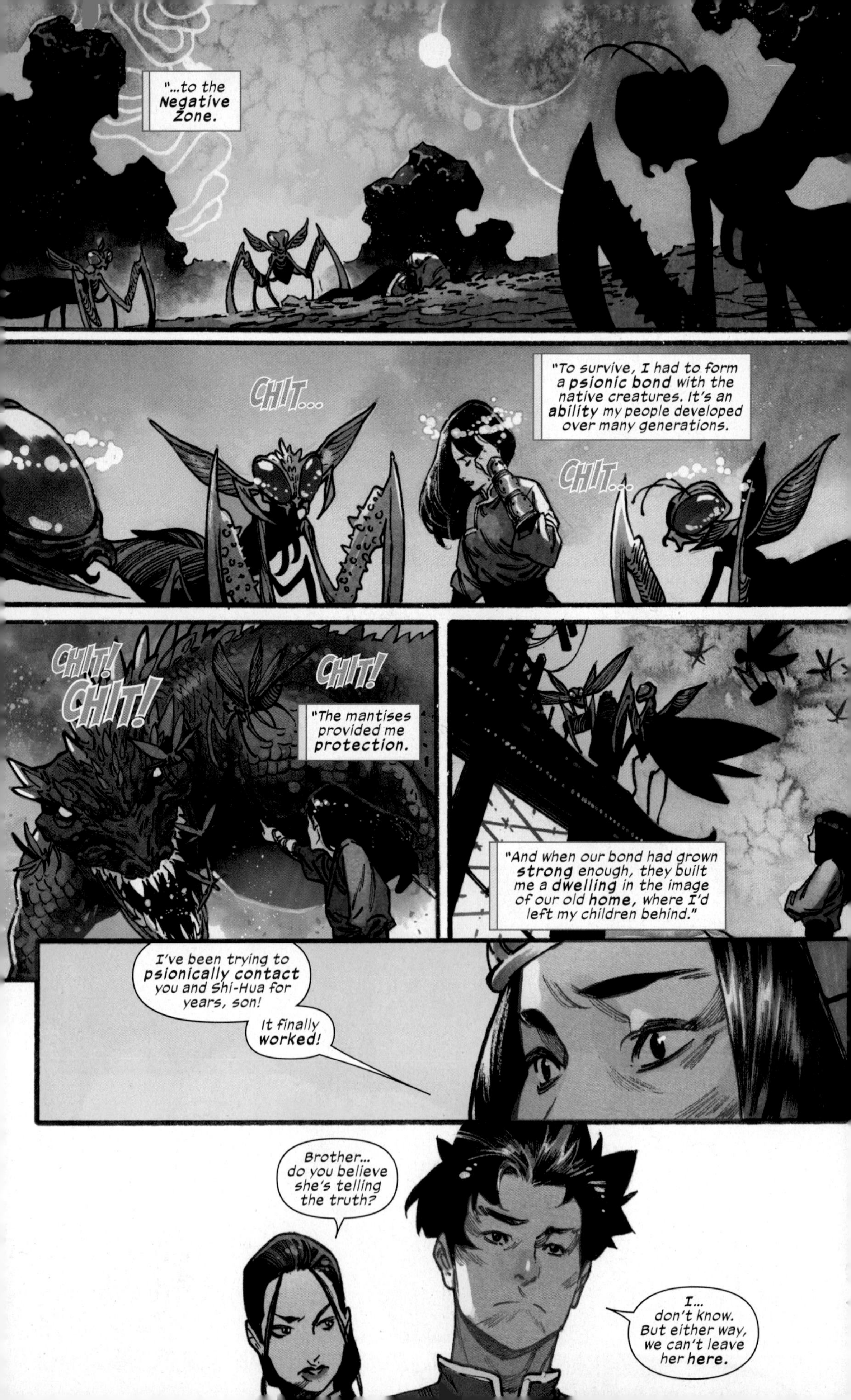

"...to the Negative Zone.
CHIT...
"To survive, I had to form a psionic bond with the native creatures. It's an ability my people developed over many generations.
CHIT...
CHIT! CHIT!
CHIT!
"The mantises provided me protection.
"And when our bond had grown strong enough, they built me a dwelling in the image of our old home, where I'd left my children behind."
I've been trying to psionically contact you and Shi-Hua for years, son!
It finally worked!
Brother... do you believe she's telling the truth?
I... don't know. But either way, we can't leave her here.

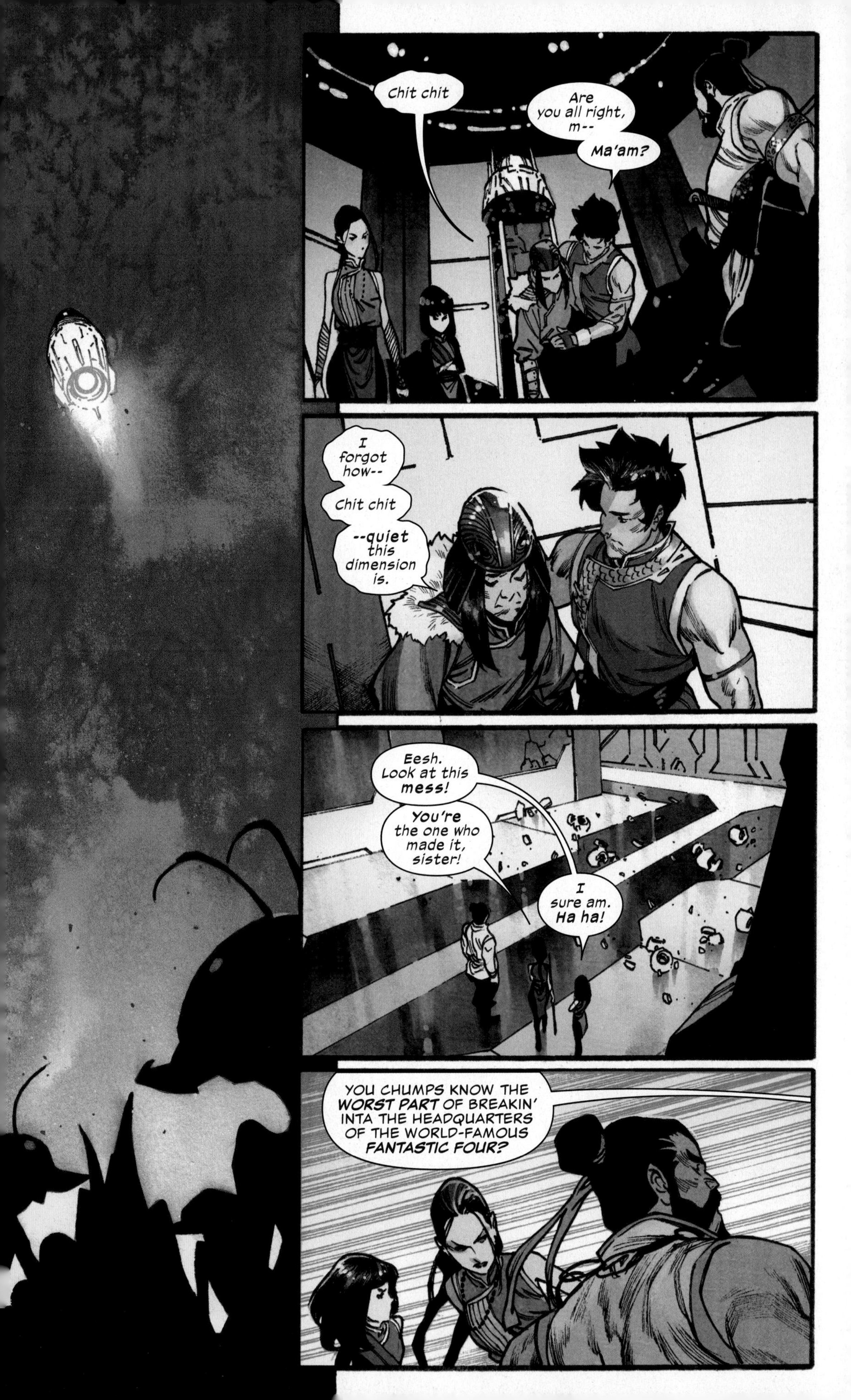
Chit chit
Are you all right, m--
Ma'am?
I forgot how--
Chit chit
--quiet this dimension is.
Eesh. Look at this mess!
You're the one who made it, sister!
I sure am. Ha ha!
YOU CHUMPS KNOW THE WORST PART OF BREAKIN' INTA THE HEADQUARTERS OF THE WORLD-FAMOUS FANTASTIC FOUR?

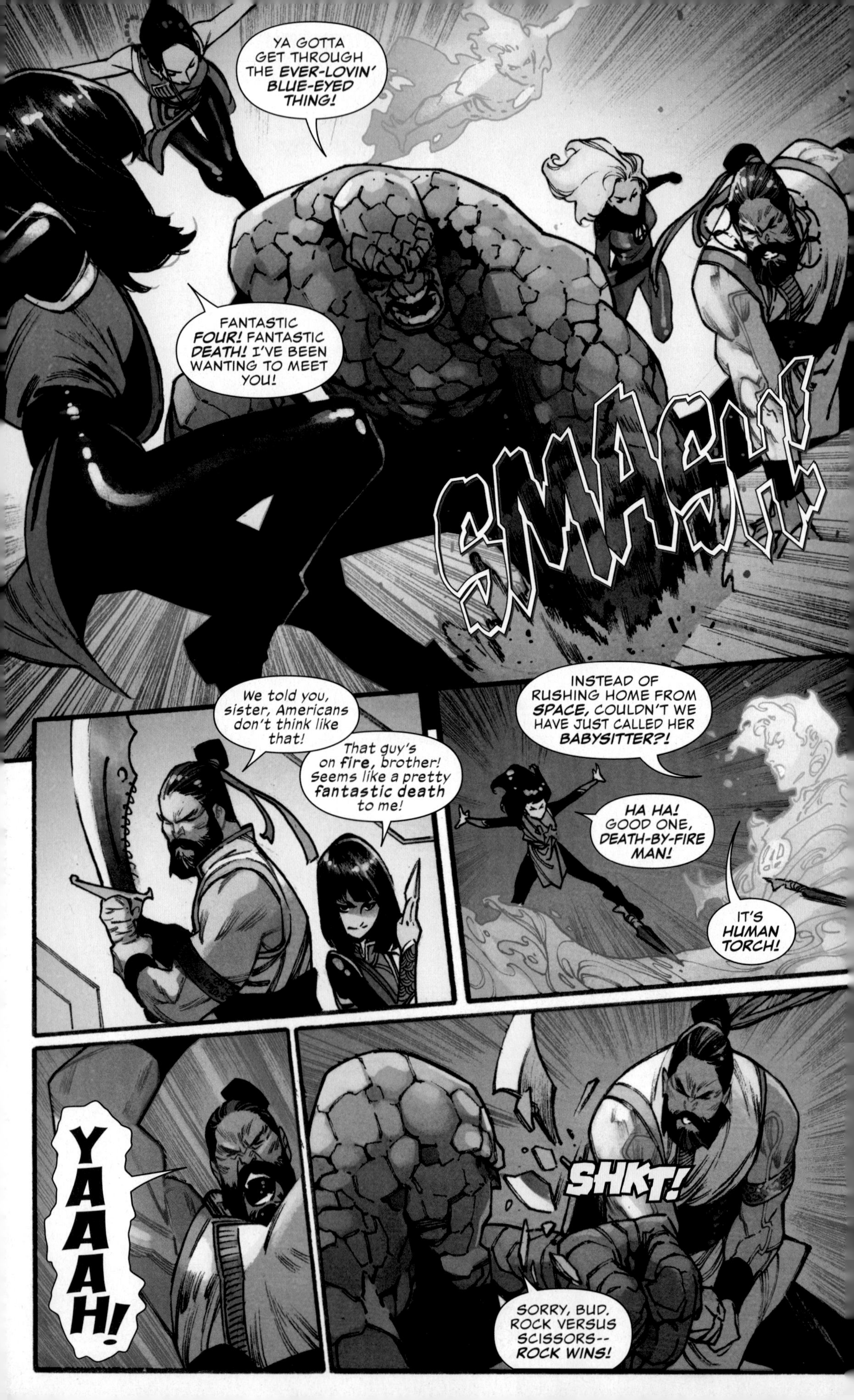
YA GOTTA GET THROUGH THE EVER-LOVIN' BLUE-EYED THING!
FANTASTIC FOUR! FANTASTIC DEATH! I'VE BEEN WANTING TO MEET YOU!
SMASH!
We told you, sister, Americans don't think like that!
That guy's on fire, brother! Seems like a pretty fantastic death to me!
INSTEAD OF RUSHING HOME FROM SPACE, COULDN'T WE HAVE JUST CALLED HER BABYSITTER?!
HA HA! GOOD ONE, DEATH-BY-FIRE MAN!
IT'S HUMAN TORCH!
YAAAH!
SHKT!
SORRY, BUD. ROCK VERSUS SCISSORS-- ROCK WINS!

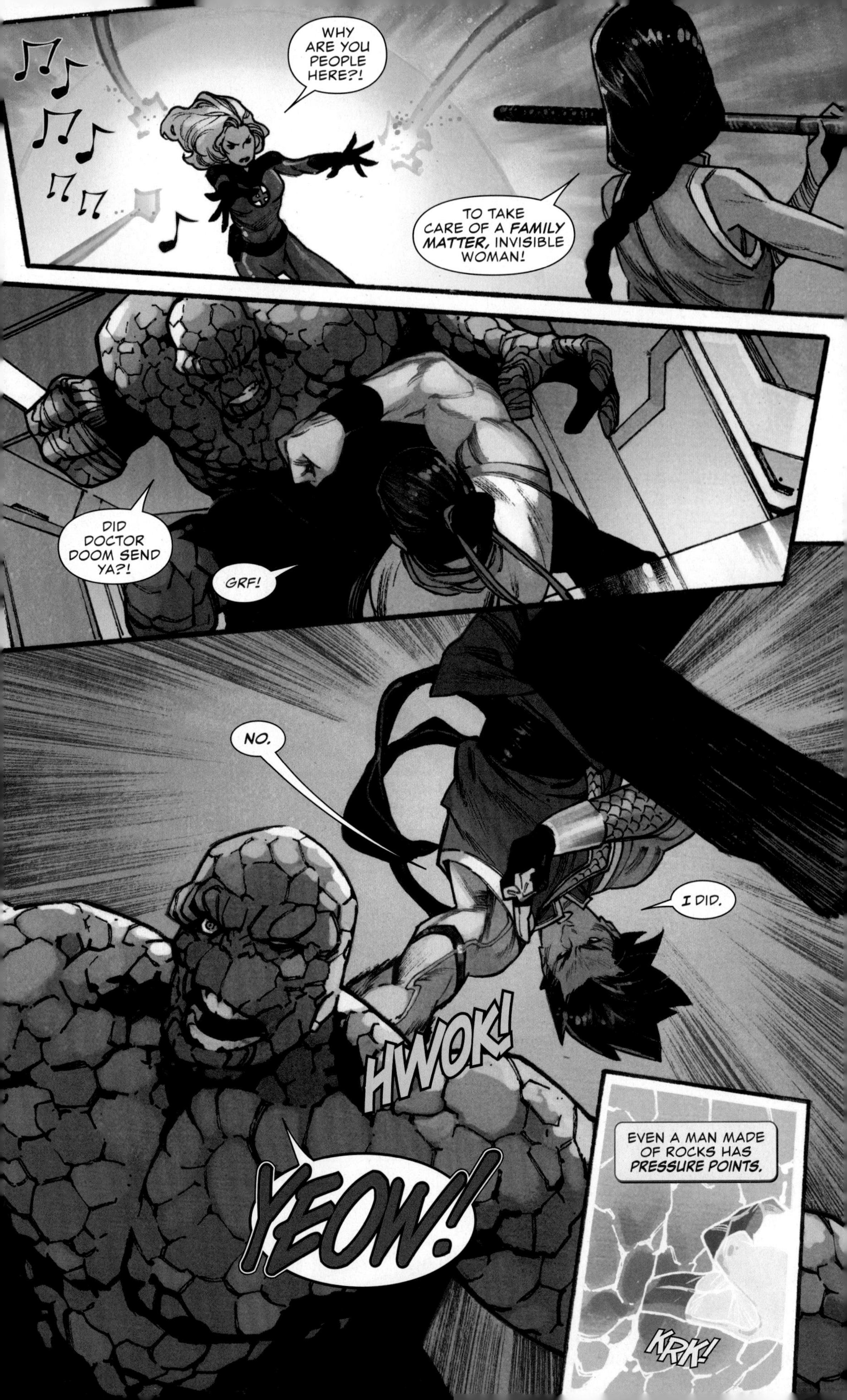
WHY ARE YOU PEOPLE HERE?!
TO TAKE CARE OF A FAMILY MATTER, INVISIBLE WOMAN!
DID DOCTOR DOOM SEND YA?!
GRF!
NO.
I DID.
HWOK!
YEOW!
EVEN A MAN MADE OF ROCKS HAS PRESSURE POINTS.
KRK!

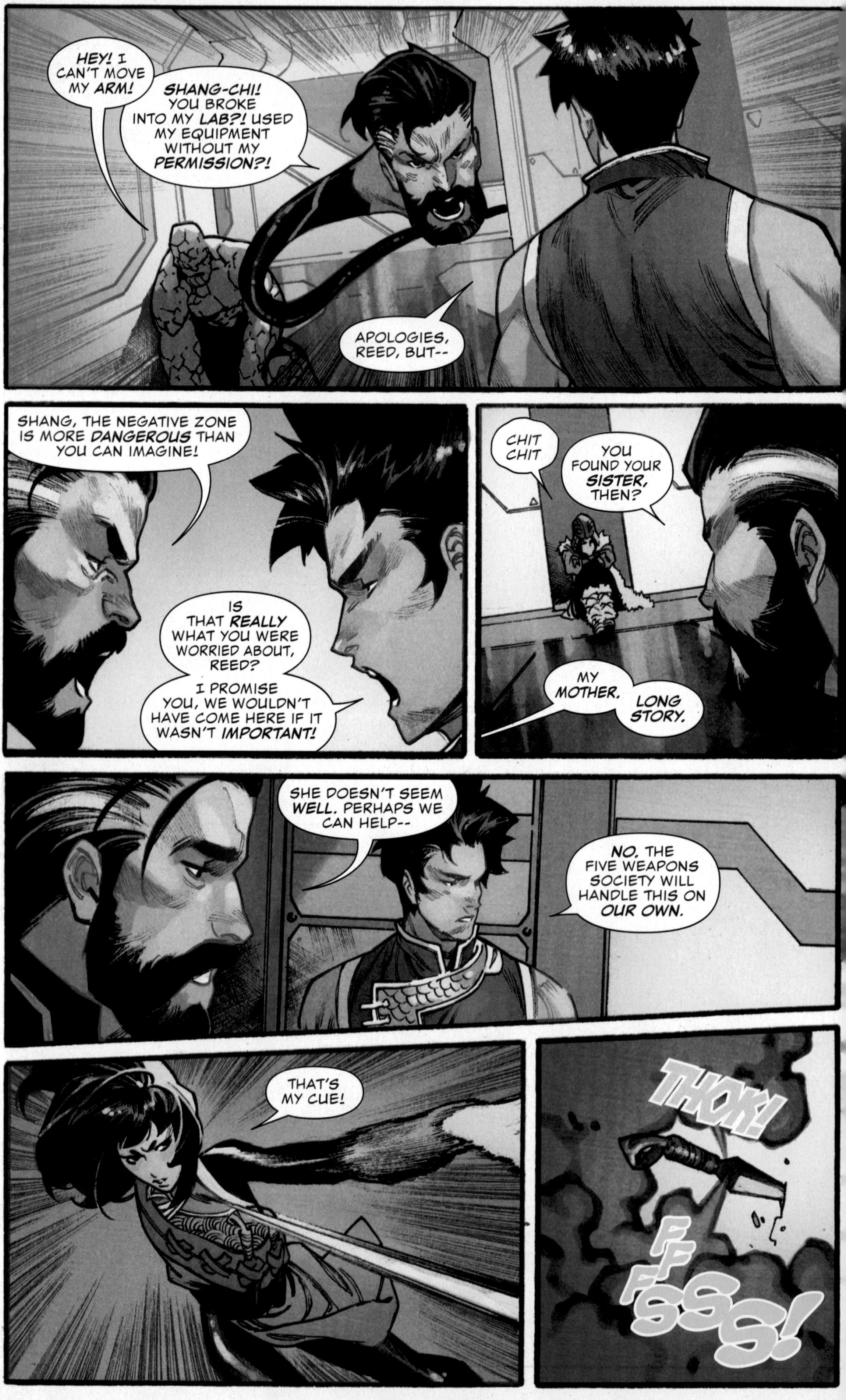
HEY! I CAN'T MOVE MY ARM!
SHANG-CHI! YOU BROKE INTO MY LAB?! USED MY EQUIPMENT WITHOUT MY PERMISSION?!
APOLOGIES, REED, BUT--
SHANG, THE NEGATIVE ZONE IS MORE DANGEROUS THAN YOU CAN IMAGINE!
IS THAT REALLY WHAT YOU WERE WORRIED ABOUT, REED?
I PROMISE YOU, WE WOULDN'T HAVE COME HERE IF IT WASN'T IMPORTANT!
CHIT CHIT
YOU FOUND YOUR SISTER, THEN?
MY MOTHER.
LONG STORY.
SHE DOESN'T SEEM WELL. PERHAPS WE CAN HELP--
NO. THE FIVE WEAPONS SOCIETY WILL HANDLE THIS ON OUR OWN.
THAT'S MY CUE!
THOK!
FFFSSS!

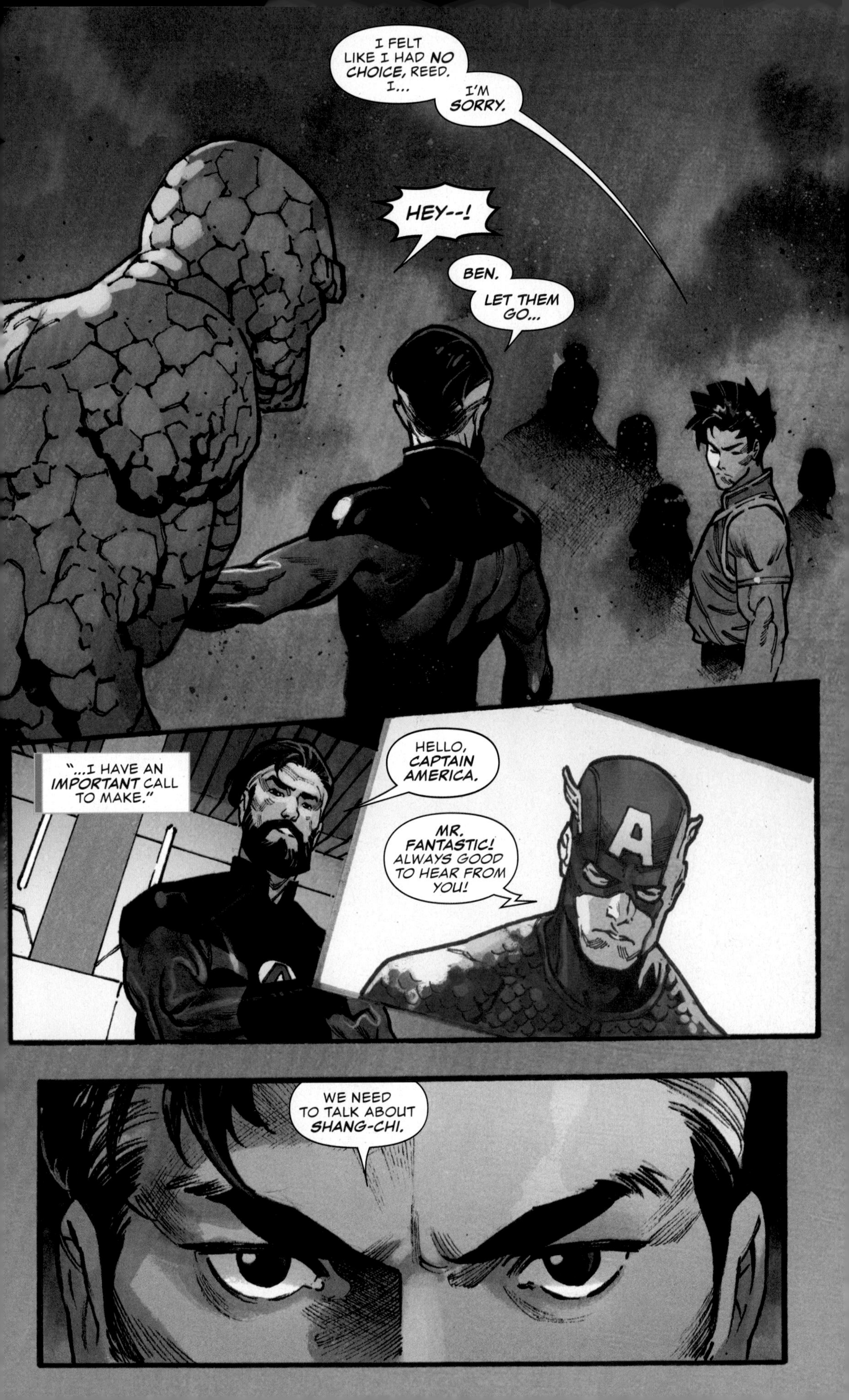
I FELT LIKE I HAD NO CHOICE, REED. I...
I'M SORRY.
HEY--!
BEN.
LET THEM GO...
"...I HAVE AN IMPORTANT CALL TO MAKE."
HELLO, CAPTAIN AMERICA.
MR. FANTASTIC! ALWAYS GOOD TO HEAR FROM YOU!
WE NEED TO TALK ABOUT SHANG-CHI.

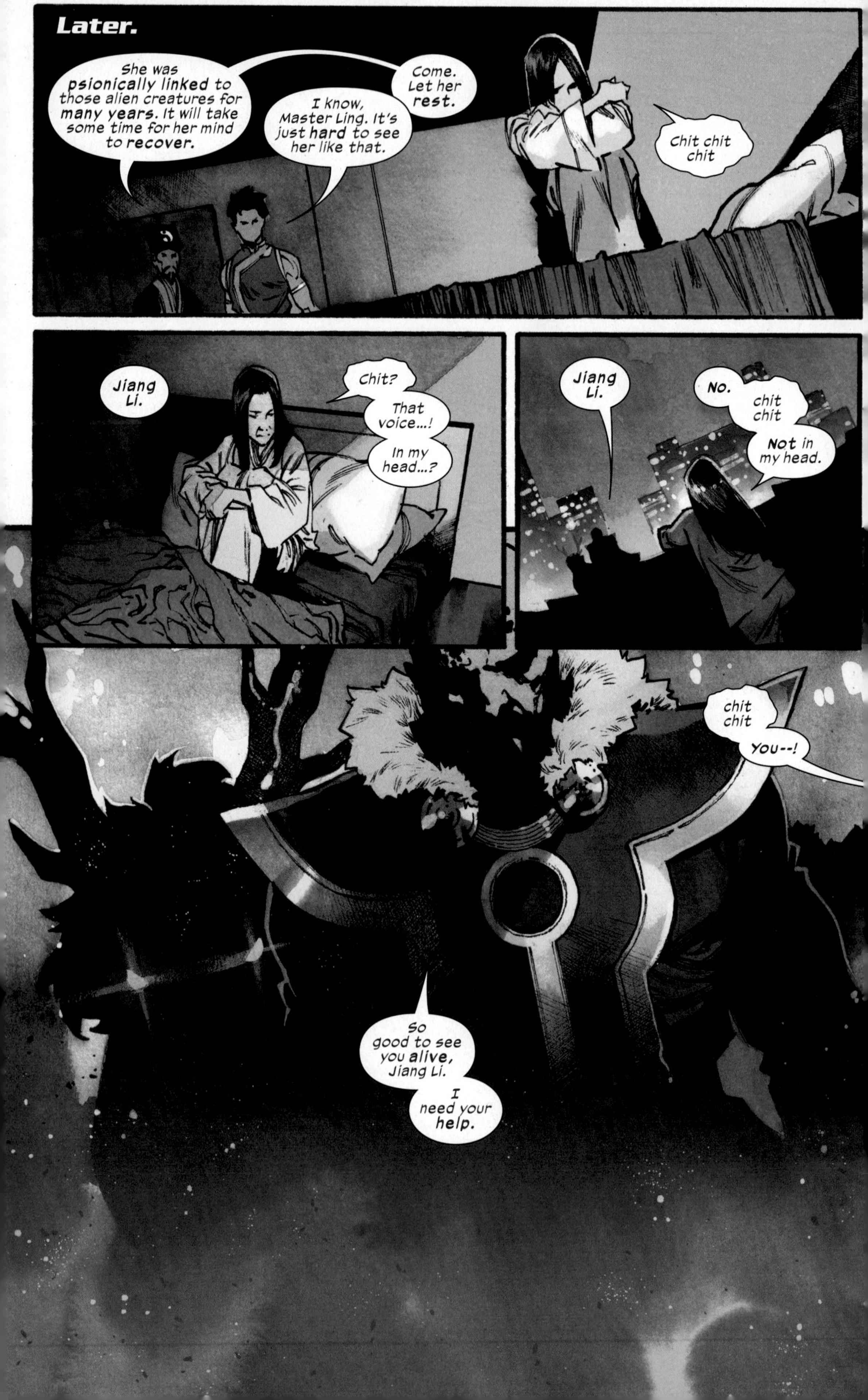
Later.
She was psionically linked to those alien creatures for many years. It will take some time for her mind to recover.
Come. Let her rest.
I know, Master Ling. It's just hard to see her like that.
Chit chit chit
Jiang Li.
Chit?
That voice...!
In my head...?
Jiang Li.
No.
chit chit
Not in my head.
chit chit
YOU--!
So good to see you alive, Jiang Li.
I need your help.

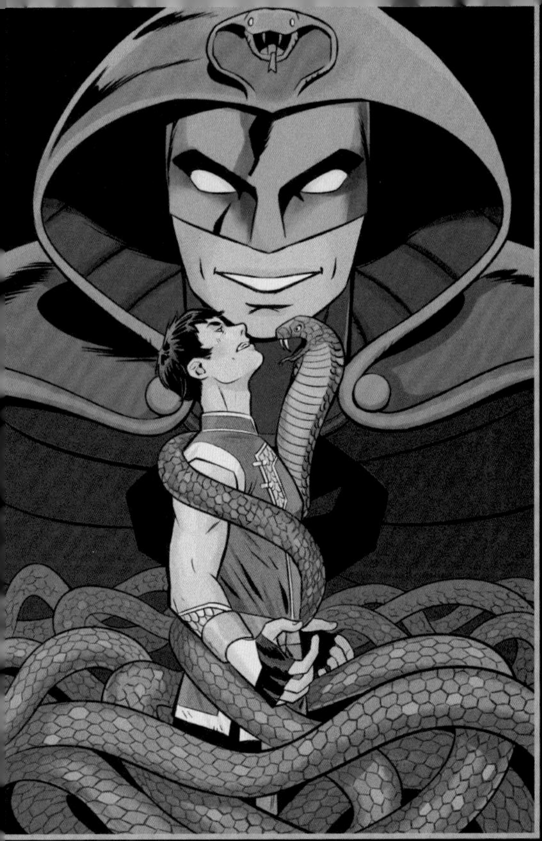

#2 SPIDER-MAN VILLAINS VARIANT BY
NATACHA BUSTOS

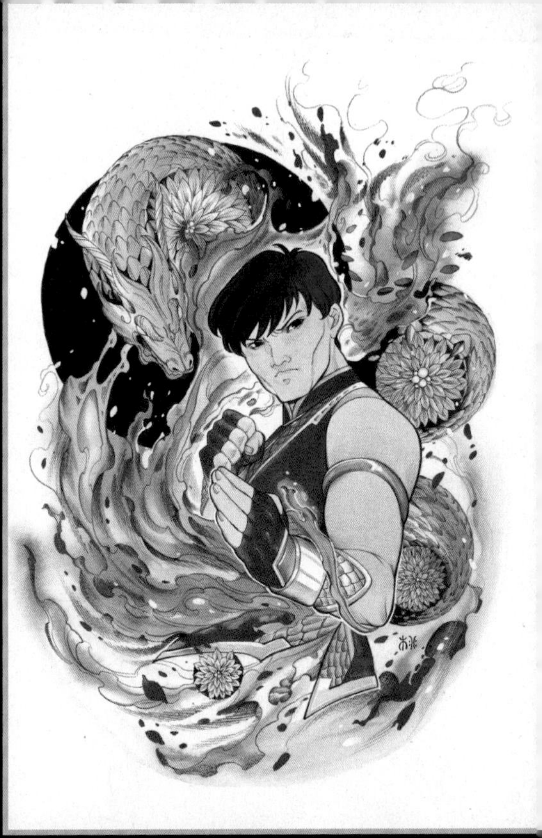

#2 VARIANT BY
PEACH MOMOKO

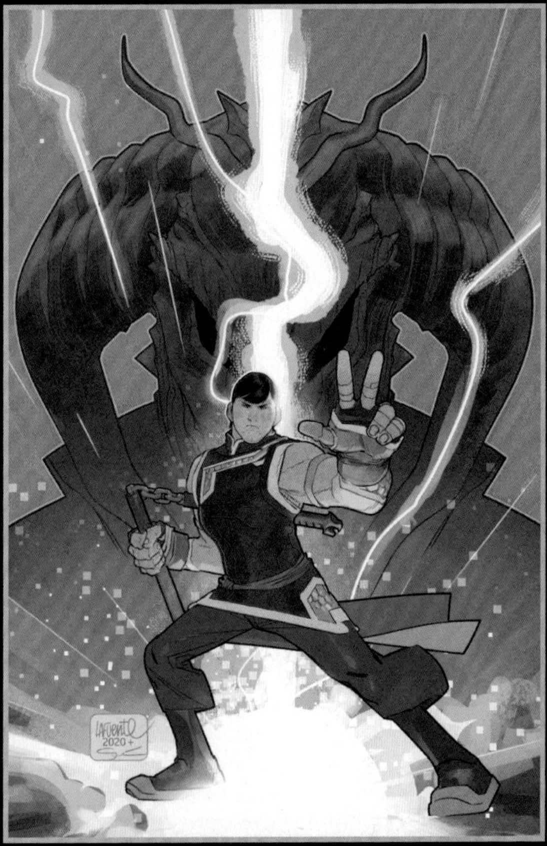

#3 VARIANT BY
DAVID LAFUENTE & GERMÁN GARCÍA

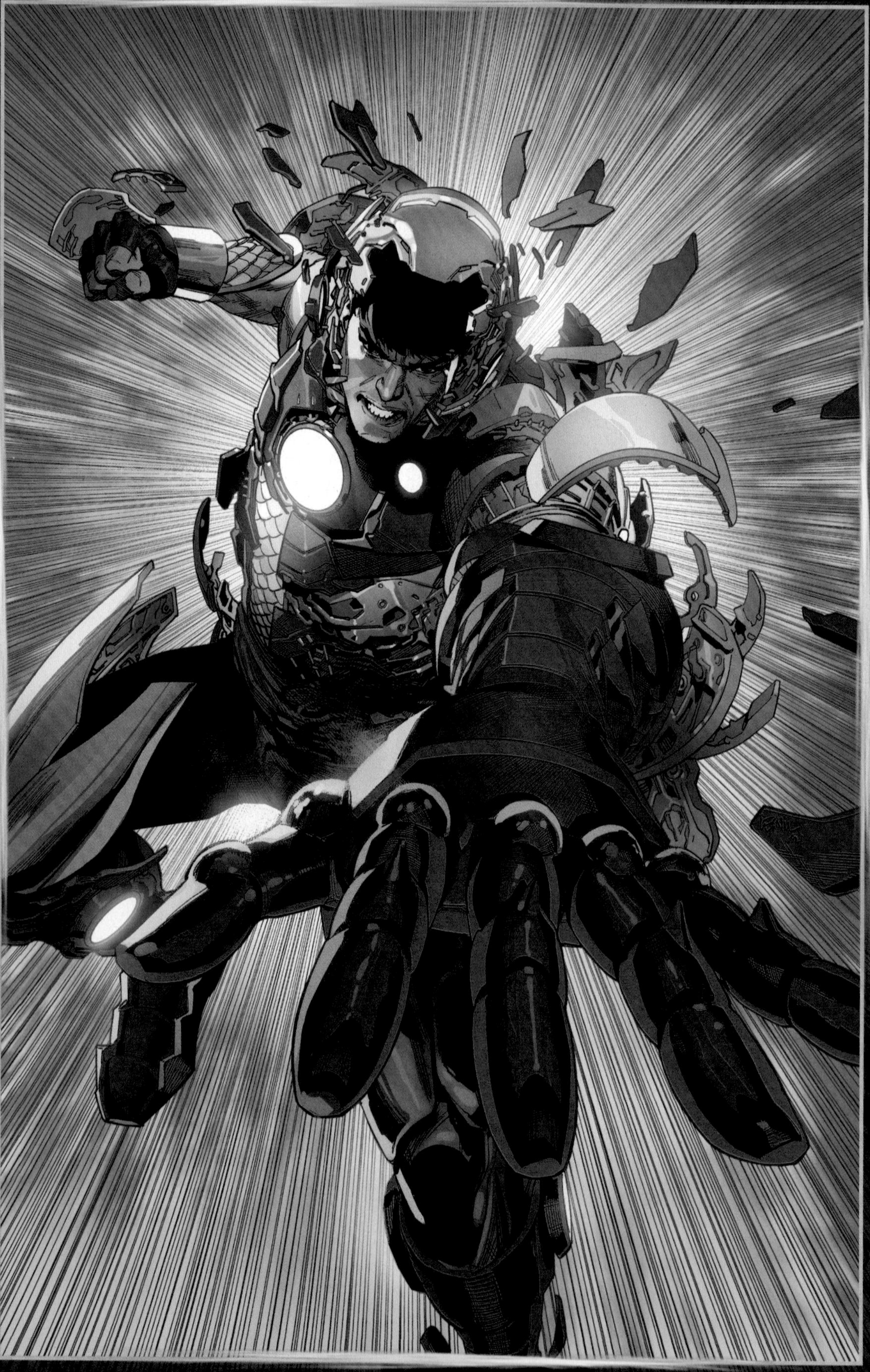

FIVE

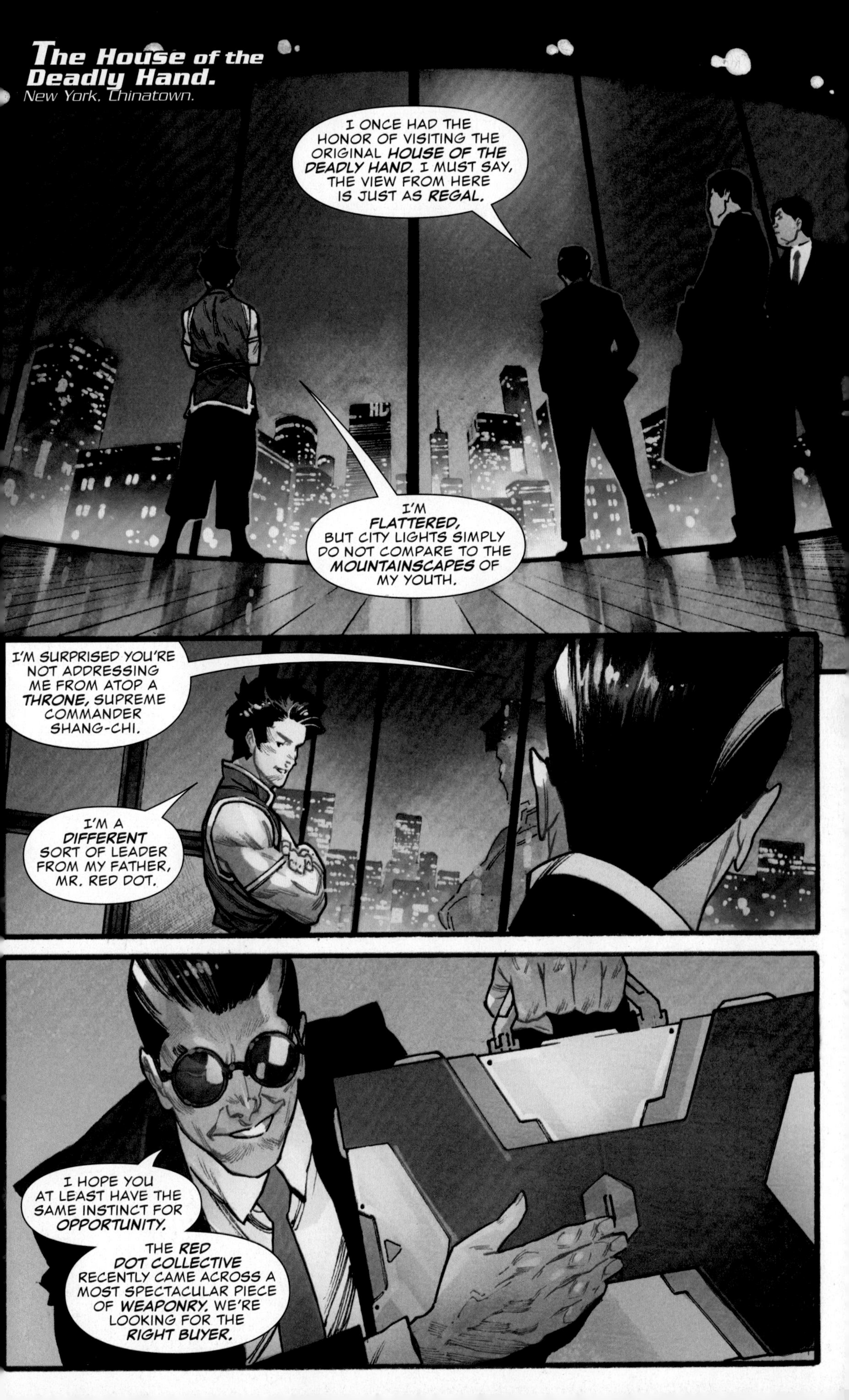
The House of the Deadly Hand.
New York, Chinatown.
I ONCE HAD THE HONOR OF VISITING THE ORIGINAL HOUSE OF THE DEADLY HAND. I MUST SAY, THE VIEW FROM HERE IS JUST AS REGAL.
I'M FLATTERED, BUT CITY LIGHTS SIMPLY DO NOT COMPARE TO THE MOUNTAINSCAPES OF MY YOUTH.
I'M SURPRISED YOU'RE NOT ADDRESSING ME FROM ATOP A THRONE, SUPREME COMMANDER SHANG-CHI.
I'M A DIFFERENT SORT OF LEADER FROM MY FATHER, MR. RED DOT.
I HOPE YOU AT LEAST HAVE THE SAME INSTINCT FOR OPPORTUNITY.
THE RED DOT COLLECTIVE RECENTLY CAME ACROSS A MOST SPECTACULAR PIECE OF WEAPONRY. WE'RE LOOKING FOR THE RIGHT BUYER.

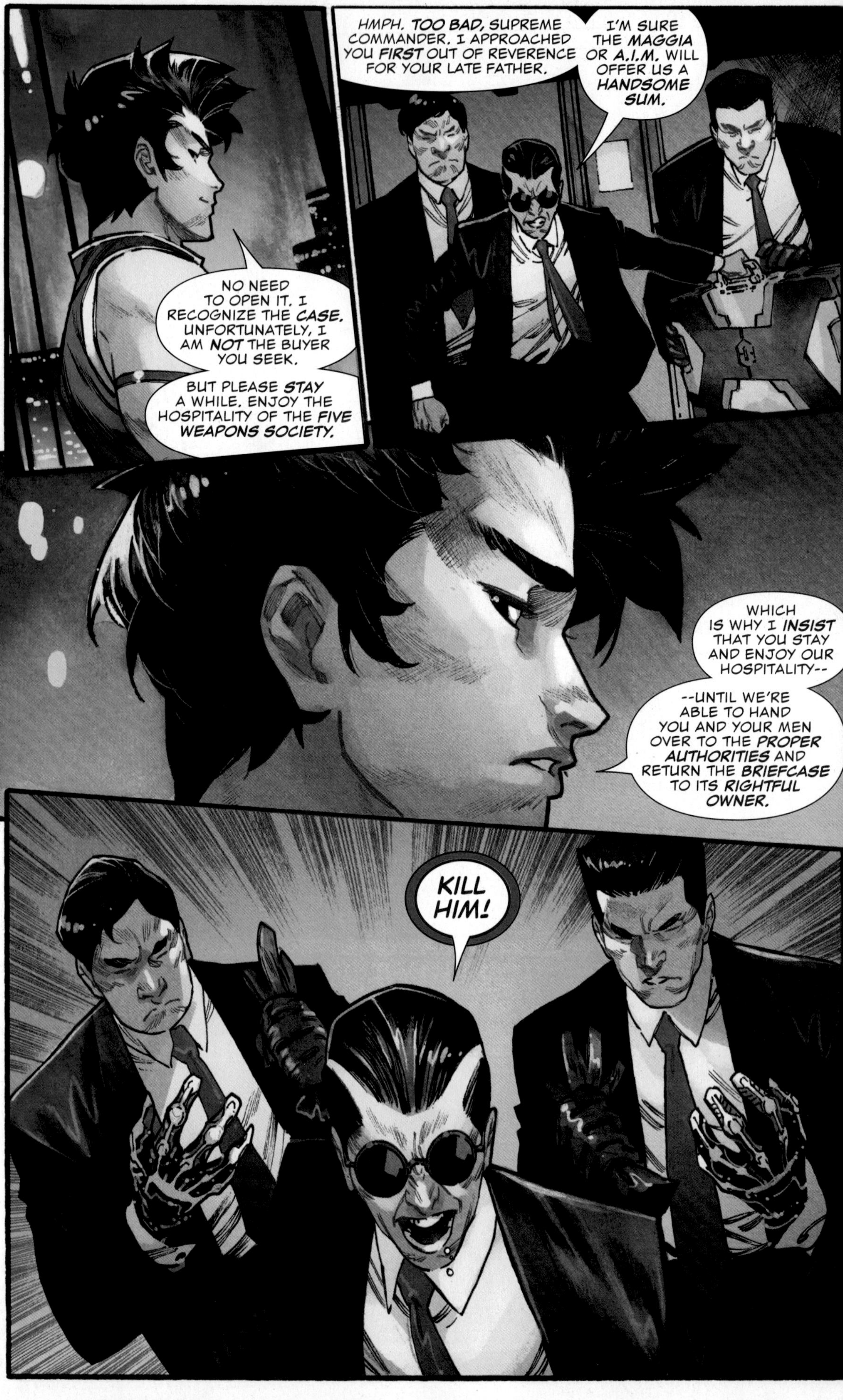
NO NEED TO OPEN IT. I RECOGNIZE THE CASE. UNFORTUNATELY, I AM NOT THE BUYER YOU SEEK.
BUT PLEASE STAY A WHILE. ENJOY THE HOSPITALITY OF THE FIVE WEAPONS SOCIETY.
HMPH. TOO BAD, SUPREME COMMANDER. I APPROACHED YOU FIRST OUT OF REVERENCE FOR YOUR LATE FATHER.
I'M SURE THE MAGGIA OR A.I.M. WILL OFFER US A HANDSOME SUM.
WHICH IS WHY I INSIST THAT YOU STAY AND ENJOY OUR HOSPITALITY--
--UNTIL WE'RE ABLE TO HAND YOU AND YOUR MEN OVER TO THE PROPER AUTHORITIES AND RETURN THE BRIEFCASE TO ITS RIGHTFUL OWNER.
KILL HIM!

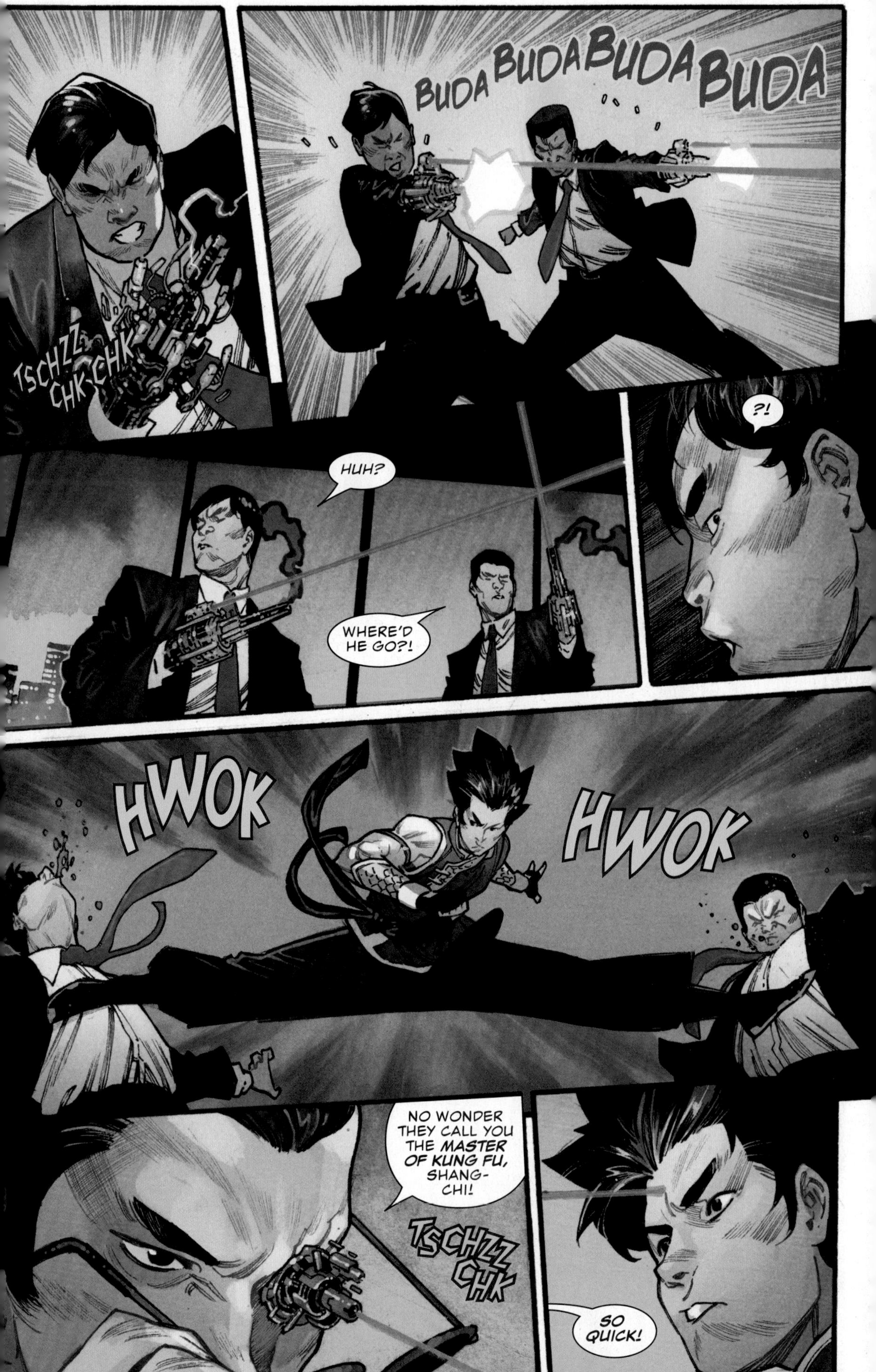
TSCHZZ CHK CHK
BUDA BUDA BUDA BUDA
?!
HUH?
WHERE'D HE GO?!
HWOK
HWOK
NO WONDER THEY CALL YOU THE *MASTER OF KUNG FU,* SHANG-CHI!
TSCHZZ CHK
SO QUICK!

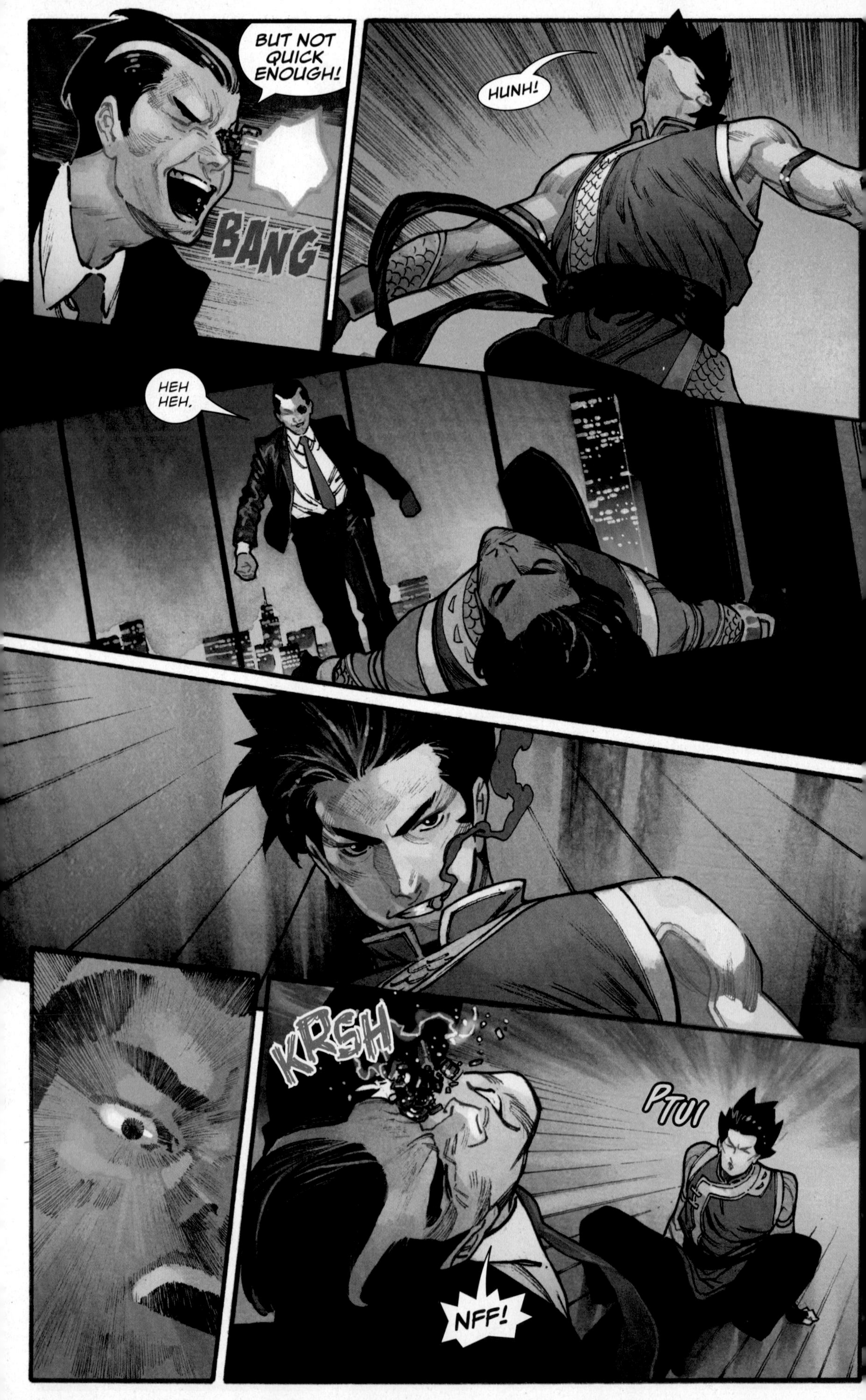

BUT NOT QUICK ENOUGH!
BANG
HUNH!
HEH HEH.
KRSH
PTUI
NFF!

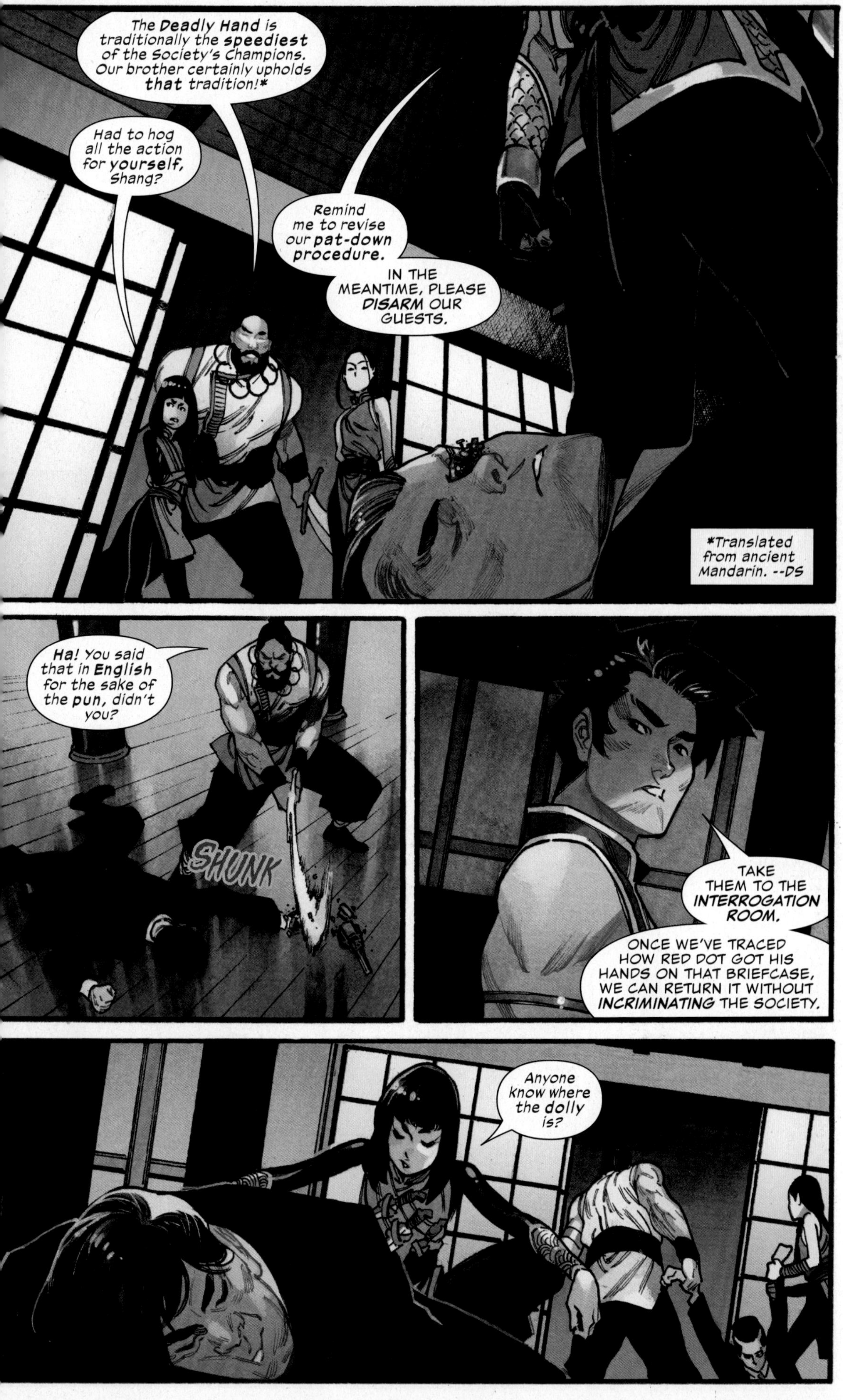
The Deadly Hand is traditionally the speediest of the Society's Champions. Our brother certainly upholds that tradition!*
Had to hog all the action for yourself, Shang?
Remind me to revise our pat-down procedure.
IN THE MEANTIME, PLEASE DISARM OUR GUESTS.
*Translated from ancient Mandarin. --DS
Ha! You said that in English for the sake of the pun, didn't you?
SHUNK
TAKE THEM TO THE INTERROGATION ROOM.
ONCE WE'VE TRACED HOW RED DOT GOT HIS HANDS ON THAT BRIEFCASE, WE CAN RETURN IT WITHOUT INCRIMINATING THE SOCIETY.
Anyone know where the dolly is?

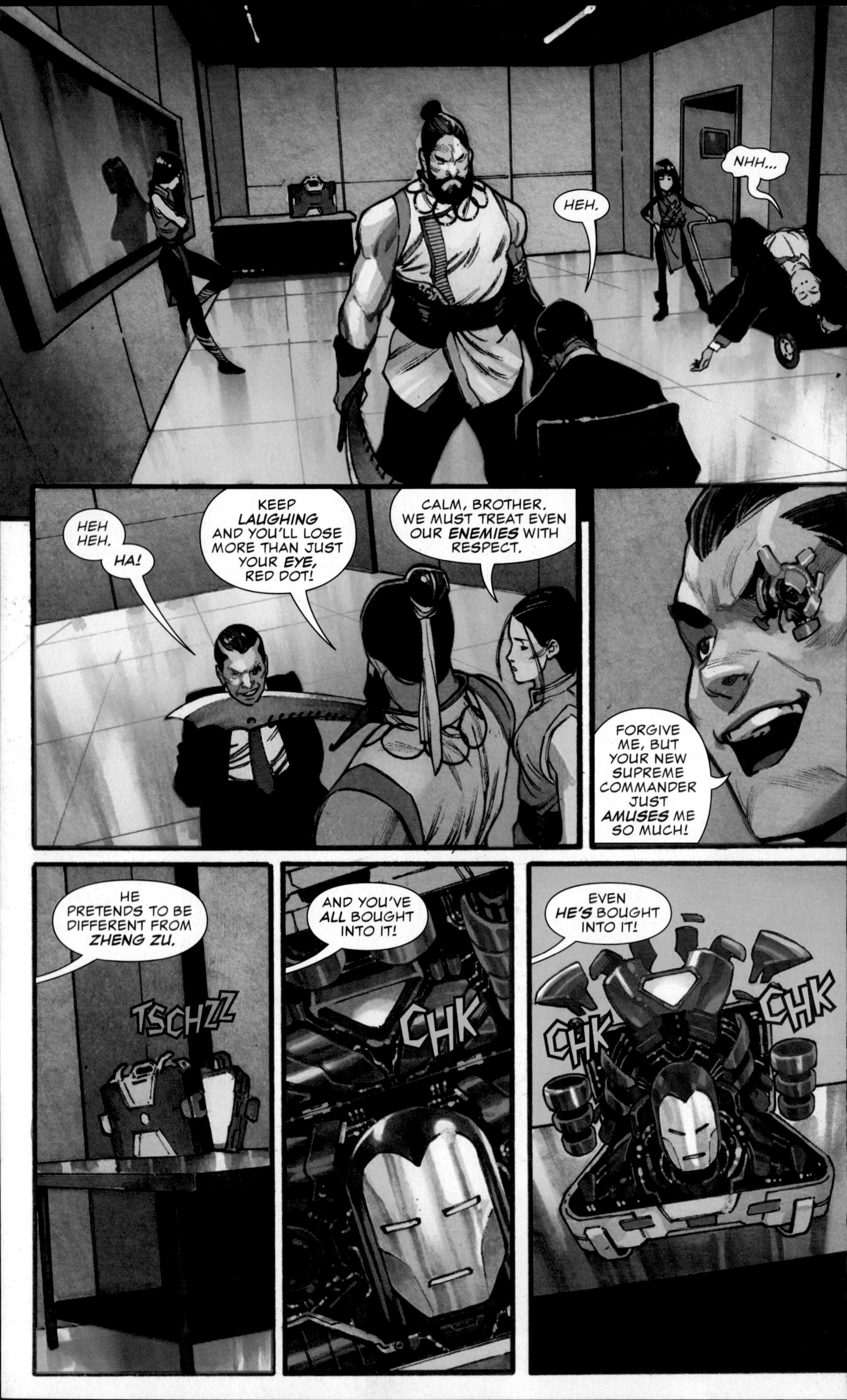
HEH.
NHH...
HEH HEH. HA!
KEEP LAUGHING AND YOU'LL LOSE MORE THAN JUST YOUR EYE, RED DOT!
CALM, BROTHER. WE MUST TREAT EVEN OUR ENEMIES WITH RESPECT.
FORGIVE ME, BUT YOUR NEW SUPREME COMMANDER JUST AMUSES ME SO MUCH!
HE PRETENDS TO BE DIFFERENT FROM ZHENG ZU.
TSCHZZZ
AND YOU'VE ALL BOUGHT INTO IT!
CHK
EVEN HE'S BOUGHT INTO IT!
CHK
CHK

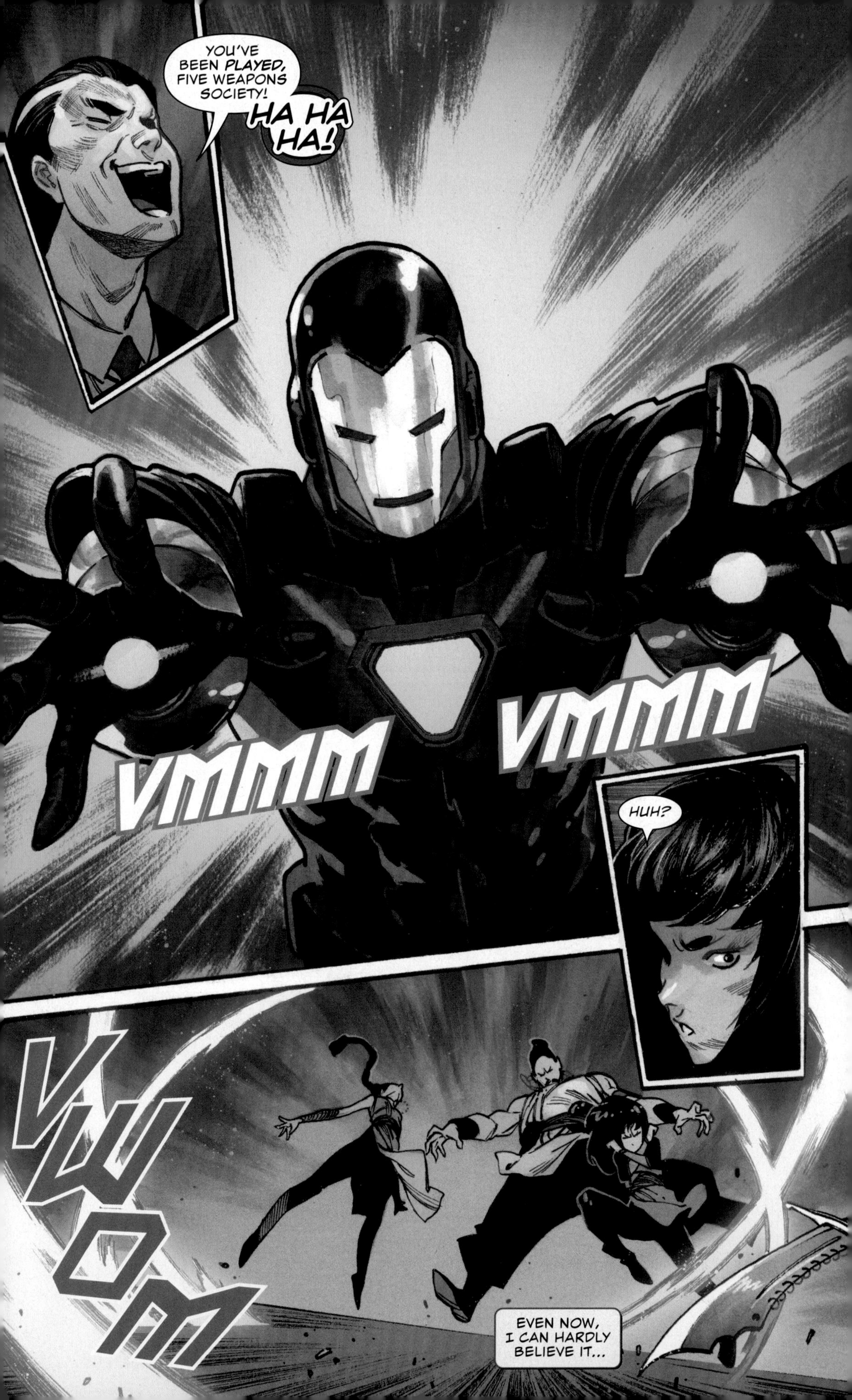

YOU'VE BEEN PLAYED, FIVE WEAPONS SOCIETY!
HA HA HA!
VMMM
VMMM
HUH?
VWOM
EVEN NOW, I CAN HARDLY BELIEVE IT...

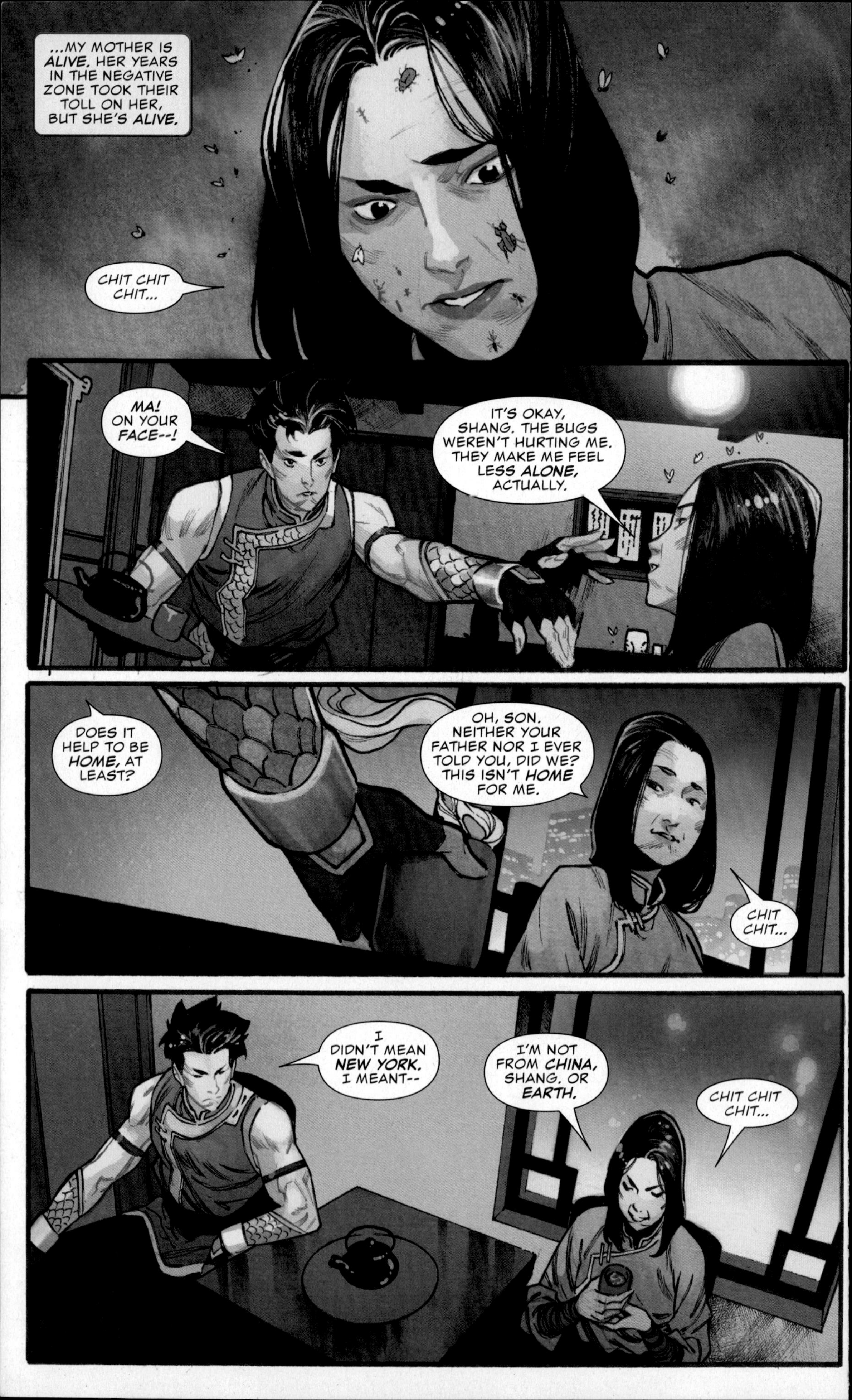
...MY MOTHER IS ALIVE. HER YEARS IN THE NEGATIVE ZONE TOOK THEIR TOLL ON HER, BUT SHE'S ALIVE.
CHIT CHIT CHIT...
MA! ON YOUR FACE--!
IT'S OKAY, SHANG. THE BUGS WEREN'T HURTING ME. THEY MAKE ME FEEL LESS ALONE, ACTUALLY.
DOES IT HELP TO BE HOME, AT LEAST?
OH, SON. NEITHER YOUR FATHER NOR I EVER TOLD YOU, DID WE? THIS ISN'T HOME FOR ME.
CHIT CHIT...
I DIDN'T MEAN NEW YORK. I MEANT--
I'M NOT FROM CHINA, SHANG. OR EARTH.
CHIT CHIT CHIT...

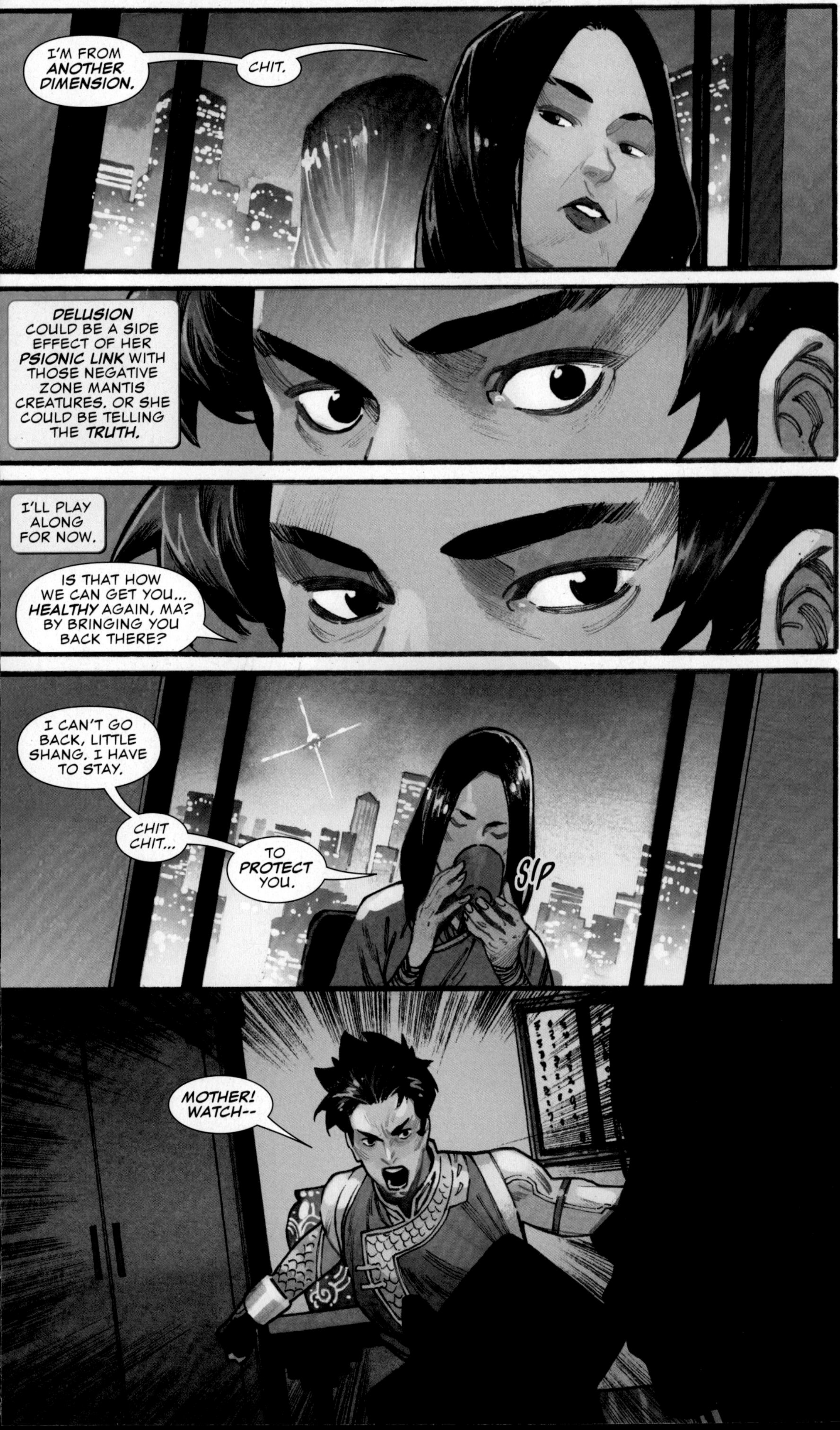
I'M FROM ANOTHER DIMENSION.
CHIT.
DELUSION COULD BE A SIDE EFFECT OF HER PSIONIC LINK WITH THOSE NEGATIVE ZONE MANTIS CREATURES. OR SHE COULD BE TELLING THE TRUTH.
I'LL PLAY ALONG FOR NOW.
IS THAT HOW WE CAN GET YOU... HEALTHY AGAIN, MA? BY BRINGING YOU BACK THERE?
I CAN'T GO BACK, LITTLE SHANG. I HAVE TO STAY.
CHIT CHIT...
TO PROTECT YOU.
SIP
MOTHER! WATCH--

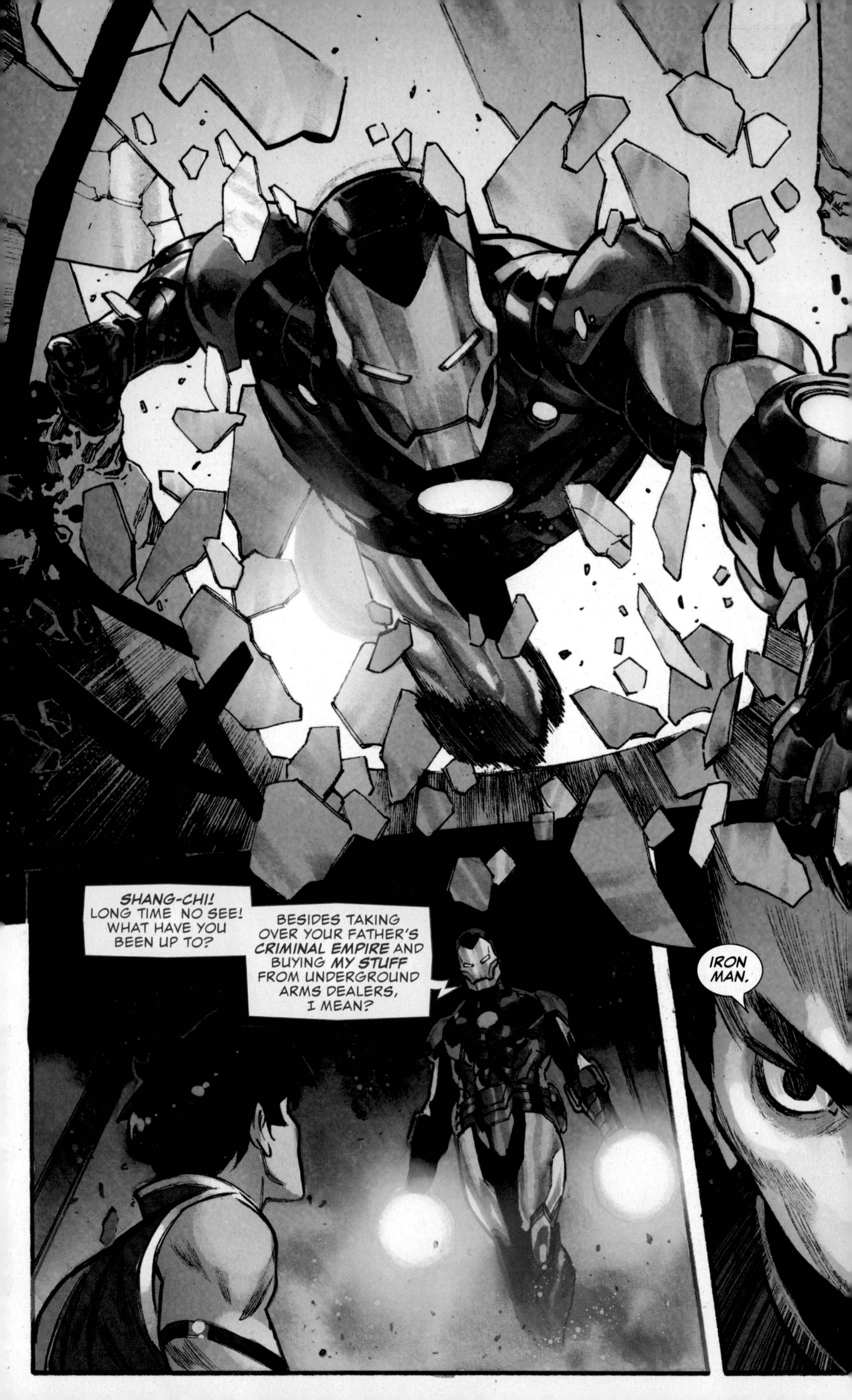
SHANG-CHI! LONG TIME NO SEE! WHAT HAVE YOU BEEN UP TO?
BESIDES TAKING OVER YOUR FATHER'S CRIMINAL EMPIRE AND BUYING MY STUFF FROM UNDERGROUND ARMS DEALERS, I MEAN?
IRON MAN.

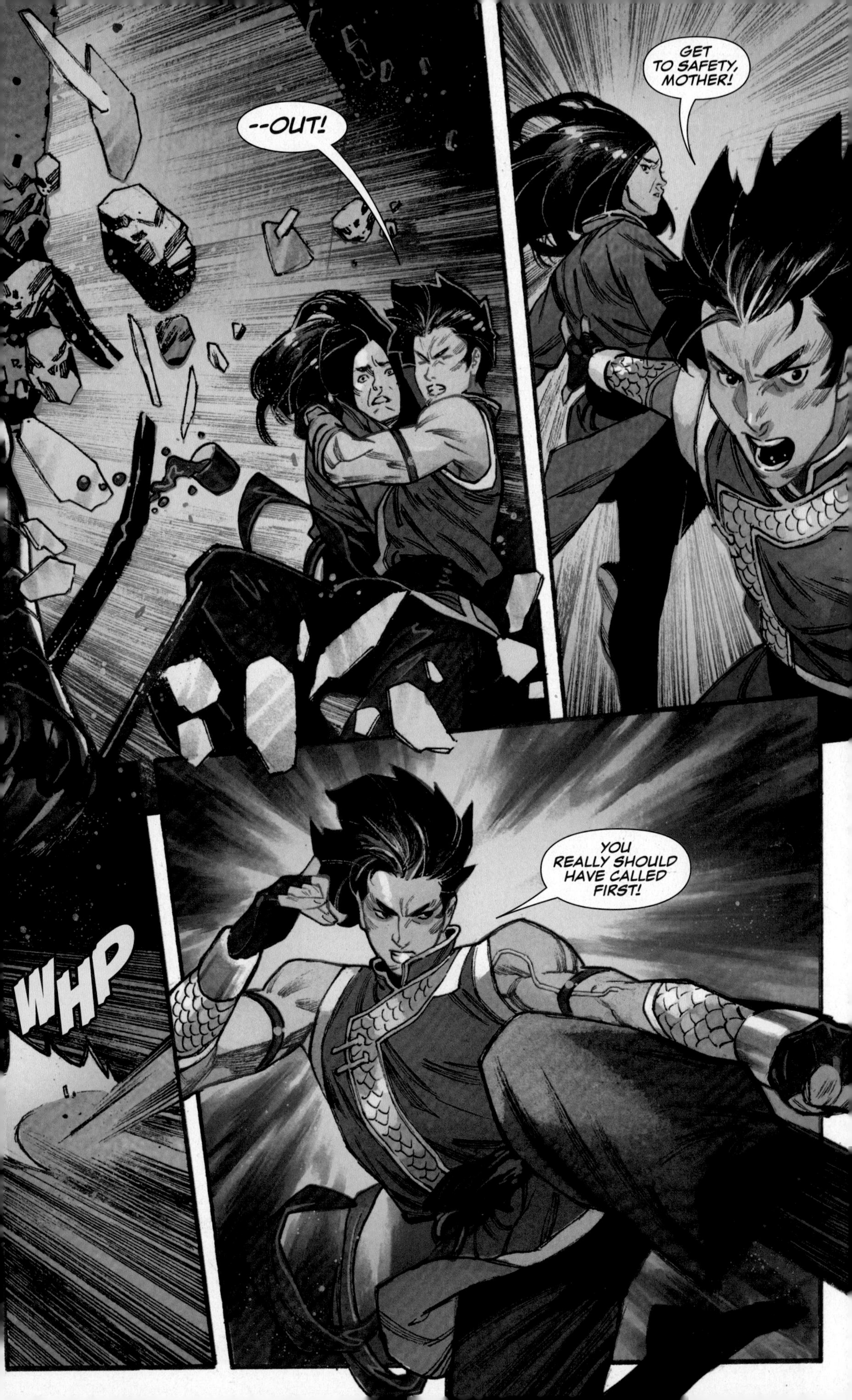
--OUT!
GET TO SAFETY, MOTHER!
YOU REALLY SHOULD HAVE CALLED FIRST!
WHP

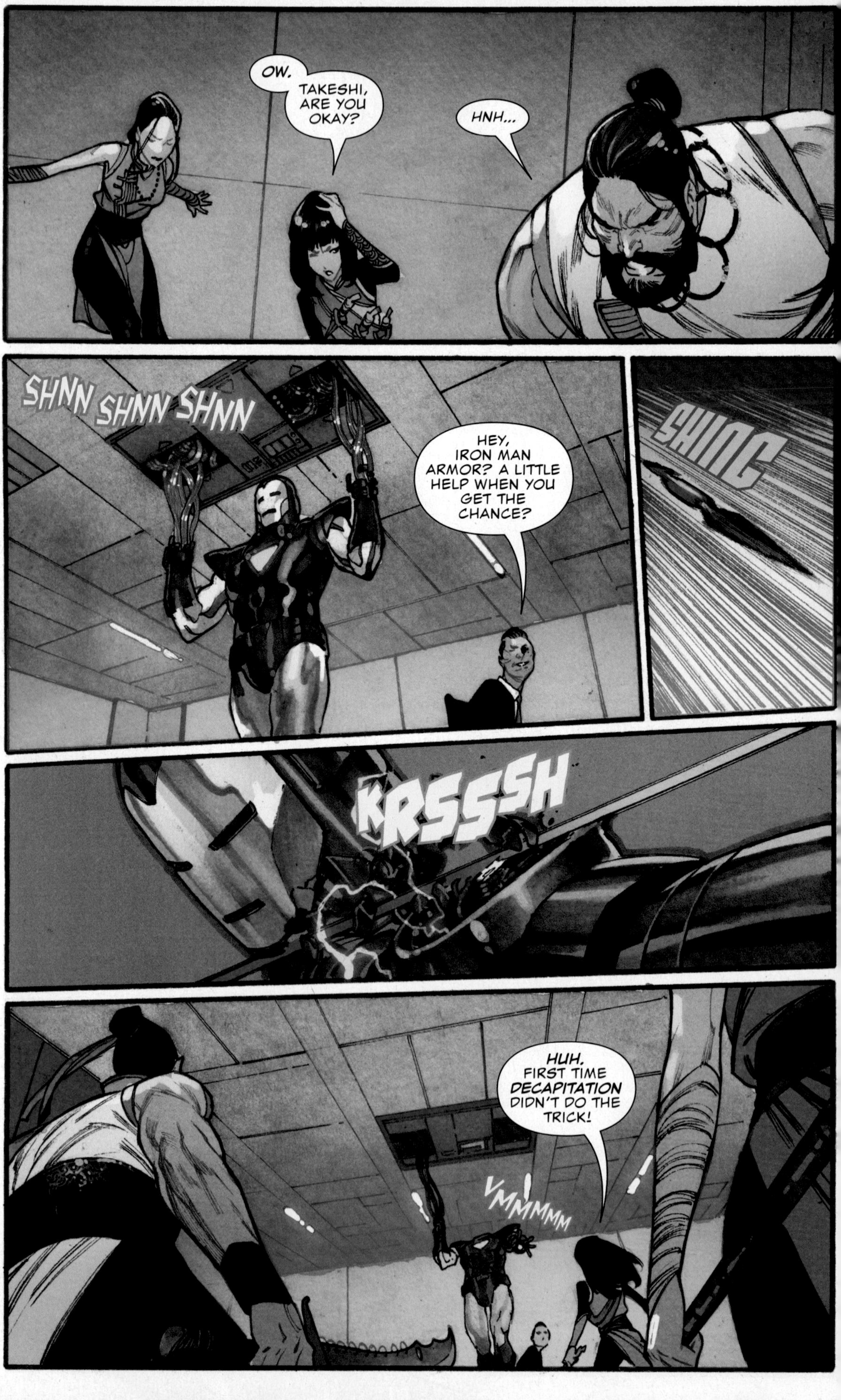
OW.
TAKESHI, ARE YOU OKAY?
HNH...
SHNN SHNN SHNN
HEY, IRON MAN ARMOR? A LITTLE HELP WHEN YOU GET THE CHANCE?
SHING
KRSSSH
HUH. FIRST TIME DECAPITATION DIDN'T DO THE TRICK!
VMMMMM

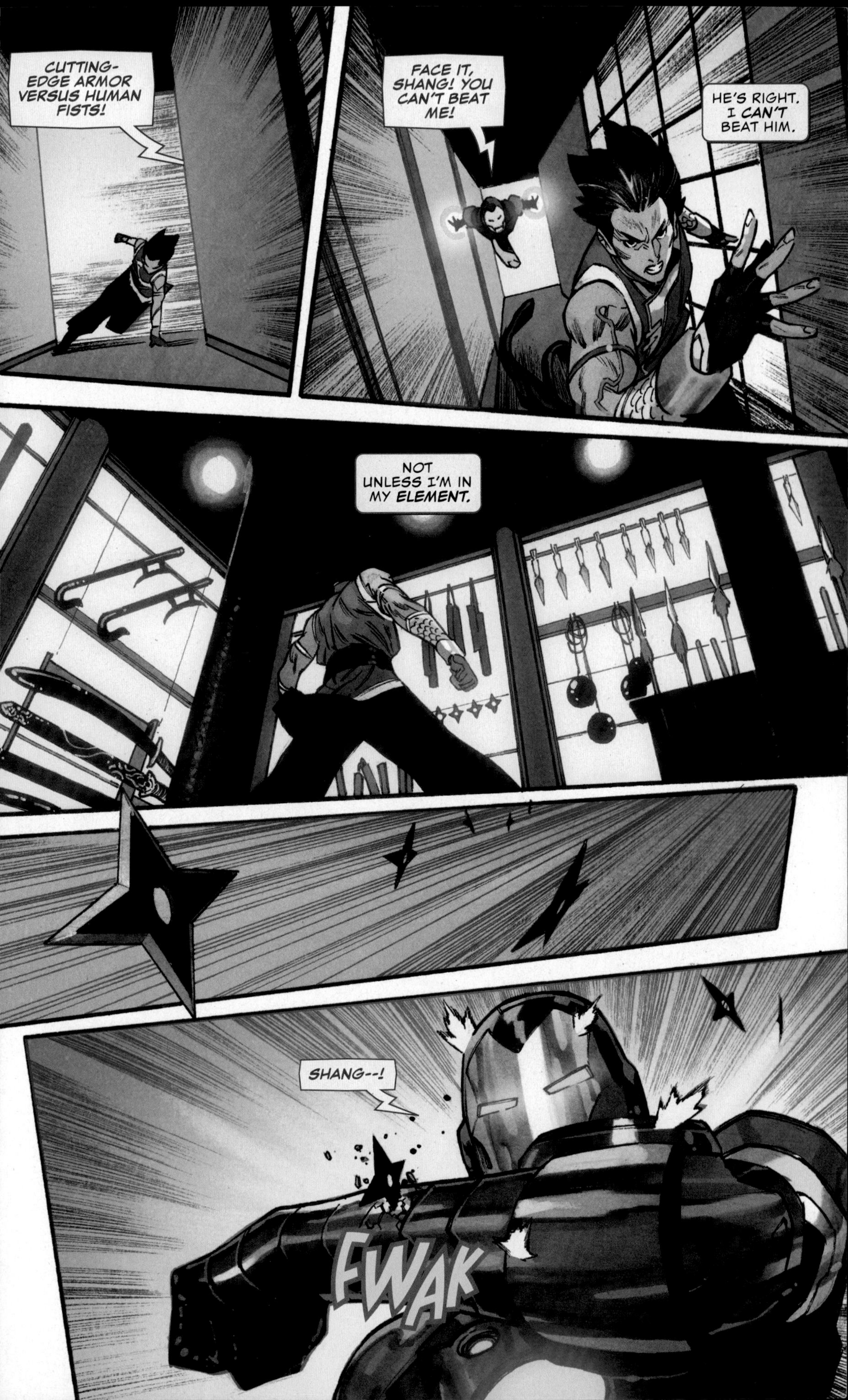
CUTTING-EDGE ARMOR VERSUS HUMAN FISTS!
FACE IT, SHANG! YOU CAN'T BEAT ME!
HE'S RIGHT. I CAN'T BEAT HIM.
NOT UNLESS I'M IN MY ELEMENT.
SHANG--!
FWAK

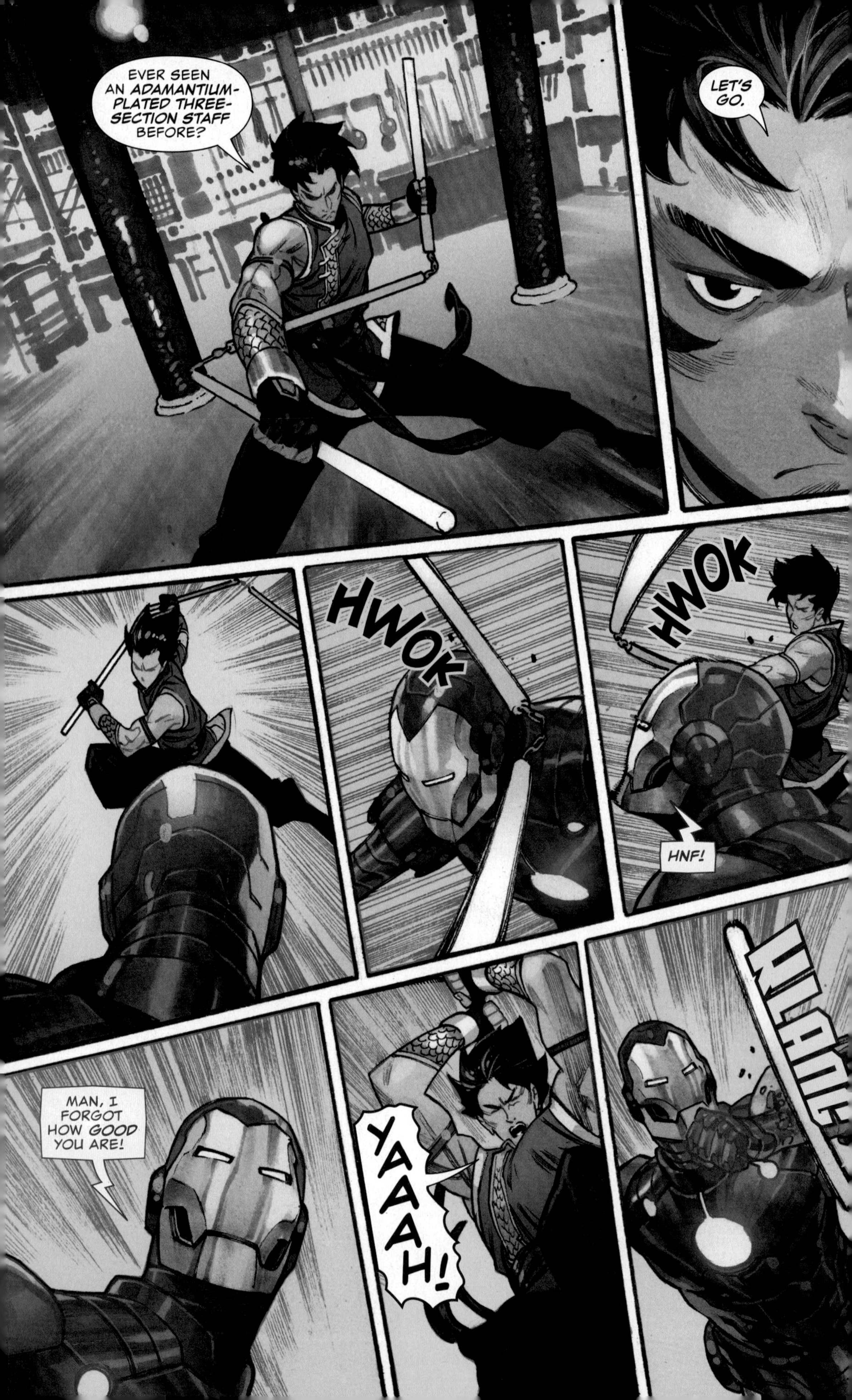
EVER SEEN AN ADAMANTIUM-PLATED THREE-SECTION STAFF BEFORE?
LET'S GO.
HWOK
HWOK
HNF!
MAN, I FORGOT HOW GOOD YOU ARE!
YAAAAH!

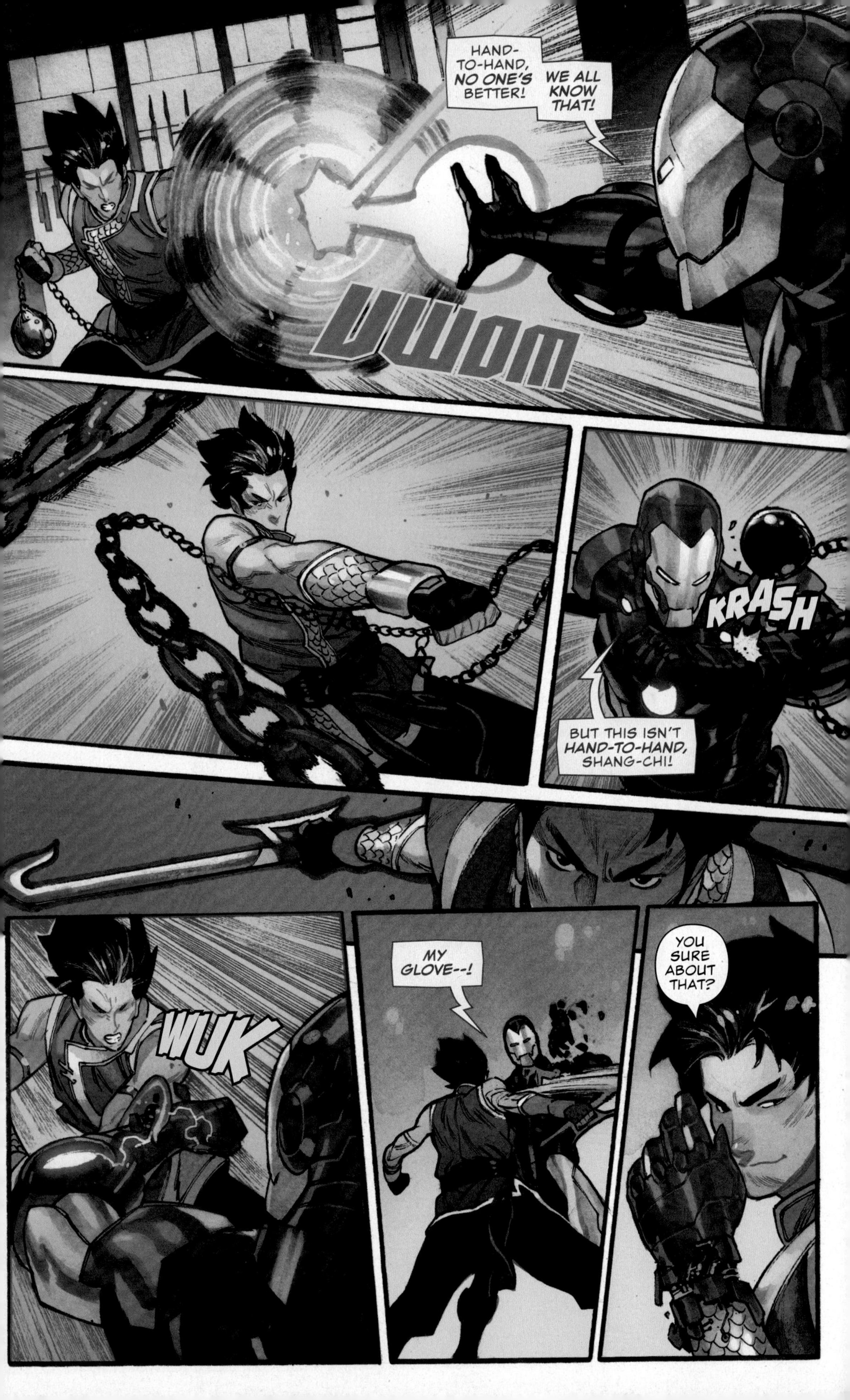
HAND-TO-HAND, NO ONE'S BETTER!
WE ALL KNOW THAT!
UWOM
KRASH
BUT THIS ISN'T HAND-TO-HAND, SHANG-CHI!
WUK
MY GLOVE--!
YOU SURE ABOUT THAT?

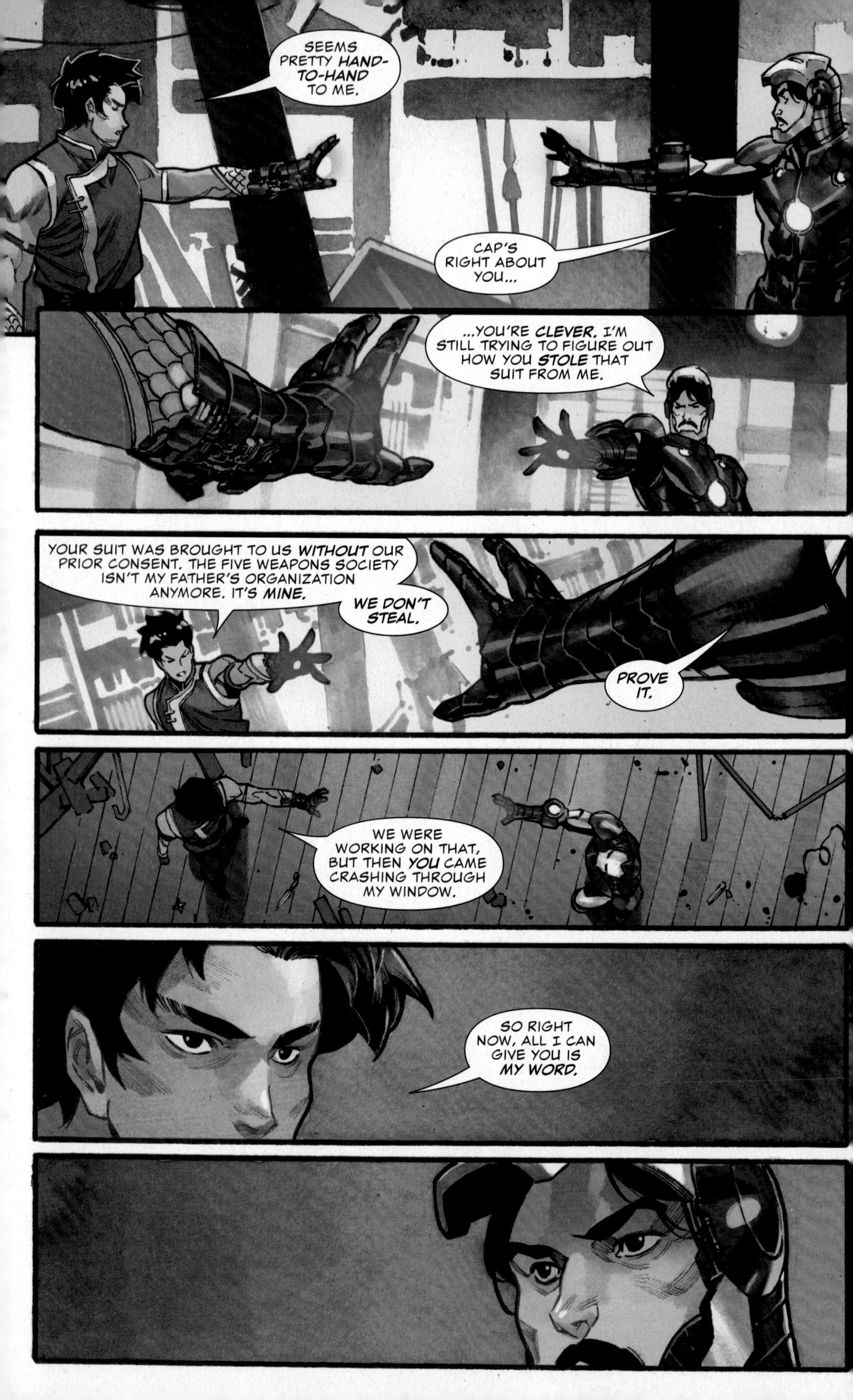
SEEMS PRETTY HAND-TO-HAND TO ME.
CAP'S RIGHT ABOUT YOU...
...YOU'RE CLEVER. I'M STILL TRYING TO FIGURE OUT HOW YOU STOLE THAT SUIT FROM ME.
YOUR SUIT WAS BROUGHT TO US WITHOUT OUR PRIOR CONSENT. THE FIVE WEAPONS SOCIETY ISN'T MY FATHER'S ORGANIZATION ANYMORE. IT'S MINE.
WE DON'T STEAL.
PROVE IT.
WE WERE WORKING ON THAT, BUT THEN YOU CAME CRASHING THROUGH MY WINDOW.
SO RIGHT NOW, ALL I CAN GIVE YOU IS MY WORD.

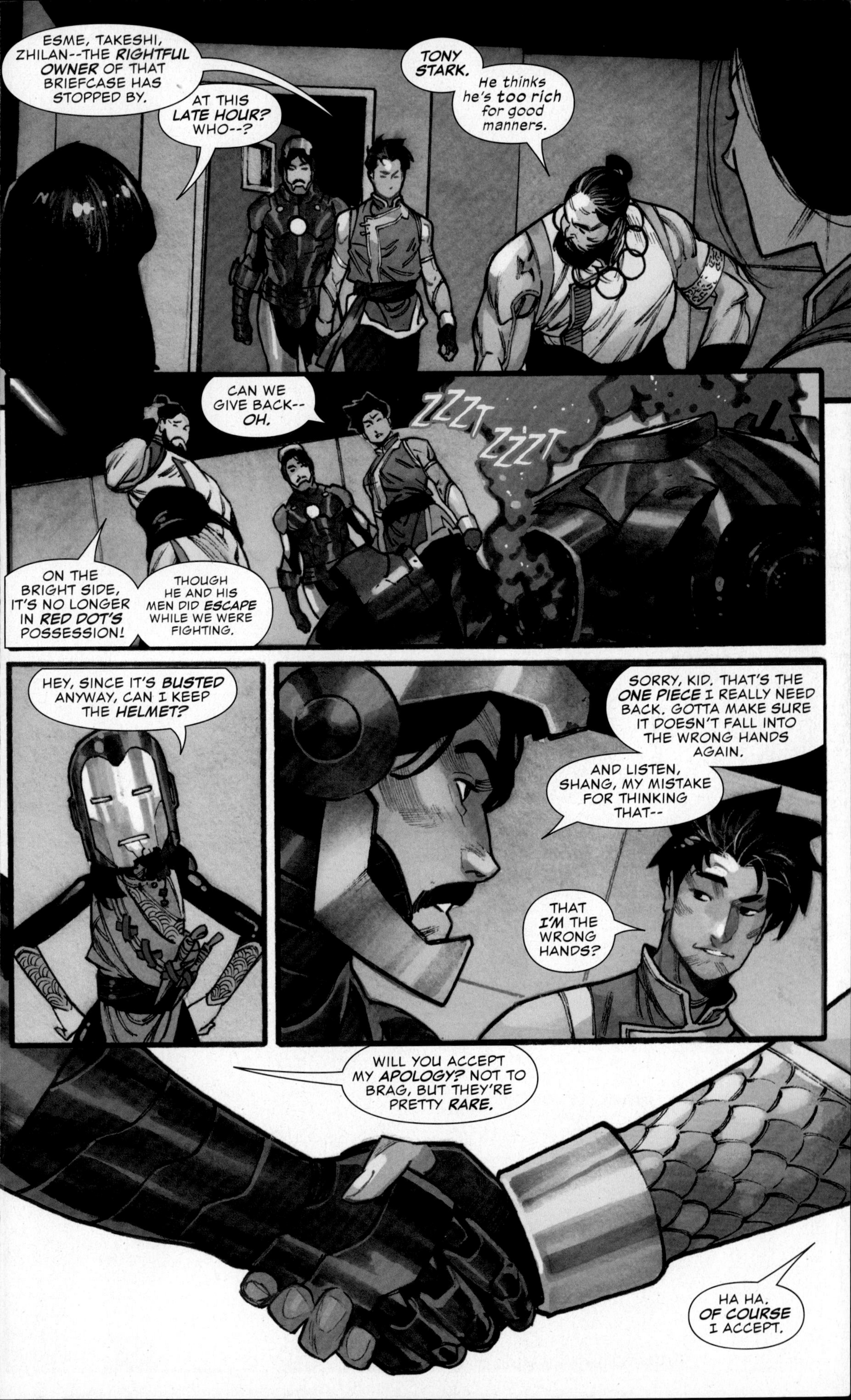
ESME, TAKESHI, ZHILAN--THE RIGHTFUL OWNER OF THAT BRIEFCASE HAS STOPPED BY.
AT THIS LATE HOUR? WHO--?
TONY STARK.
He thinks he's too rich for good manners.
CAN WE GIVE BACK-- OH.
ZZZT ZZZT
ON THE BRIGHT SIDE, IT'S NO LONGER IN RED DOT'S POSSESSION!
THOUGH HE AND HIS MEN DID ESCAPE WHILE WE WERE FIGHTING.
HEY, SINCE IT'S BUSTED ANYWAY, CAN I KEEP THE HELMET?
SORRY, KID. THAT'S THE ONE PIECE I REALLY NEED BACK. GOTTA MAKE SURE IT DOESN'T FALL INTO THE WRONG HANDS AGAIN.
AND LISTEN, SHANG, MY MISTAKE FOR THINKING THAT--
THAT I'M THE WRONG HANDS?
WILL YOU ACCEPT MY APOLOGY? NOT TO BRAG, BUT THEY'RE PRETTY RARE.
HA HA. OF COURSE I ACCEPT.

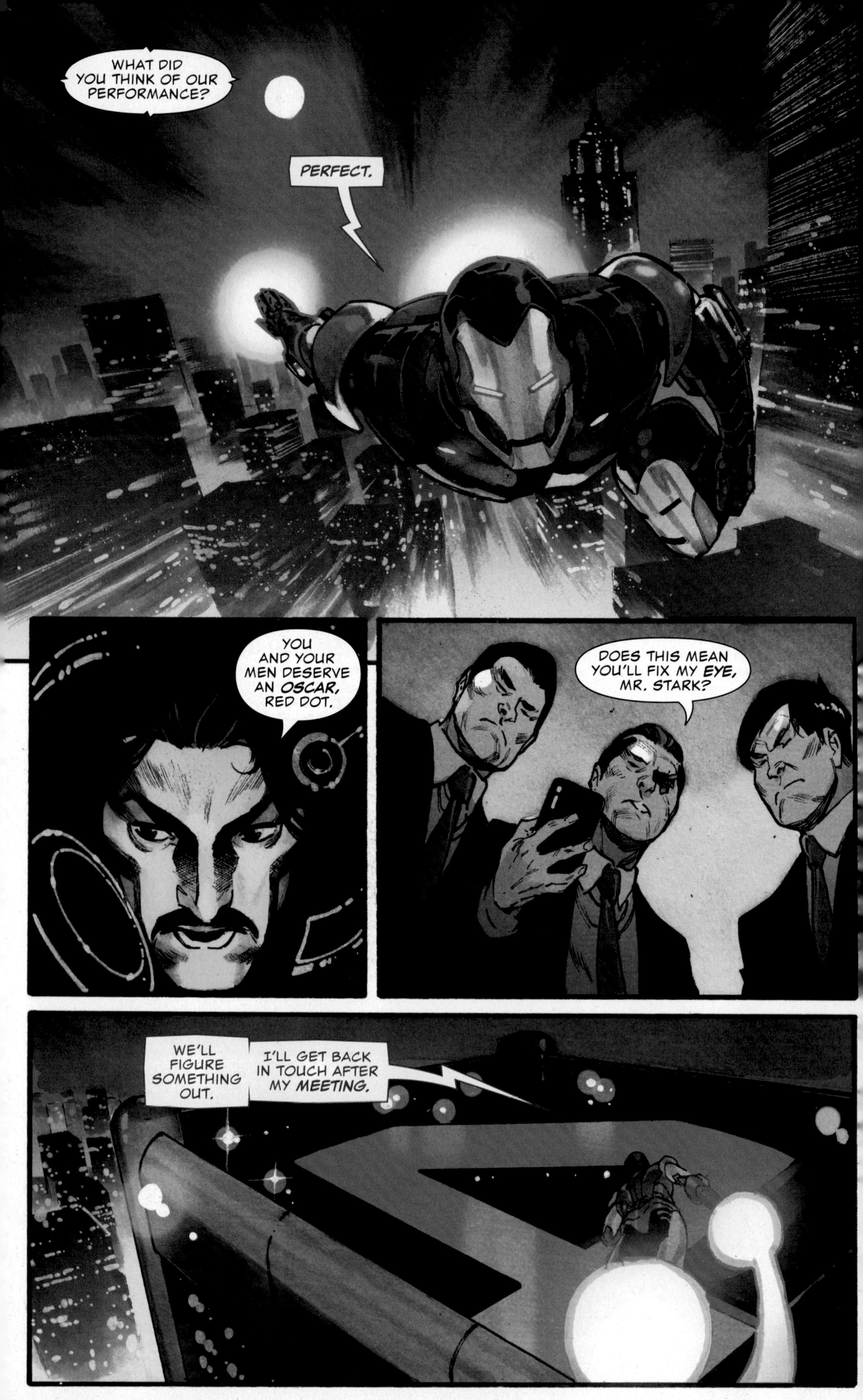
WHAT DID YOU THINK OF OUR PERFORMANCE?
PERFECT.
YOU AND YOUR MEN DESERVE AN OSCAR, RED DOT.
DOES THIS MEAN YOU'LL FIX MY EYE, MR. STARK?
WE'LL FIGURE SOMETHING OUT.
I'LL GET BACK IN TOUCH AFTER MY MEETING.

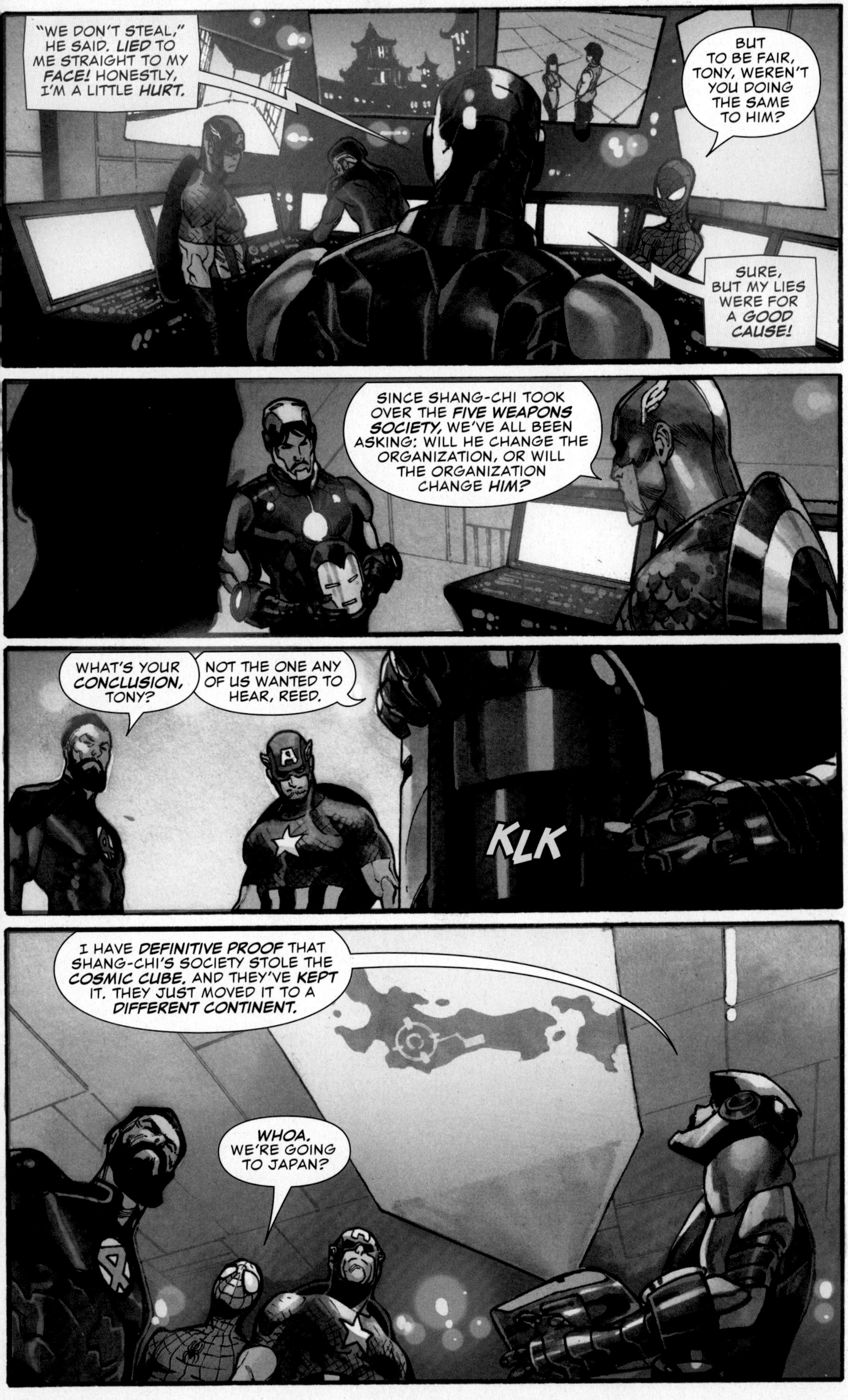
"WE DON'T STEAL," HE SAID. LIED TO ME STRAIGHT TO MY FACE! HONESTLY, I'M A LITTLE HURT.
BUT TO BE FAIR, TONY, WEREN'T YOU DOING THE SAME TO HIM?
SURE, BUT MY LIES WERE FOR A GOOD CAUSE!
SINCE SHANG-CHI TOOK OVER THE FIVE WEAPONS SOCIETY, WE'VE ALL BEEN ASKING: WILL HE CHANGE THE ORGANIZATION, OR WILL THE ORGANIZATION CHANGE HIM?
WHAT'S YOUR CONCLUSION, TONY?
NOT THE ONE ANY OF US WANTED TO HEAR, REED.
KLK
I HAVE DEFINITIVE PROOF THAT SHANG-CHI'S SOCIETY STOLE THE COSMIC CUBE, AND THEY'VE KEPT IT. THEY JUST MOVED IT TO A DIFFERENT CONTINENT.
WHOA. WE'RE GOING TO JAPAN?

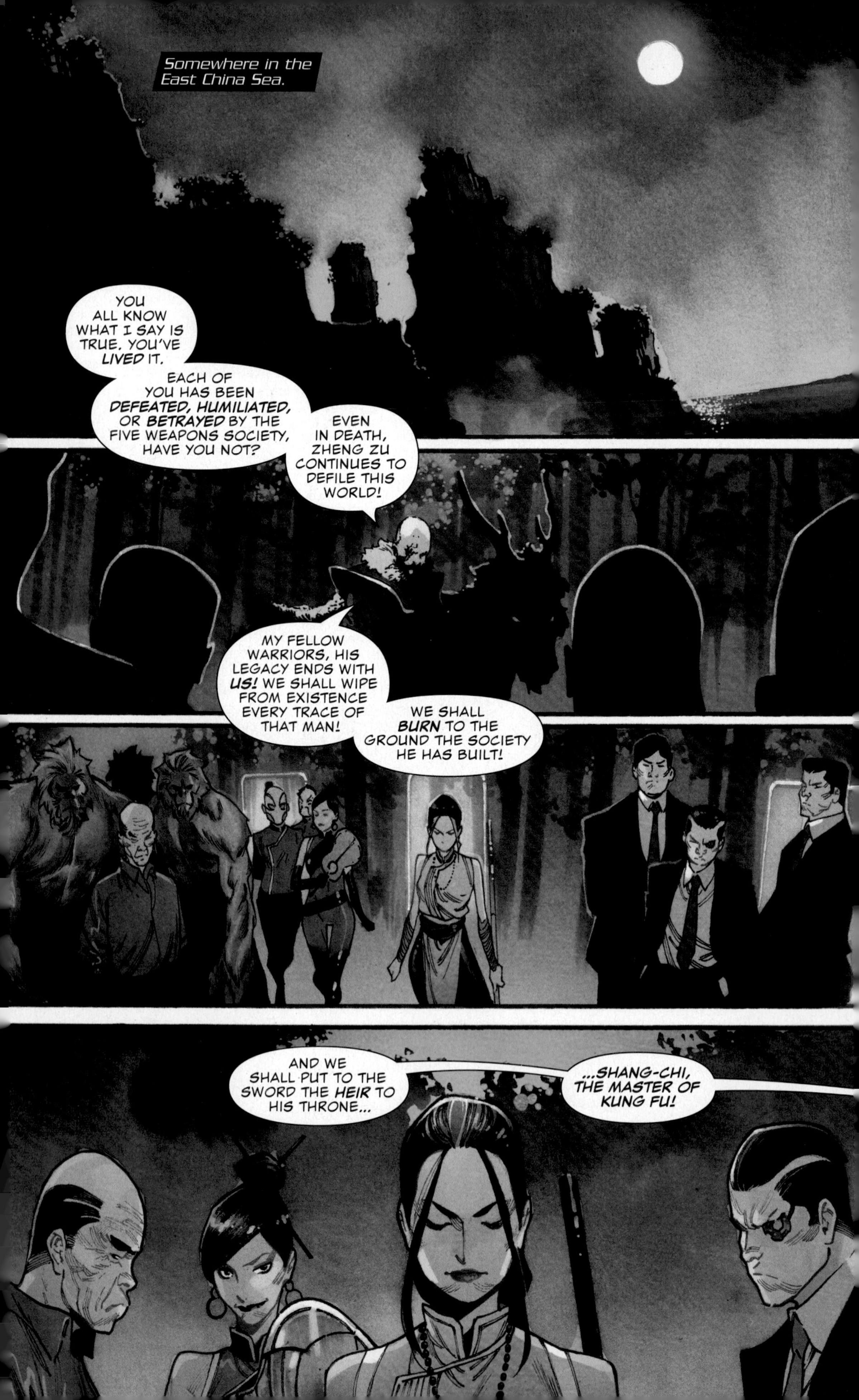
Somewhere in the East China Sea.
YOU ALL KNOW WHAT I SAY IS TRUE. YOU'VE LIVED IT.
EACH OF YOU HAS BEEN DEFEATED, HUMILIATED, OR BETRAYED BY THE FIVE WEAPONS SOCIETY, HAVE YOU NOT?
EVEN IN DEATH, ZHENG ZU CONTINUES TO DEFILE THIS WORLD!
MY FELLOW WARRIORS, HIS LEGACY ENDS WITH US! WE SHALL WIPE FROM EXISTENCE EVERY TRACE OF THAT MAN!
WE SHALL BURN TO THE GROUND THE SOCIETY HE HAS BUILT!
AND WE SHALL PUT TO THE SWORD THE HEIR TO HIS THRONE...
...SHANG-CHI, THE MASTER OF KUNG FU!

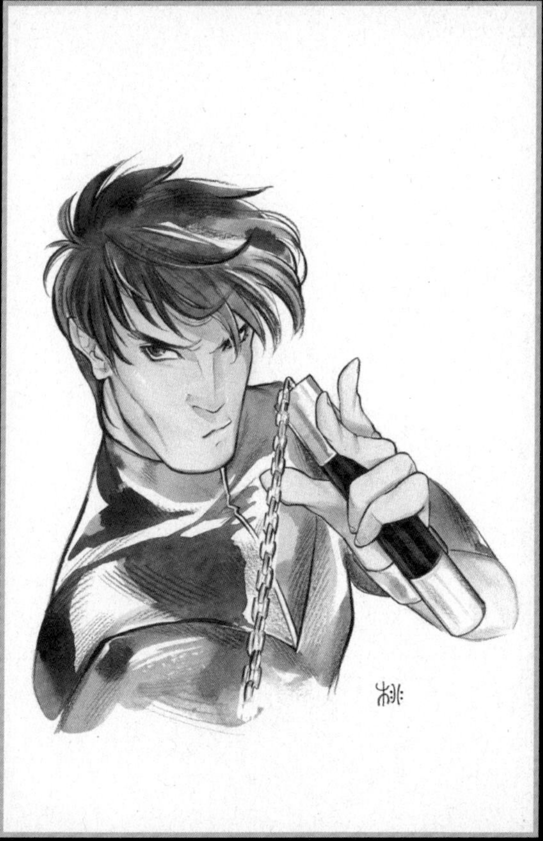

#3 ANIME VARIANT BY
PEACH MOMOKO

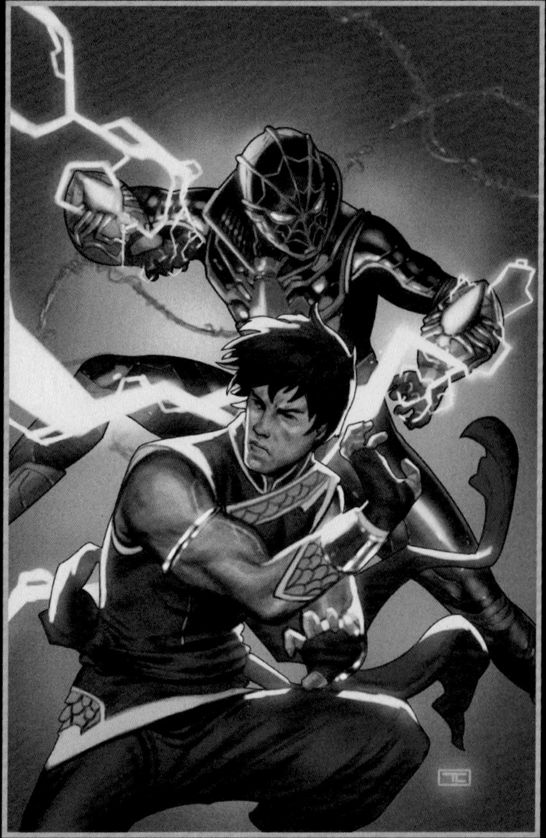

#4 MILES MORALES SPIDER-MAN 10TH ANNIVERSARY VARIANT BY
TAURIN CLARKE

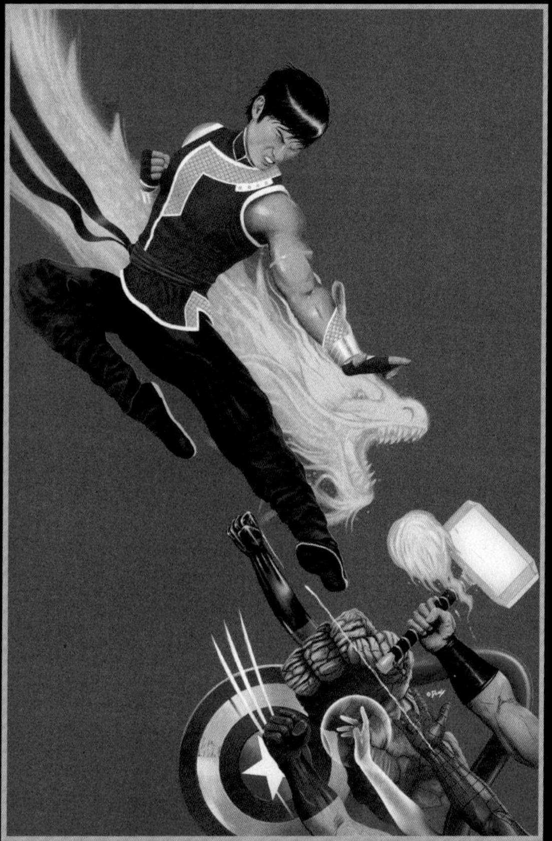

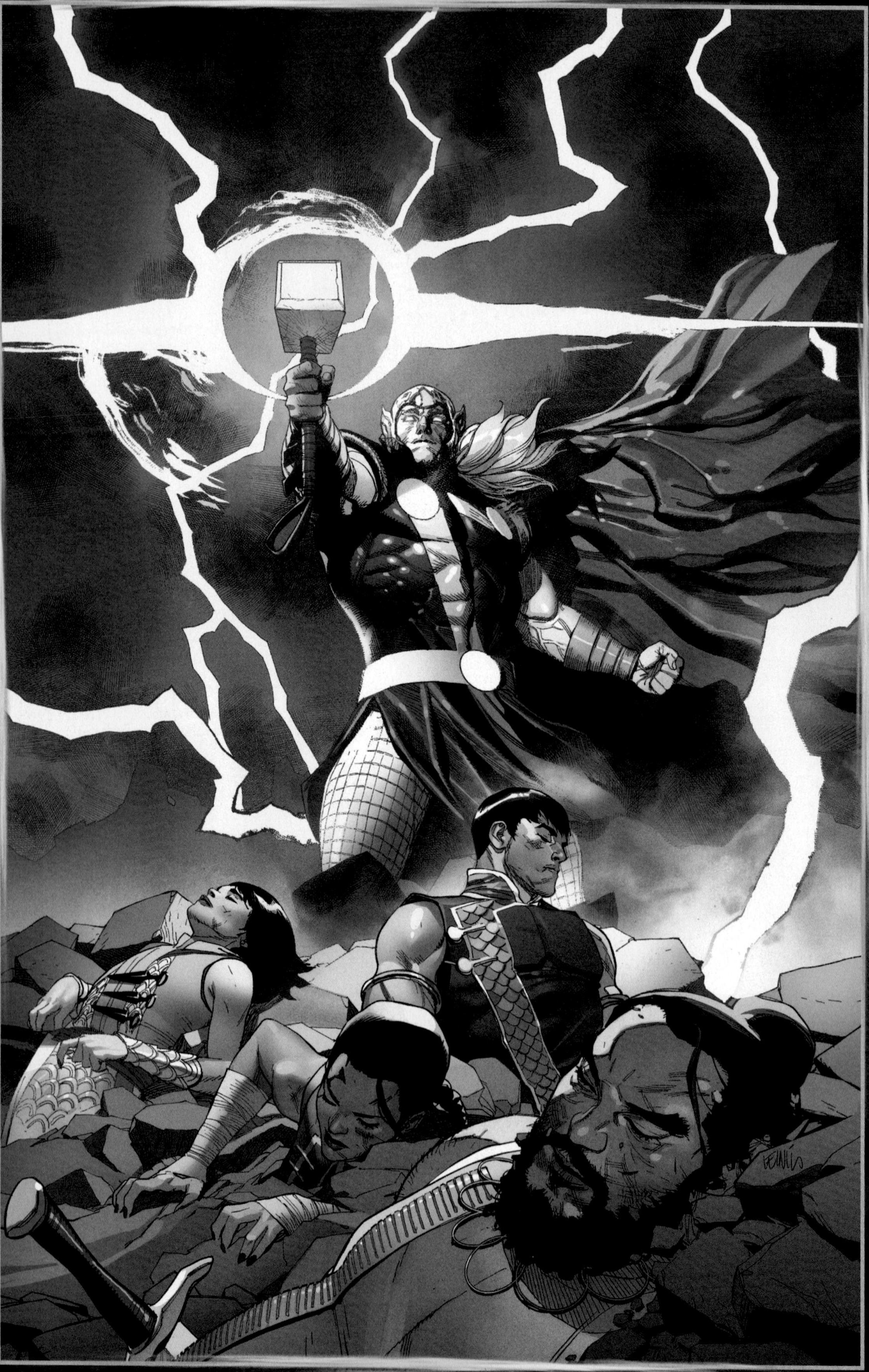

SIX

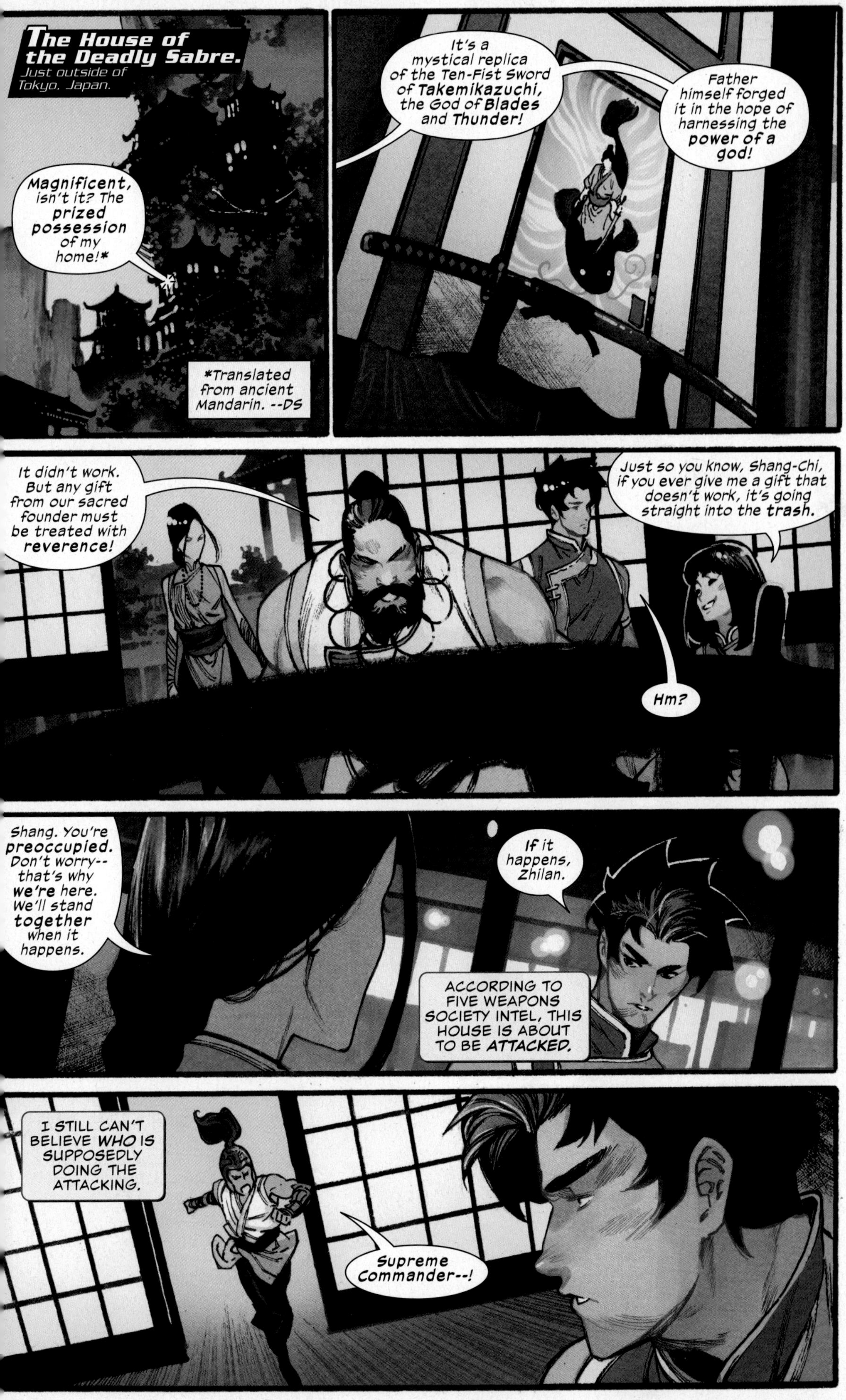

The House of the Deadly Sabre.
Just outside of Tokyo, Japan.
Magnificent, isn't it? The prized possession of my home!*
*Translated from ancient Mandarin. --DS
It's a mystical replica of the Ten-Fist Sword of Takemikazuchi, the God of Blades and Thunder!
Father himself forged it in the hope of harnessing the power of a god!
It didn't work. But any gift from our sacred founder must be treated with reverence!
Just so you know, Shang-Chi, if you ever give me a gift that doesn't work, it's going straight into the trash.
Hm?
Shang. You're preoccupied. Don't worry-- that's why we're here. We'll stand together when it happens.
If it happens, Zhilan.
ACCORDING TO FIVE WEAPONS SOCIETY INTEL, THIS HOUSE IS ABOUT TO BE ATTACKED.
I STILL CAN'T BELIEVE WHO IS SUPPOSEDLY DOING THE ATTACKING.
Supreme Commander--!

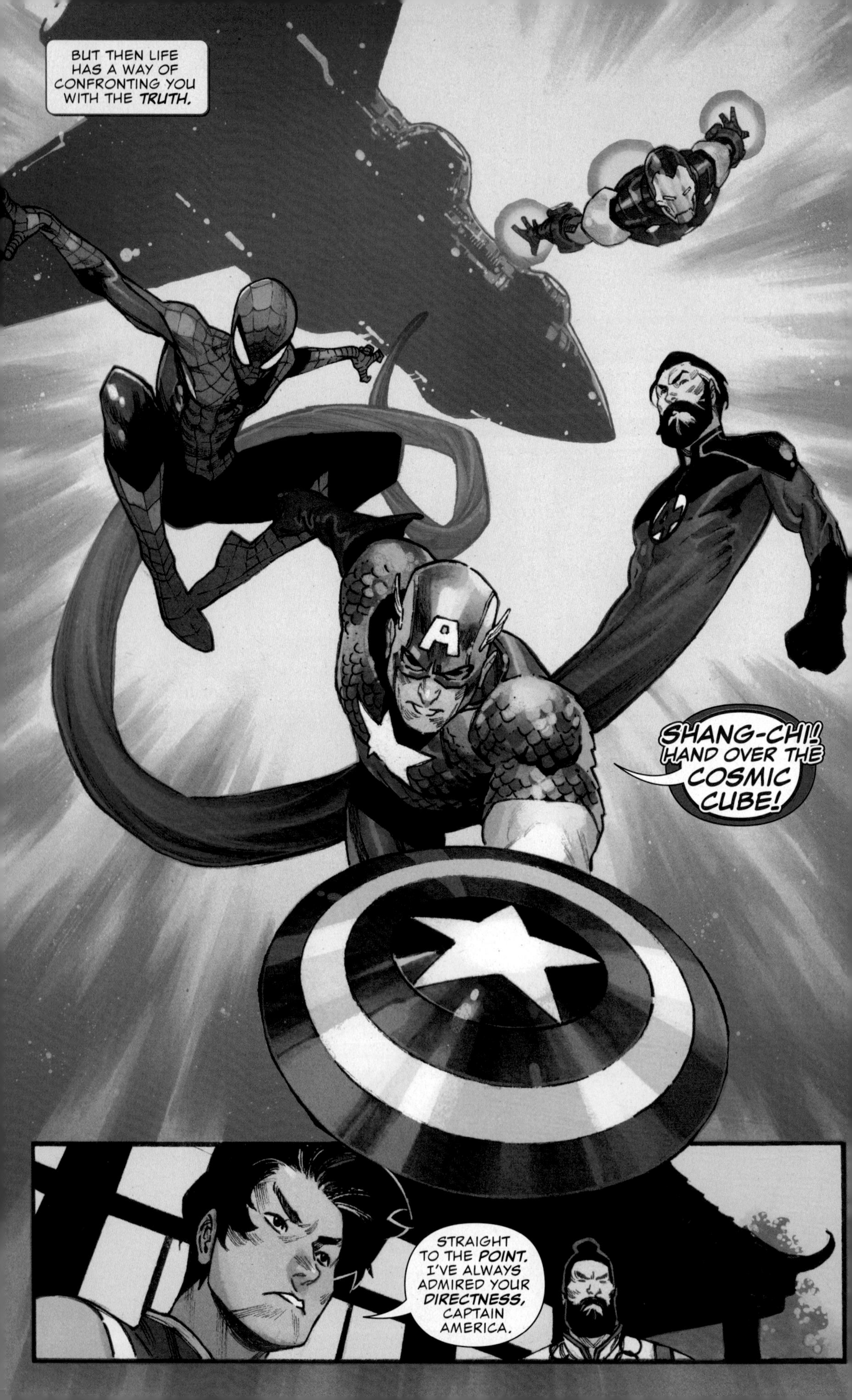
BUT THEN LIFE HAS A WAY OF CONFRONTING YOU WITH THE TRUTH.
SHANG-CHI! HAND OVER THE COSMIC CUBE!
STRAIGHT TO THE POINT. I'VE ALWAYS ADMIRED YOUR DIRECTNESS, CAPTAIN AMERICA.

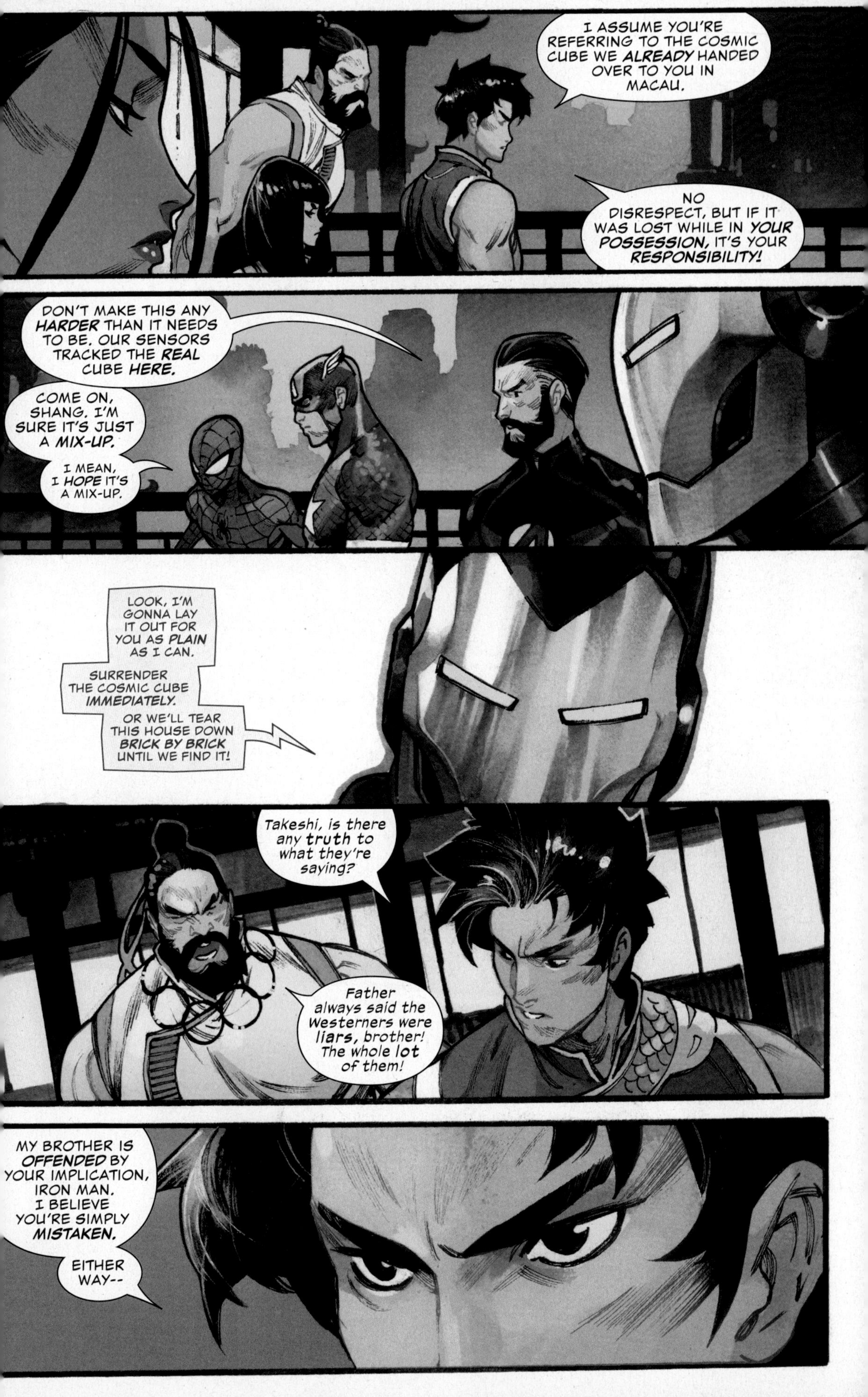

I ASSUME YOU'RE REFERRING TO THE COSMIC CUBE WE ALREADY HANDED OVER TO YOU IN MACAU.
NO DISRESPECT, BUT IF IT WAS LOST WHILE IN YOUR POSSESSION, IT'S YOUR RESPONSIBILITY!
DON'T MAKE THIS ANY HARDER THAN IT NEEDS TO BE. OUR SENSORS TRACKED THE REAL CUBE HERE.
COME ON, SHANG. I'M SURE IT'S JUST A MIX-UP.
I MEAN, I HOPE IT'S A MIX-UP.
LOOK, I'M GONNA LAY IT OUT FOR YOU AS PLAIN AS I CAN.
SURRENDER THE COSMIC CUBE IMMEDIATELY.
OR WE'LL TEAR THIS HOUSE DOWN BRICK BY BRICK UNTIL WE FIND IT!
Takeshi, is there any truth to what they're saying?
Father always said the Westerners were liars, brother! The whole lot of them!
MY BROTHER IS OFFENDED BY YOUR IMPLICATION, IRON MAN.
I BELIEVE YOU'RE SIMPLY MISTAKEN.
EITHER WAY--

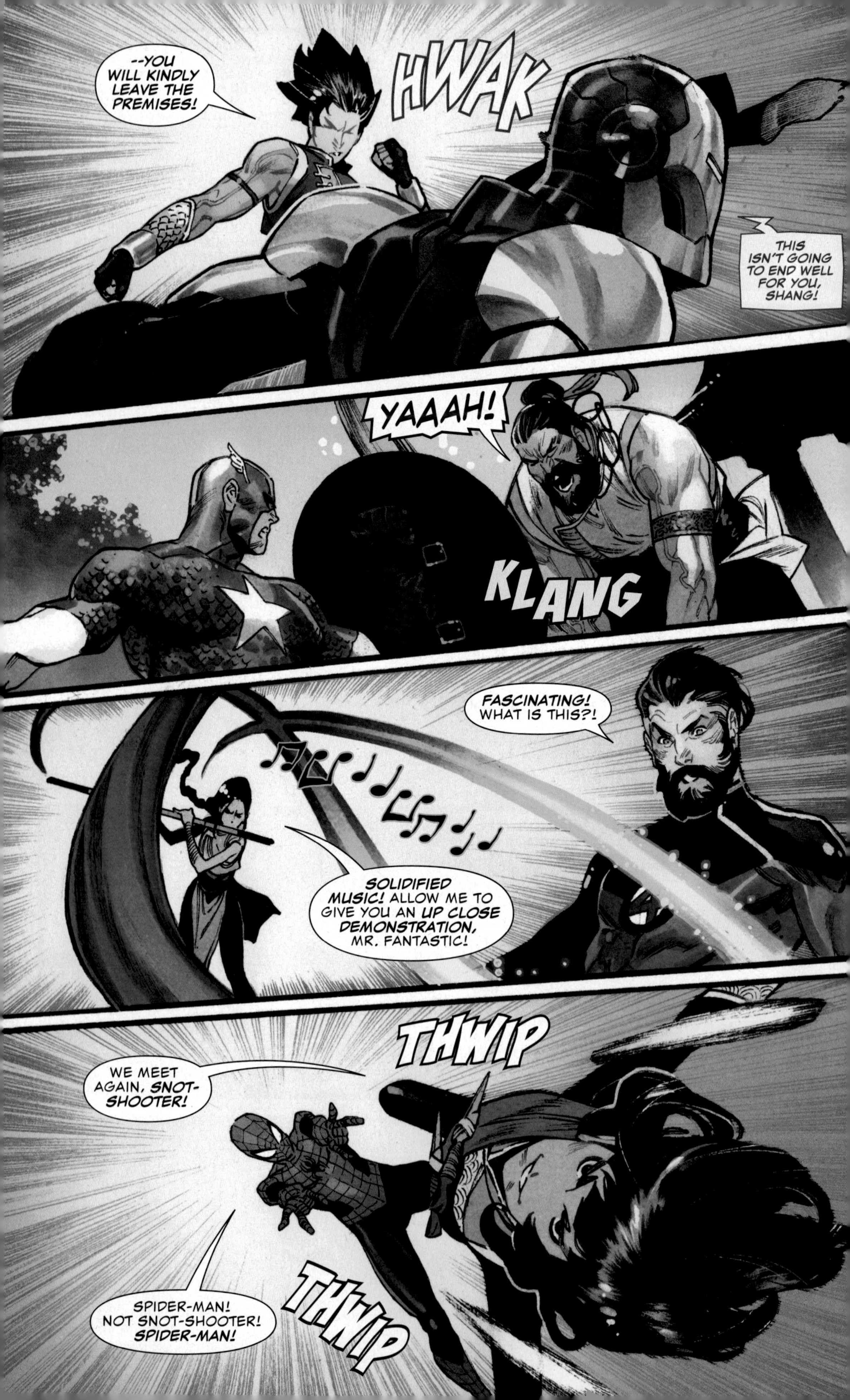
--YOU WILL KINDLY LEAVE THE PREMISES!
HWAK
THIS ISN'T GOING TO END WELL FOR YOU, SHANG!
YAAAH!
KLANG
FASCINATING! WHAT IS THIS?!
SOLIDIFIED MUSIC! ALLOW ME TO GIVE YOU AN UP CLOSE DEMONSTRATION, MR. FANTASTIC!
THWIP
WE MEET AGAIN, SNOT-SHOOTER!
THWIP
SPIDER-MAN! NOT SNOT-SHOOTER! SPIDER-MAN!

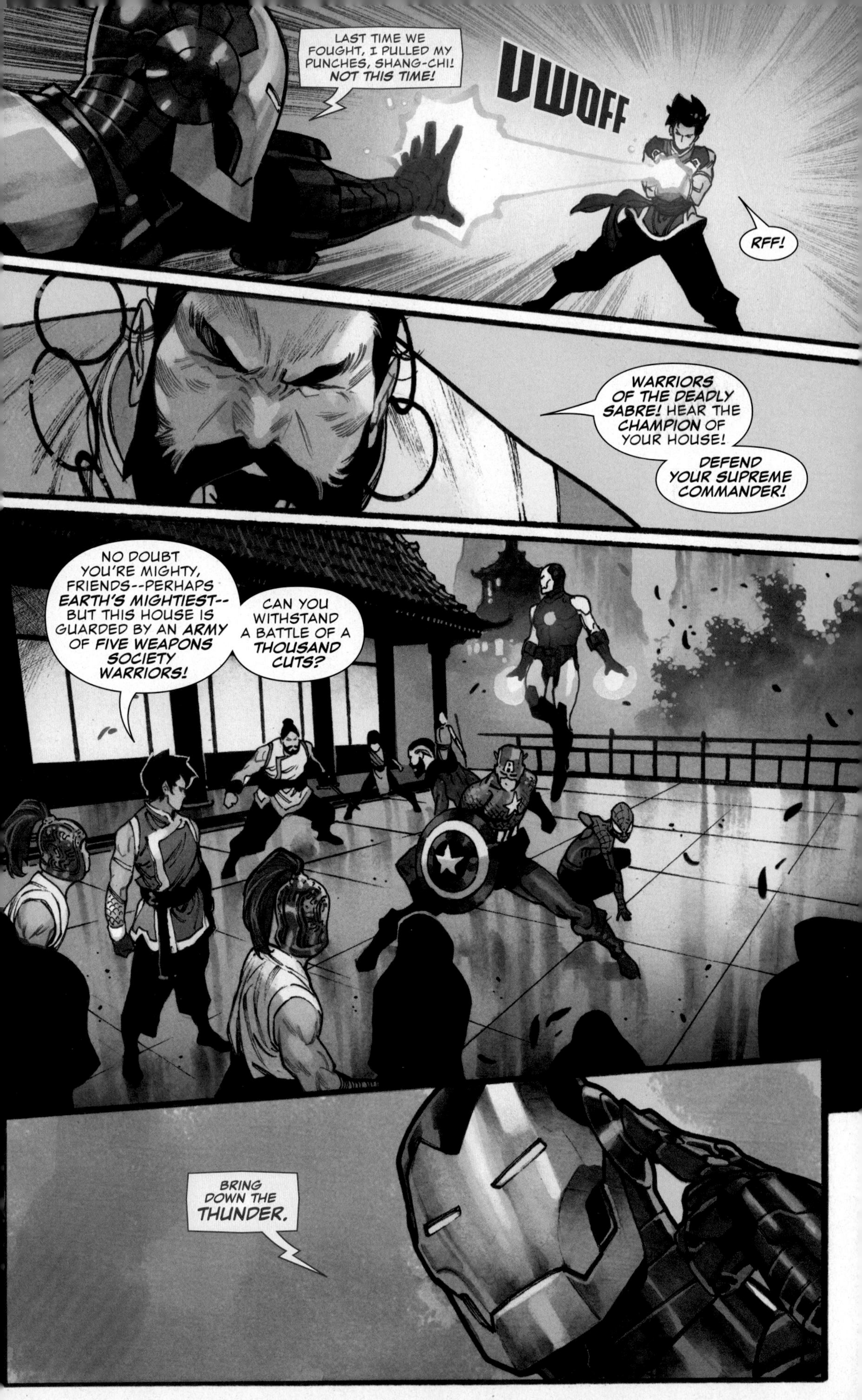
LAST TIME WE FOUGHT, I PULLED MY PUNCHES, SHANG-CHI! NOT THIS TIME!
VWOFF
RFF!
WARRIORS OF THE DEADLY SABRE! HEAR THE CHAMPION OF YOUR HOUSE!
DEFEND YOUR SUPREME COMMANDER!
NO DOUBT YOU'RE MIGHTY, FRIENDS--PERHAPS EARTH'S MIGHTIEST--BUT THIS HOUSE IS GUARDED BY AN ARMY OF FIVE WEAPONS SOCIETY WARRIORS!
CAN YOU WITHSTAND A BATTLE OF A THOUSAND CUTS?
BRING DOWN THE THUNDER.

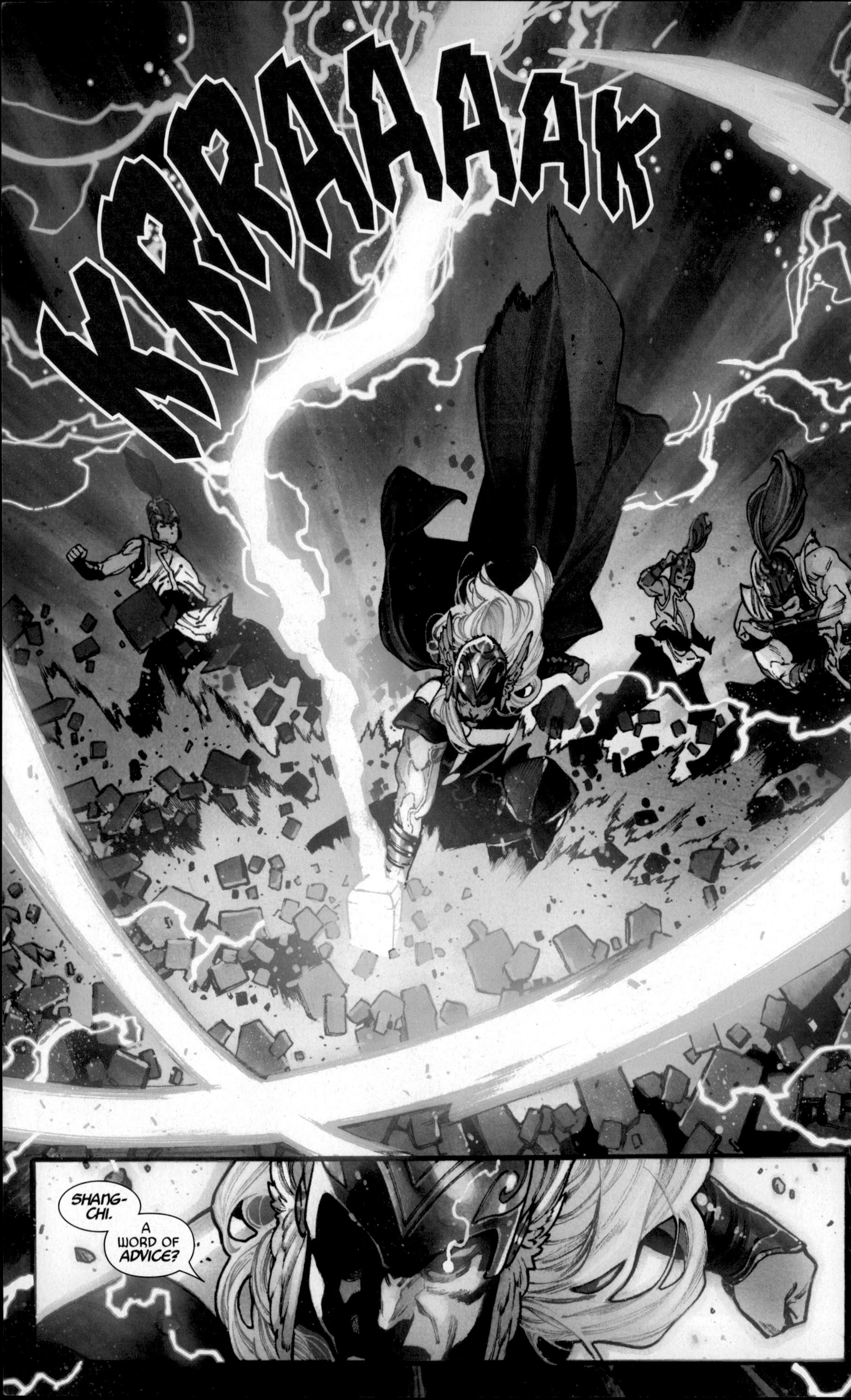
KRRAAAAK
SHANG-CHI.
A WORD OF ADVICE?

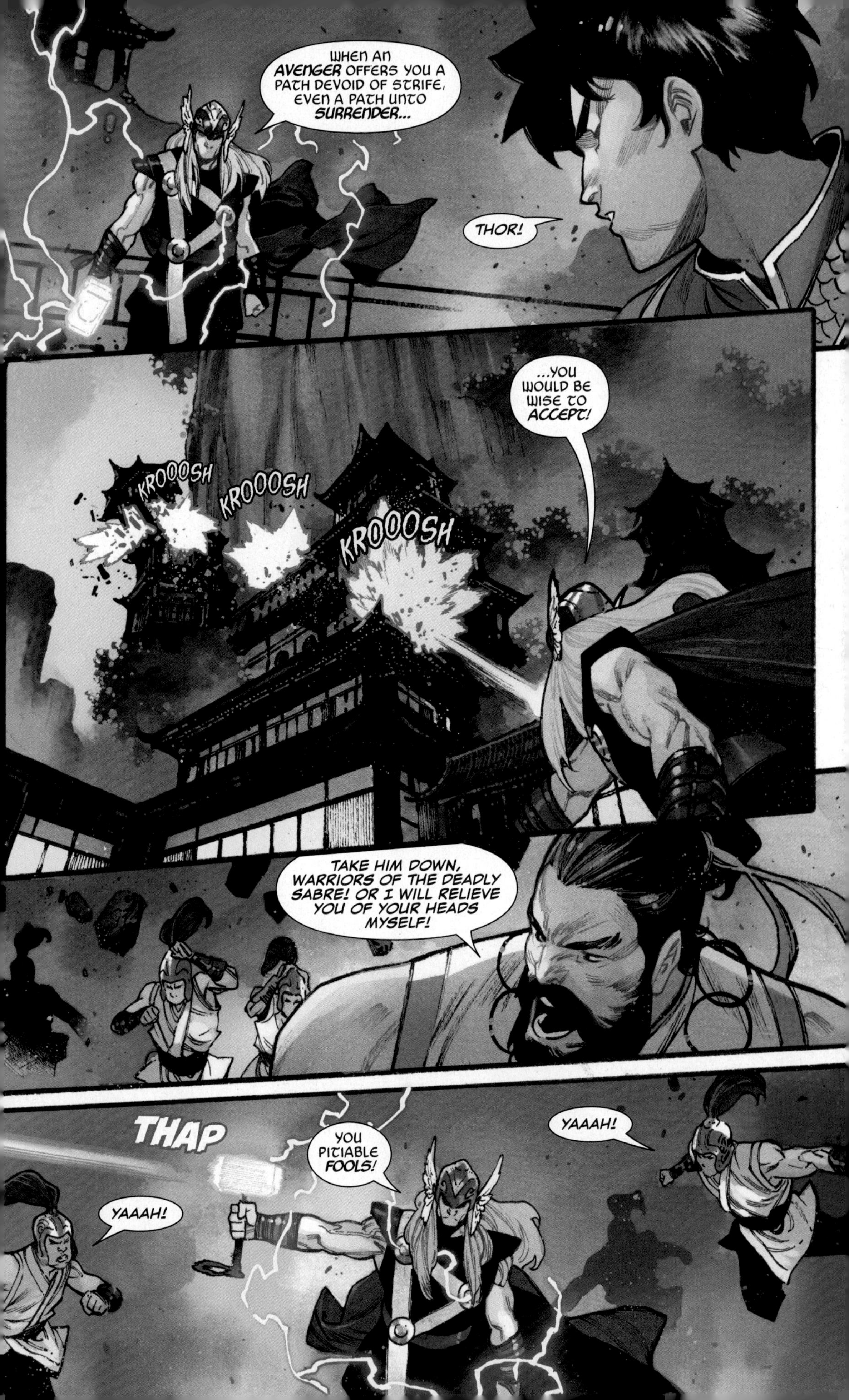
WHEN AN AVENGER OFFERS YOU A PATH DEVOID OF STRIFE, EVEN A PATH UNTO SURRENDER...
THOR!
...YOU WOULD BE WISE TO ACCEPT!
KROOOSH
KROOOSH
KROOOSH
TAKE HIM DOWN, WARRIORS OF THE DEADLY SABRE! OR I WILL RELIEVE YOU OF YOUR HEADS MYSELF!
THAP
YOU PITIABLE FOOLS!
YAAAH!
YAAAH!

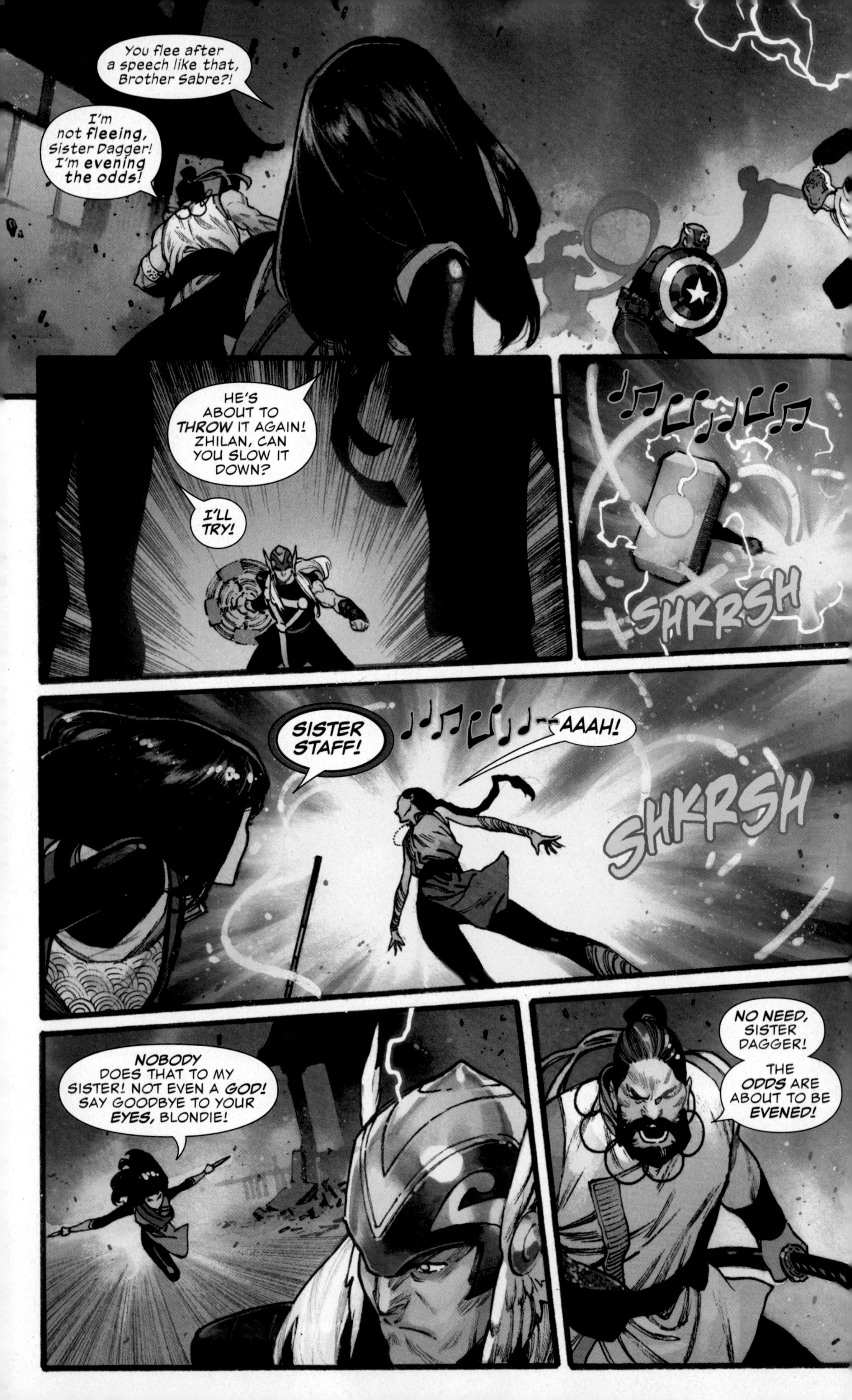
You flee after a speech like that, Brother Sabre?!
I'm not fleeing, Sister Dagger! I'm evening the odds!
HE'S ABOUT TO THROW IT AGAIN! ZHILAN, CAN YOU SLOW IT DOWN?
I'LL TRY!
SHKRSH
SISTER STAFF!
AAAH!
SHKRSH
NOBODY DOES THAT TO MY SISTER! NOT EVEN A GOD! SAY GOODBYE TO YOUR EYES, BLONDIE!
NO NEED, SISTER DAGGER!
THE ODDS ARE ABOUT TO BE EVENED!

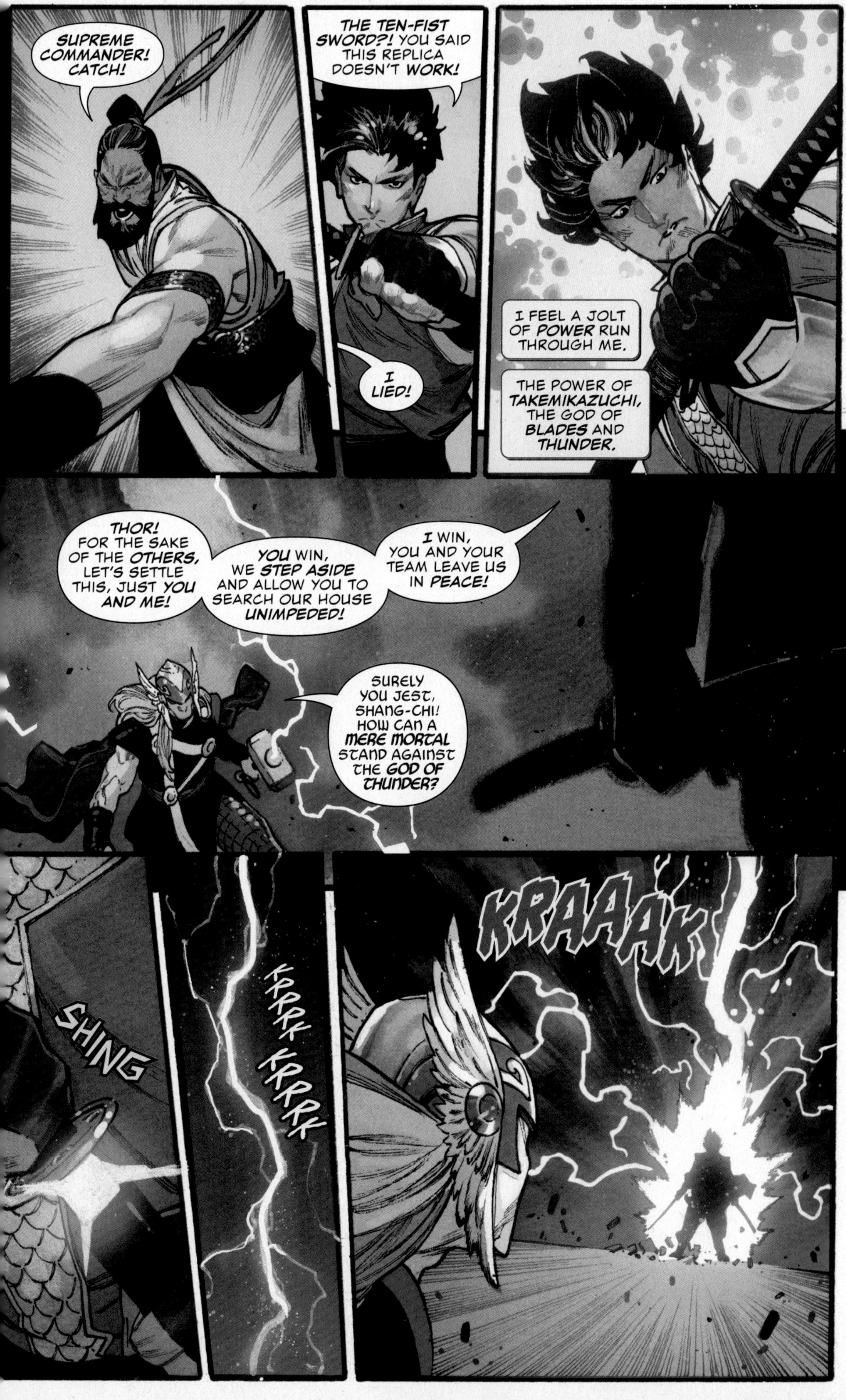
SUPREME COMMANDER! CATCH!
THE TEN-FIST SWORD?! YOU SAID THIS REPLICA DOESN'T WORK!
I LIED!
I FEEL A JOLT OF POWER RUN THROUGH ME.
THE POWER OF TAKEMIKAZUCHI, THE GOD OF BLADES AND THUNDER.
THOR! FOR THE SAKE OF THE OTHERS, LET'S SETTLE THIS, JUST YOU AND ME!
YOU WIN, WE STEP ASIDE AND ALLOW YOU TO SEARCH OUR HOUSE UNIMPEDED!
I WIN, YOU AND YOUR TEAM LEAVE US IN PEACE!
SURELY YOU JEST, SHANG-CHI! HOW CAN A MERE MORTAL STAND AGAINST THE GOD OF THUNDER?
SHING
KRRRK KRRRK
KRAAAK

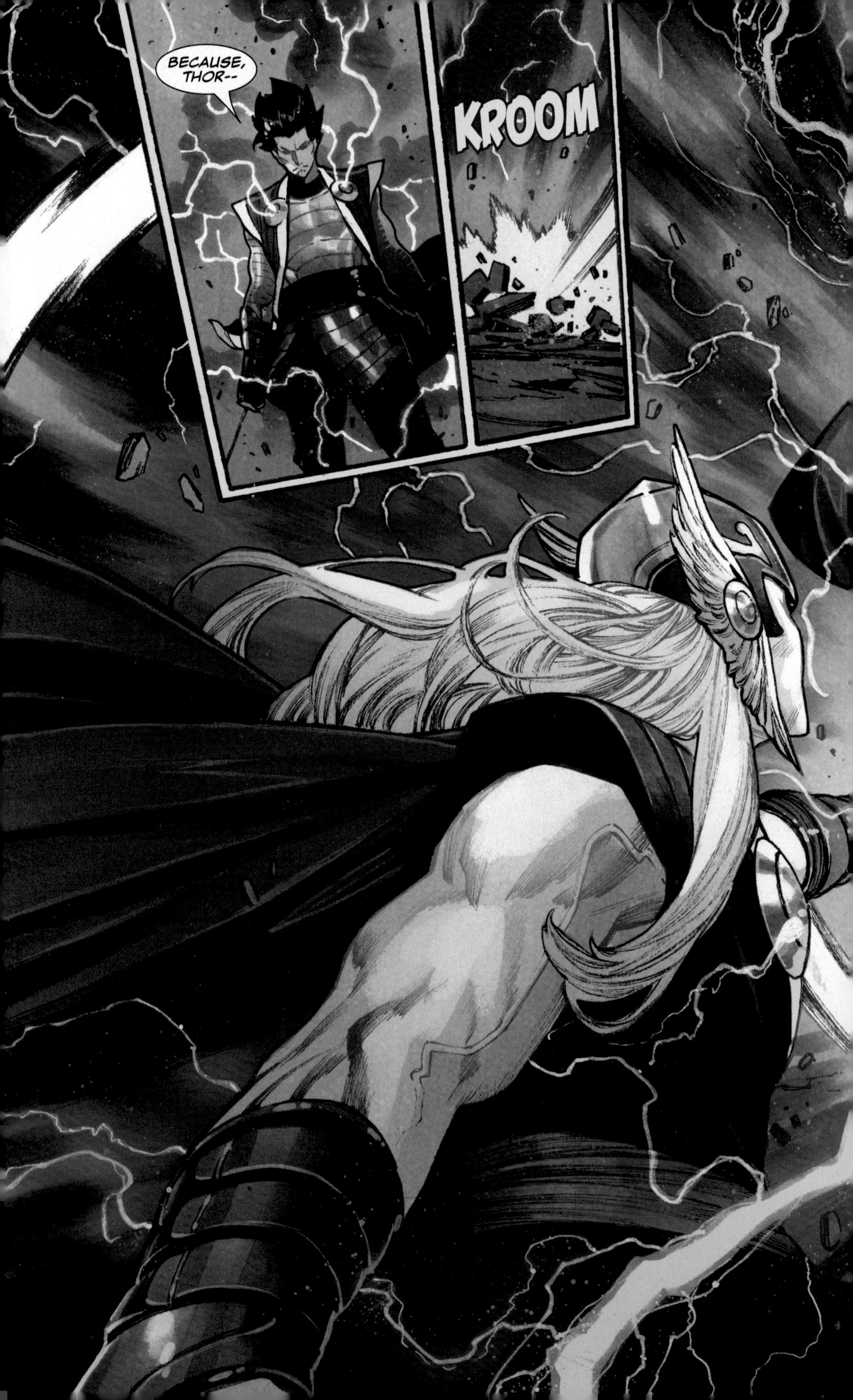
BECAUSE, THOR--
KROOM

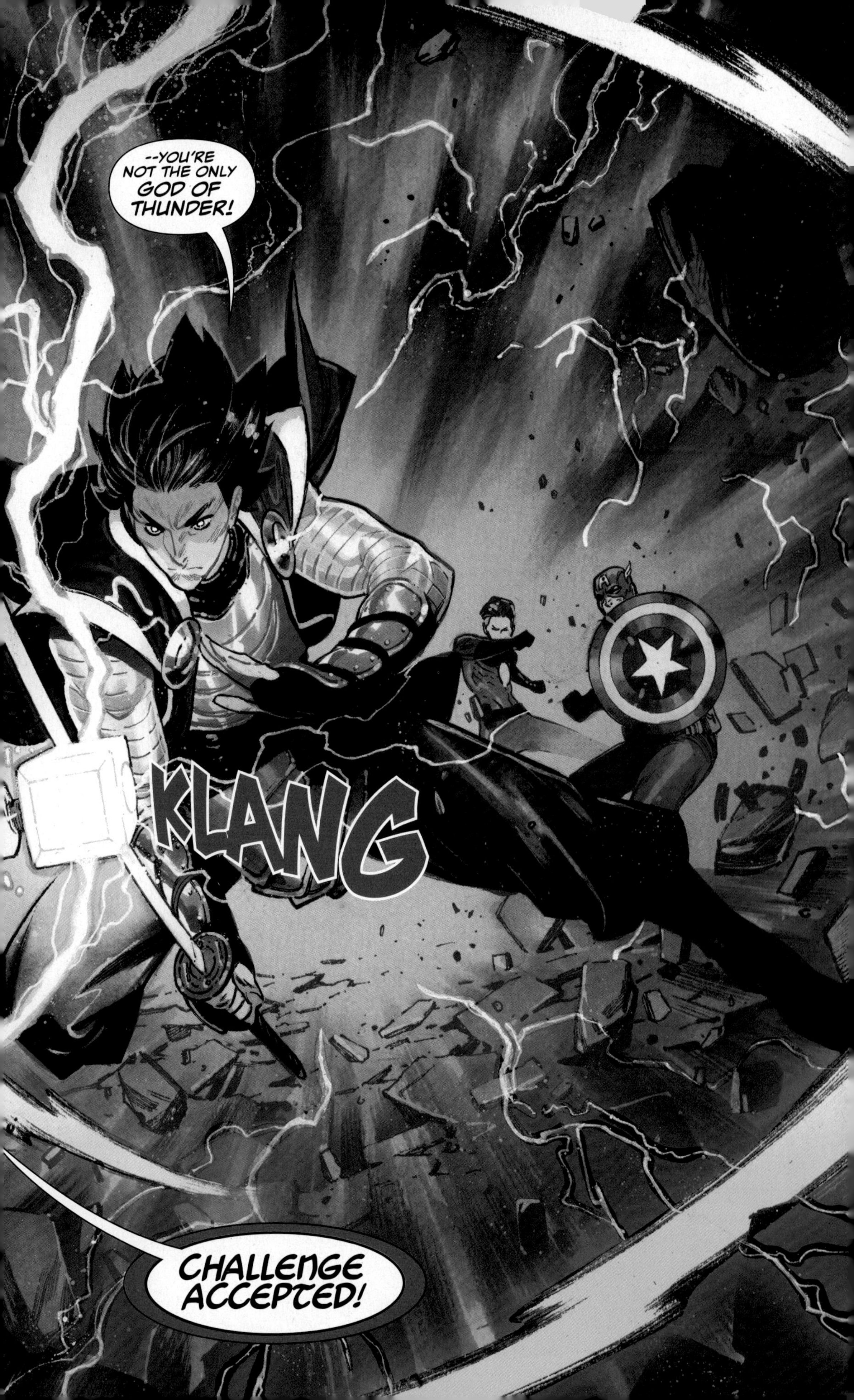
--YOU'RE NOT THE ONLY GOD OF THUNDER!
KLANG
CHALLENGE ACCEPTED!

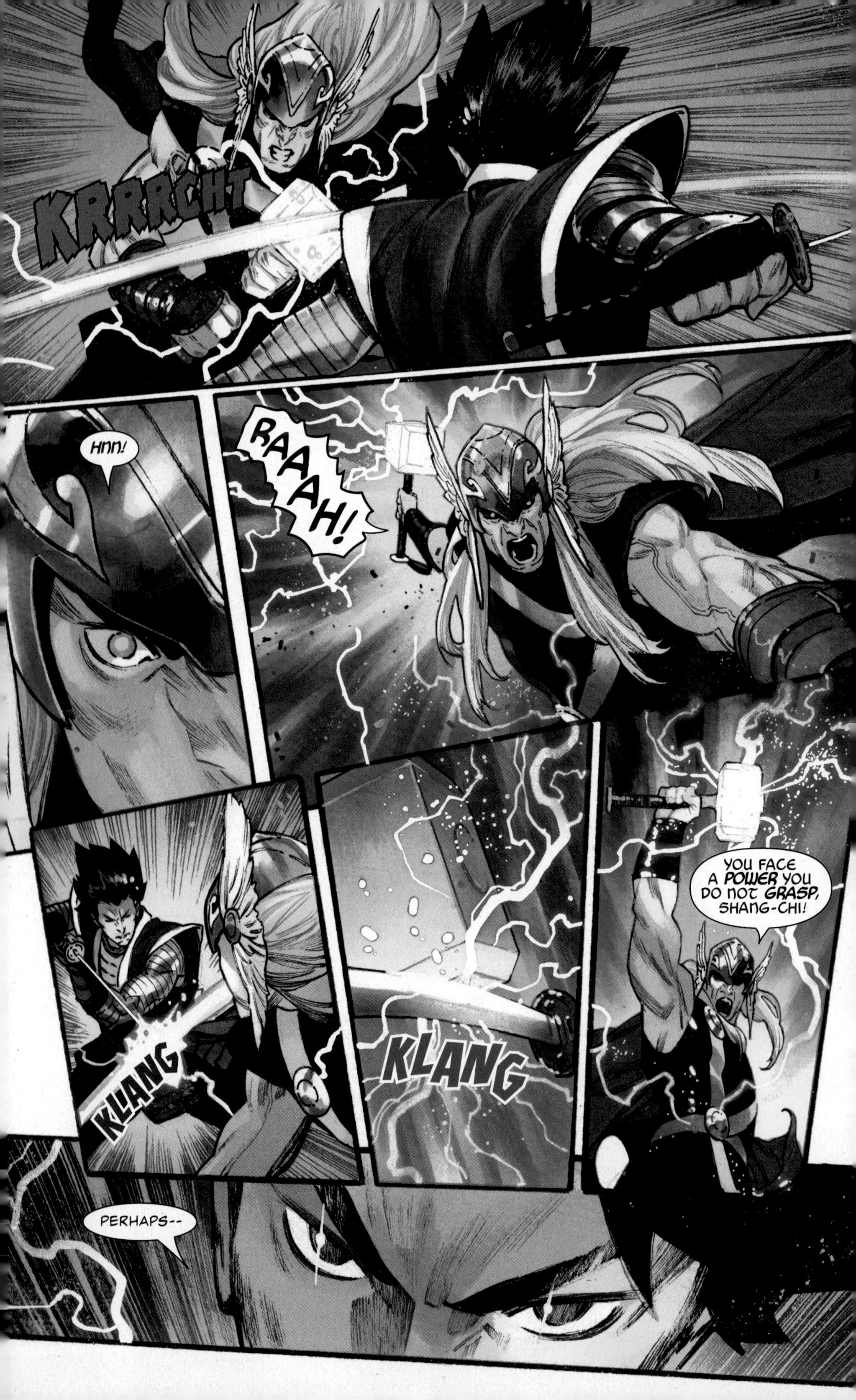
KRRRCHT
HNN!
RAAAAH!
KLANG
KLANG
YOU FACE A POWER YOU DO NOT GRASP, SHANG-CHI!
PERHAPS--

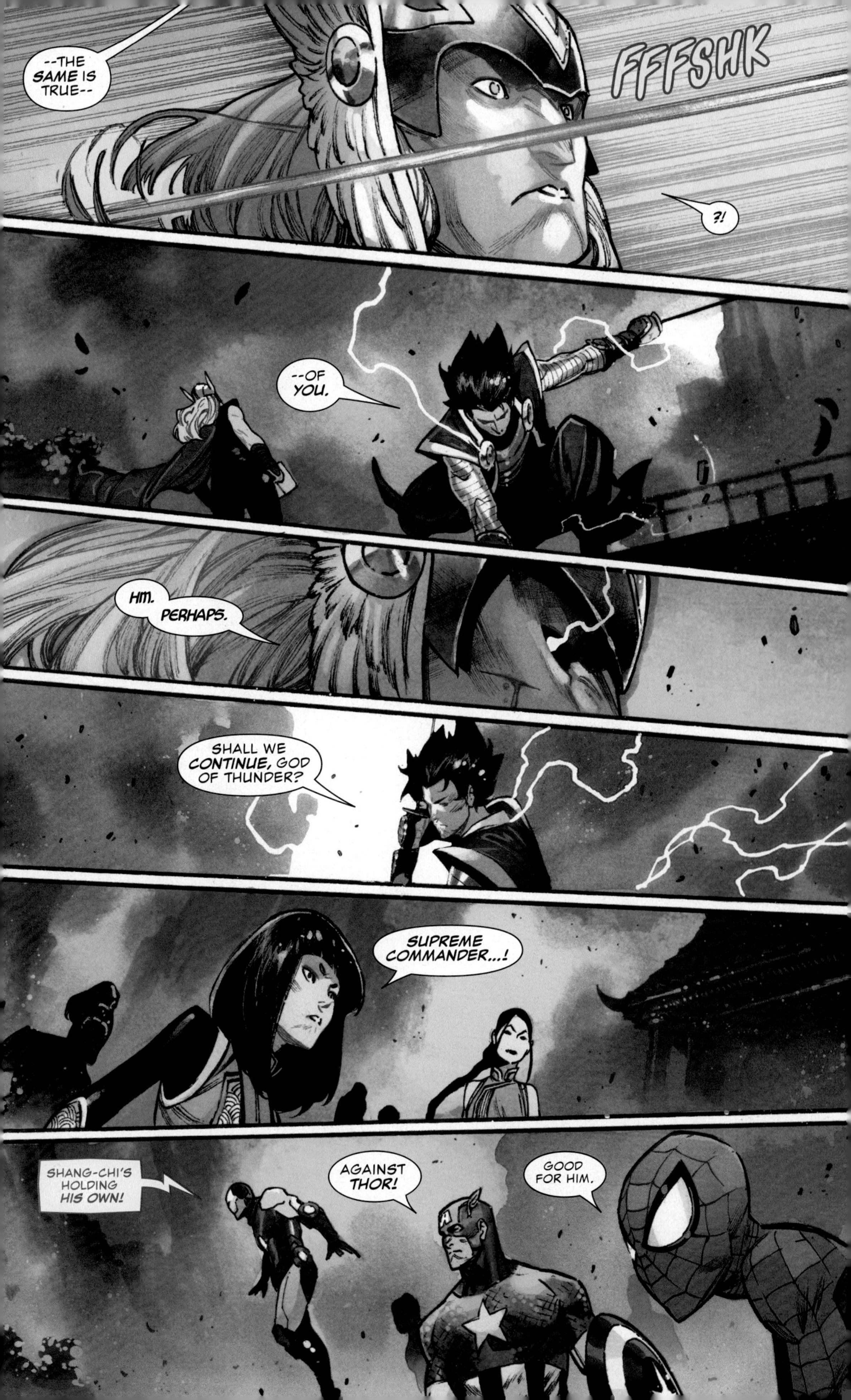
--THE SAME IS TRUE--
FFFSHK
?!
--OF YOU.
HM. PERHAPS.
SHALL WE CONTINUE, GOD OF THUNDER?
SUPREME COMMANDER...!
SHANG-CHI'S HOLDING HIS OWN!
AGAINST THOR!
GOOD FOR HIM.

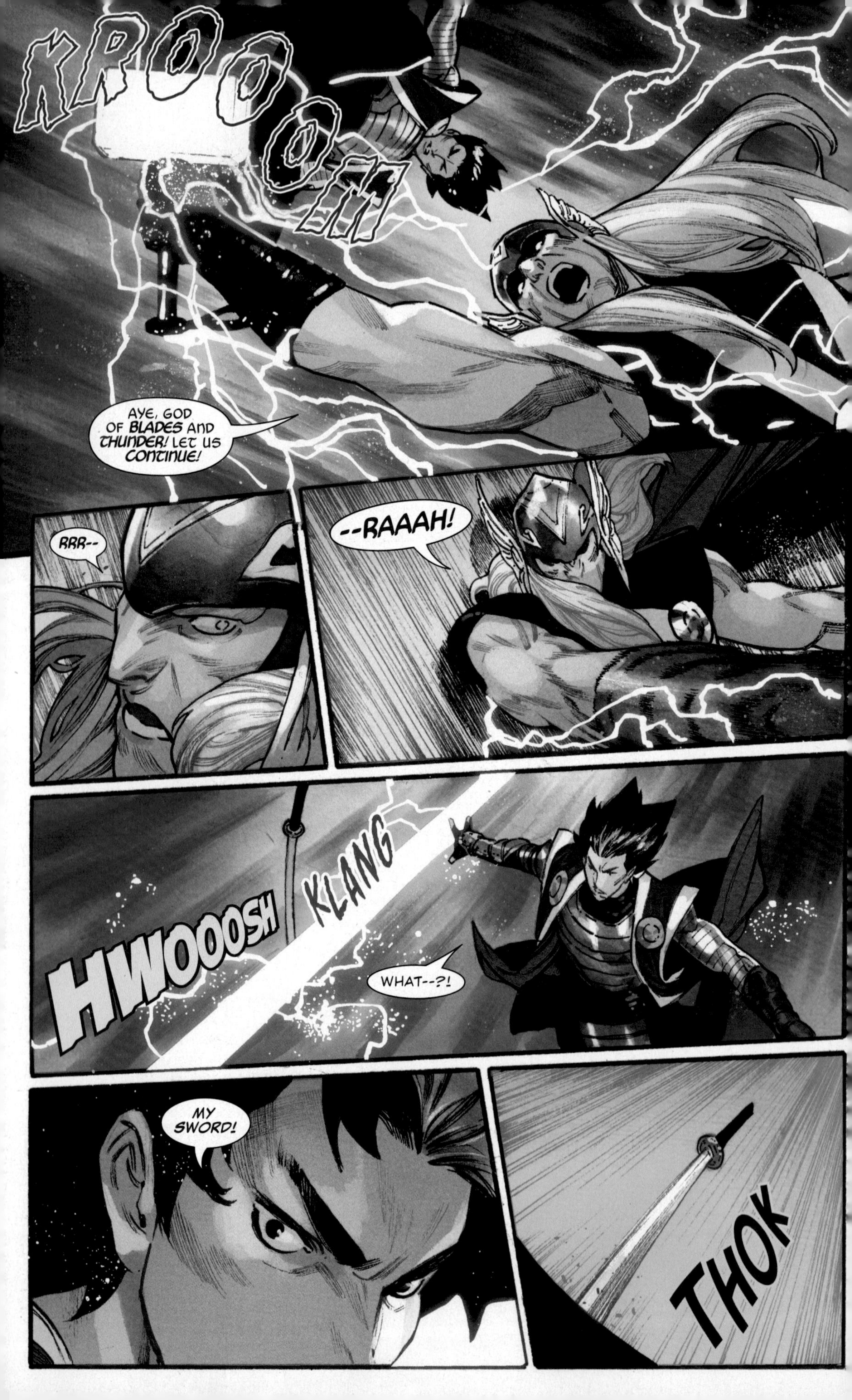
KROOOOM
AYE, GOD OF BLADES AND THUNDER! LET US CONTINUE!
RRR--
--RAAAH!
HWOOOSH
KLANG
WHAT--?!
MY SWORD!
THOK

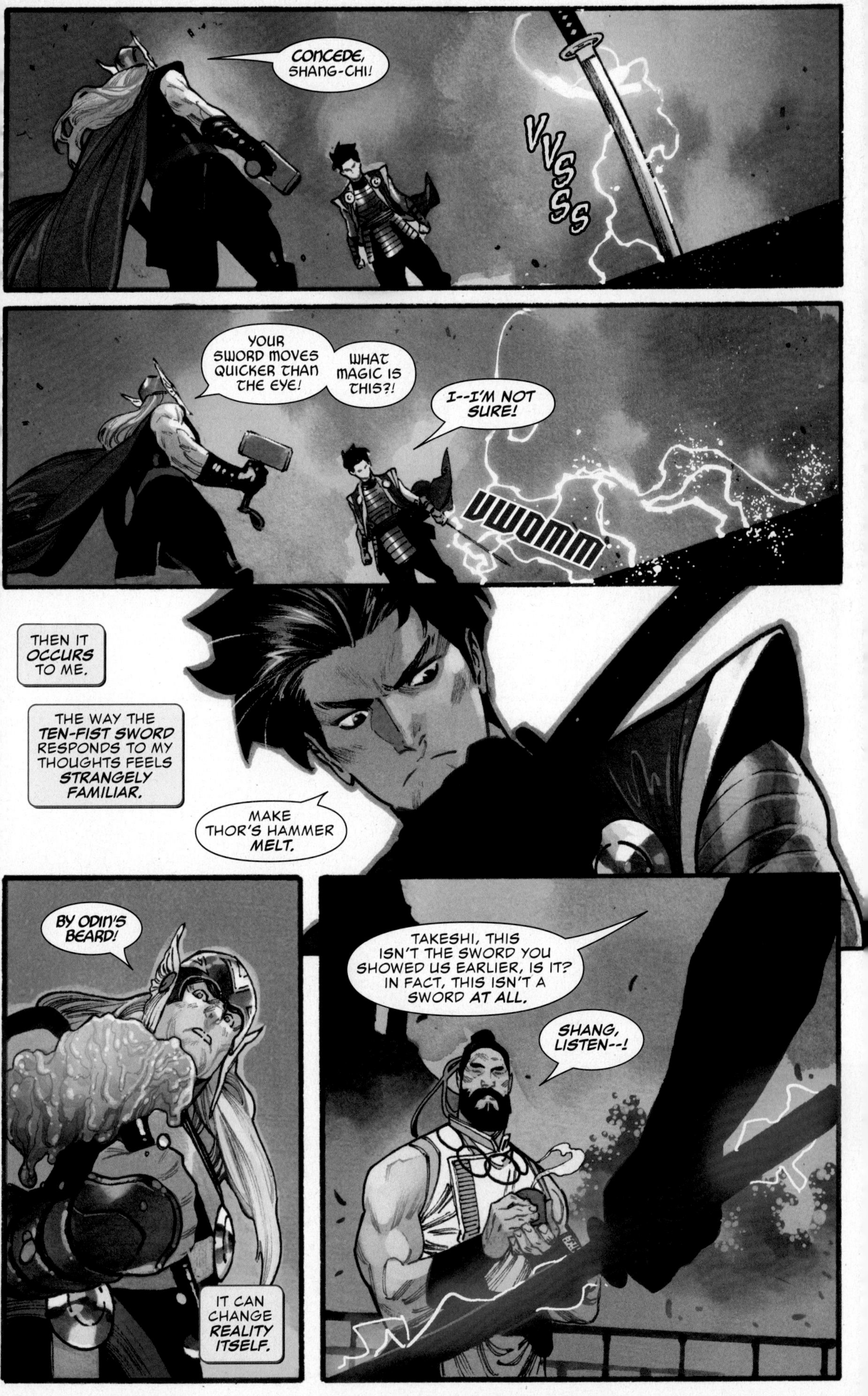
CONCEDE, SHANG-CHI!
VVSSS
YOUR SWORD MOVES QUICKER THAN THE EYE!
WHAT MAGIC IS THIS?!
I--I'M NOT SURE!
VWOMM
THEN IT OCCURS TO ME.
THE WAY THE TEN-FIST SWORD RESPONDS TO MY THOUGHTS FEELS STRANGELY FAMILIAR.
MAKE THOR'S HAMMER MELT.
BY ODIN'S BEARD!
IT CAN CHANGE REALITY ITSELF.
TAKESHI, THIS ISN'T THE SWORD YOU SHOWED US EARLIER, IS IT? IN FACT, THIS ISN'T A SWORD AT ALL.
SHANG, LISTEN--!

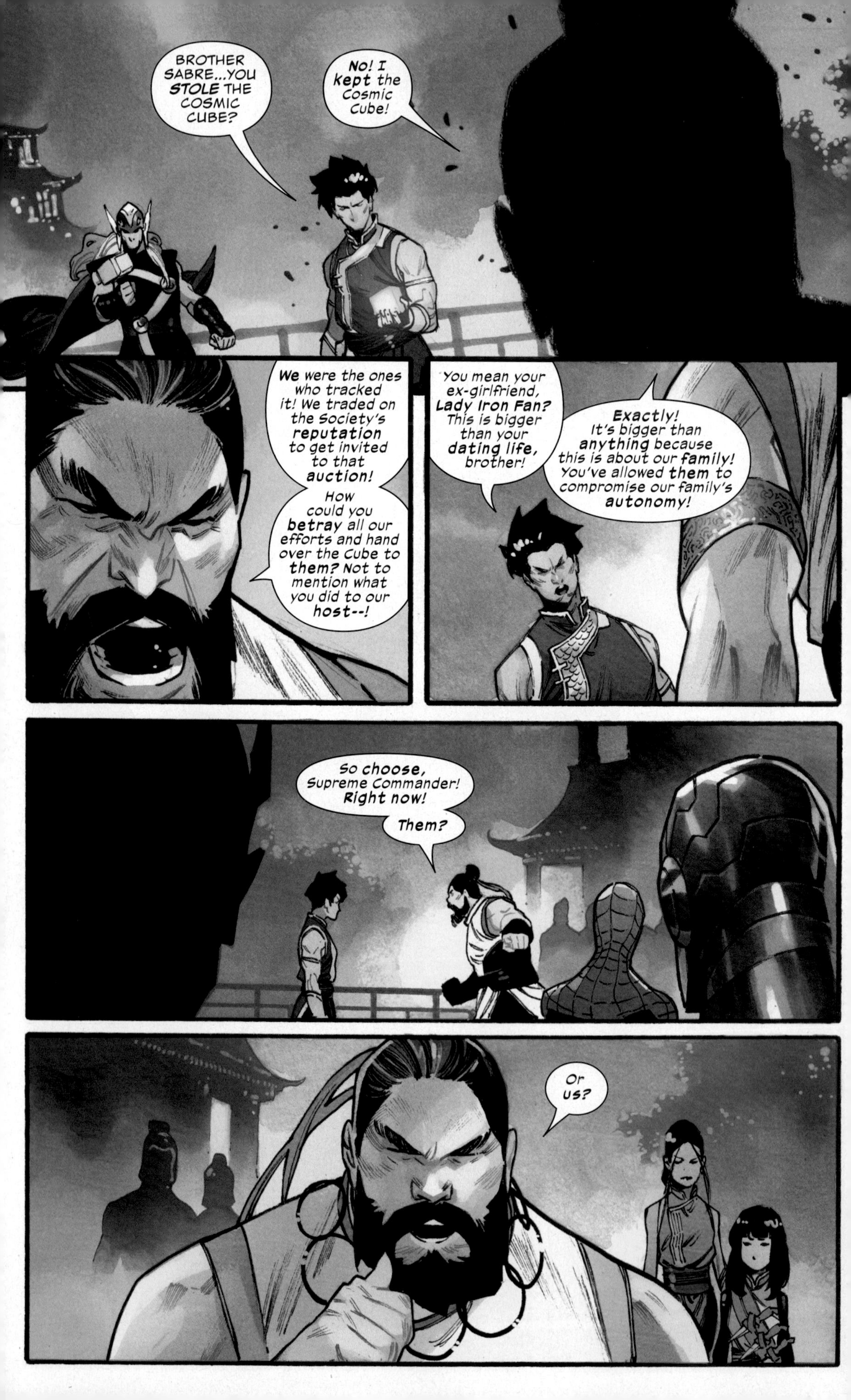
BROTHER SABRE...YOU STOLE THE COSMIC CUBE?
No! I kept the Cosmic Cube!
We were the ones who tracked it! We traded on the Society's reputation to get invited to that auction!
How could you betray all our efforts and hand over the Cube to them? Not to mention what you did to our host--!
You mean your ex-girlfriend, Lady Iron Fan? This is bigger than your dating life, brother!
Exactly! It's bigger than anything because this is about our family! You've allowed them to compromise our family's autonomy!
So choose, Supreme Commander! Right now!
Them?
Or us?

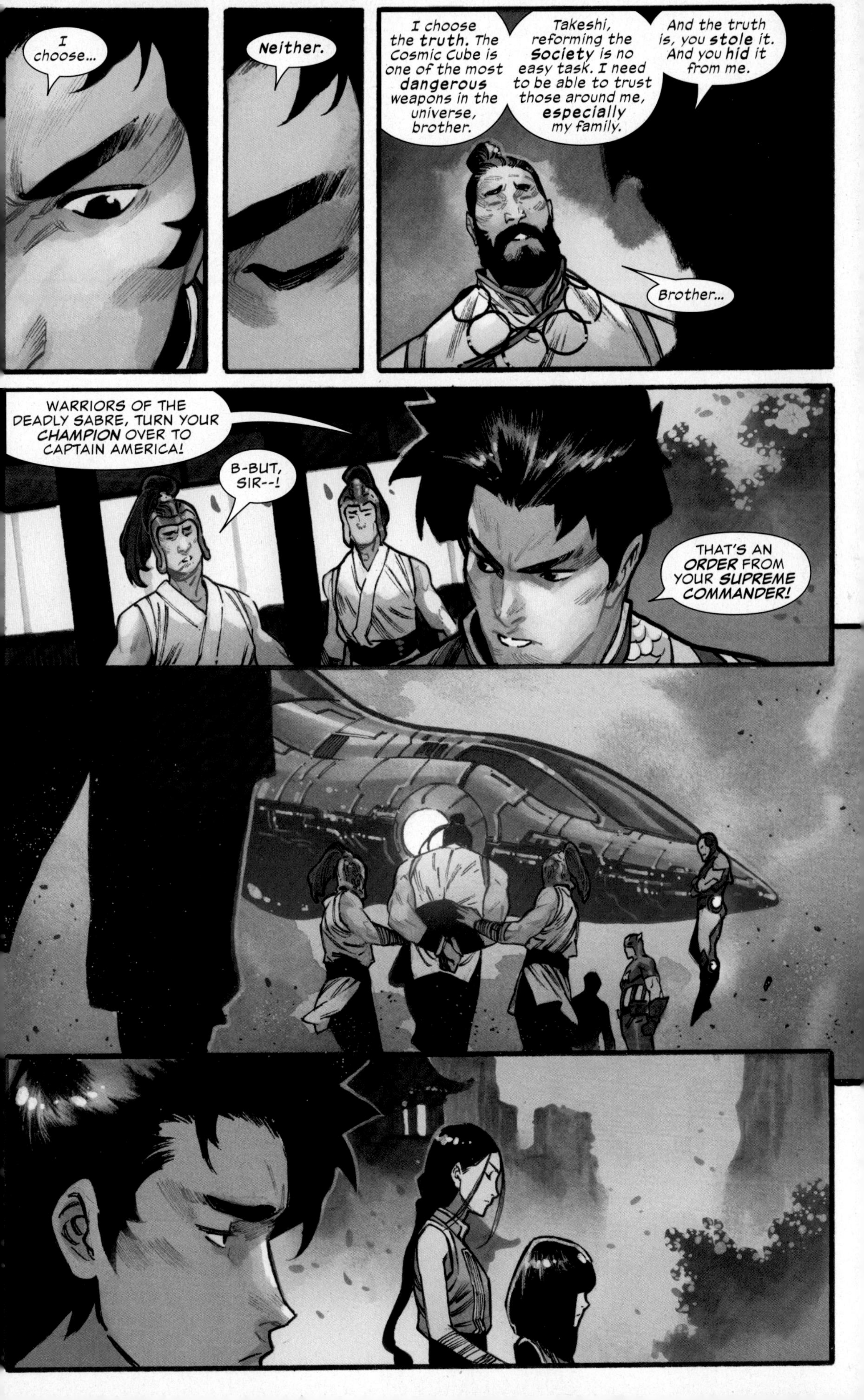
I choose...
Neither.
I choose the truth. The Cosmic Cube is one of the most dangerous weapons in the universe, brother.
Takeshi, reforming the Society is no easy task. I need to be able to trust those around me, especially my family.
And the truth is, you stole it. And you hid it from me.
Brother...
WARRIORS OF THE DEADLY SABRE, TURN YOUR CHAMPION OVER TO CAPTAIN AMERICA!
B-BUT, SIR--!
THAT'S AN ORDER FROM YOUR SUPREME COMMANDER!

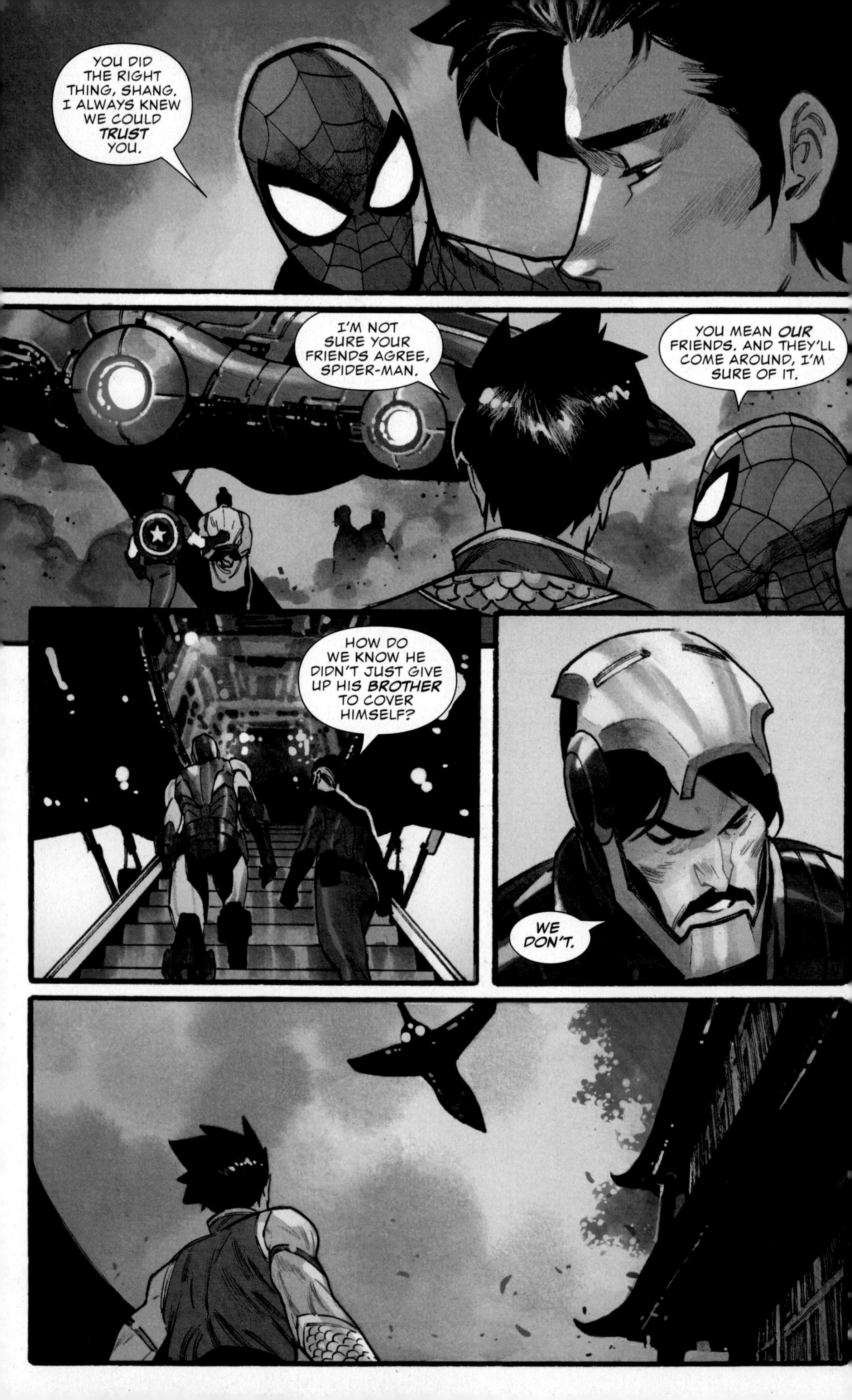
YOU DID THE RIGHT THING, SHANG. I ALWAYS KNEW WE COULD TRUST YOU.
I'M NOT SURE YOUR FRIENDS AGREE, SPIDER-MAN.
YOU MEAN OUR FRIENDS. AND THEY'LL COME AROUND, I'M SURE OF IT.
HOW DO WE KNOW HE DIDN'T JUST GIVE UP HIS BROTHER TO COVER HIMSELF?
WE DON'T.

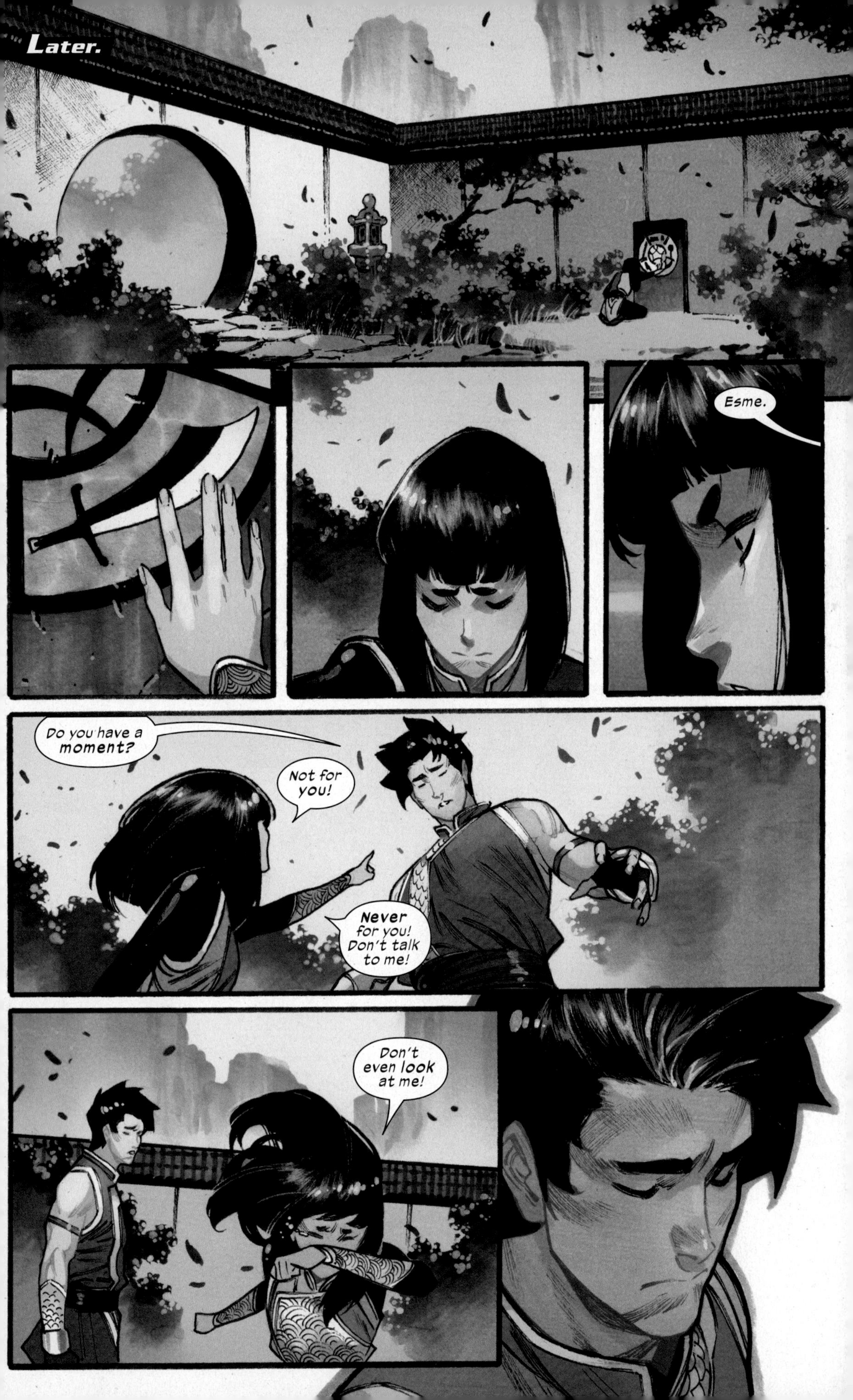
Later.
Esme.
Do you have a moment?
Not for you!
Never for you! Don't talk to me!
Don't even look at me!

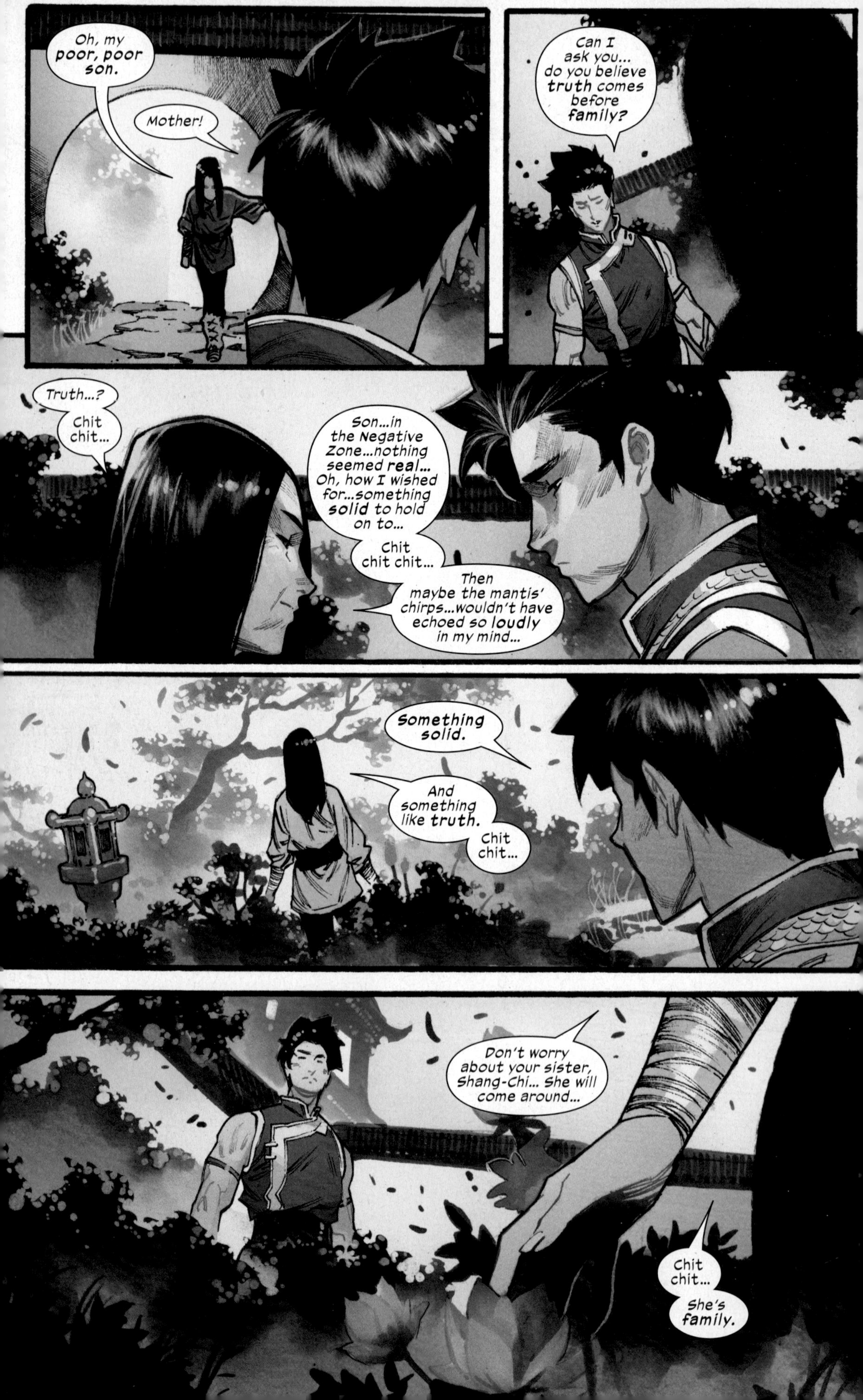
Oh, my poor, poor son.
Mother!
Can I ask you... do you believe truth comes before family?
Truth...?
Chit chit...
Son...in the Negative Zone...nothing seemed real... Oh, how I wished for...something solid to hold on to...
Chit chit chit...
Then maybe the mantis' chirps...wouldn't have echoed so loudly in my mind...
Something solid.
And something like truth.
Chit chit...
Don't worry about your sister, Shang-Chi... She will come around...
Chit chit...
She's family.

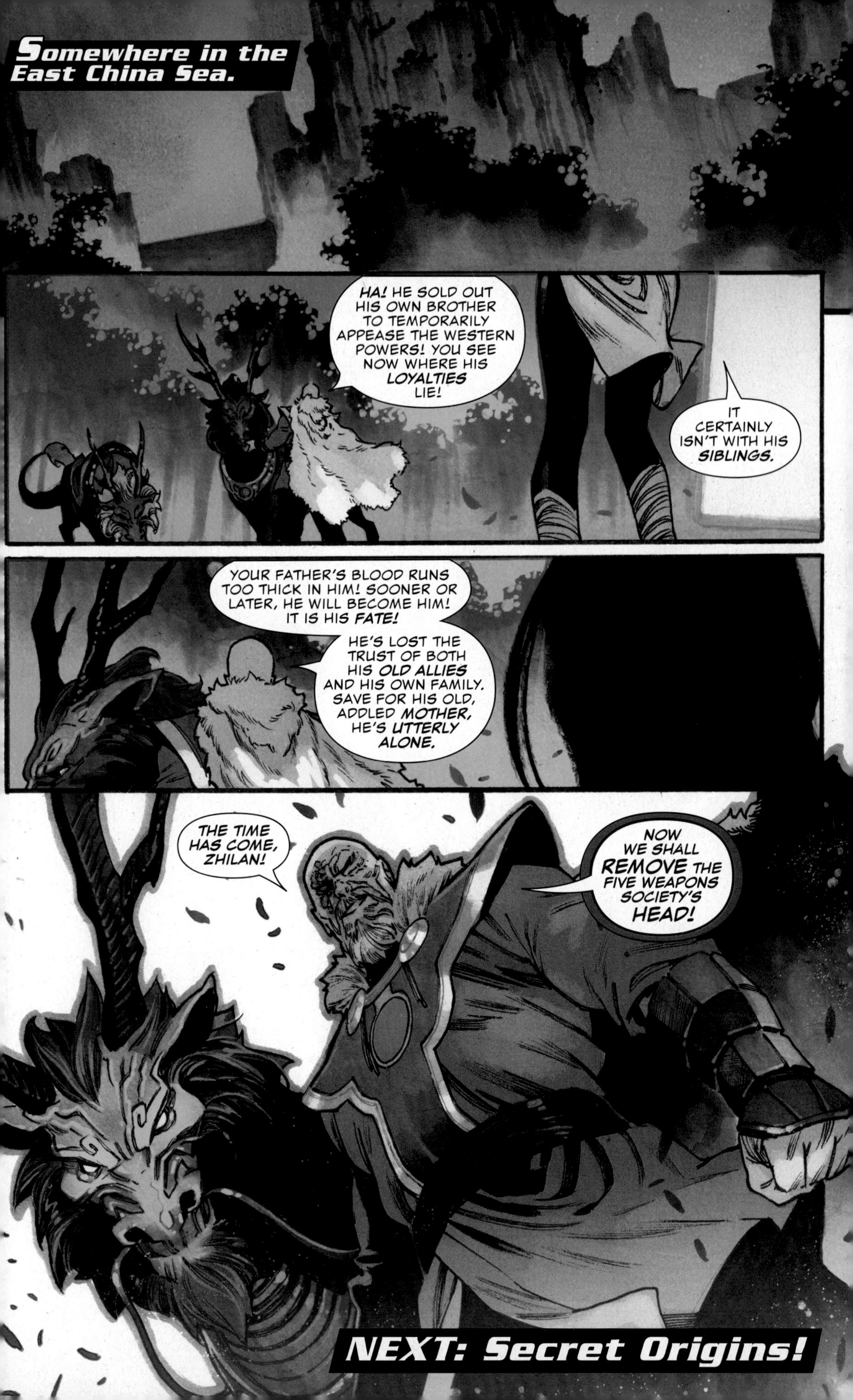
Somewhere in the East China Sea.
HA! HE SOLD OUT HIS OWN BROTHER TO TEMPORARILY APPEASE THE WESTERN POWERS! YOU SEE NOW WHERE HIS LOYALTIES LIE!
IT CERTAINLY ISN'T WITH HIS SIBLINGS.
YOUR FATHER'S BLOOD RUNS TOO THICK IN HIM! SOONER OR LATER, HE WILL BECOME HIM! IT IS HIS FATE!
HE'S LOST THE TRUST OF BOTH HIS OLD ALLIES AND HIS OWN FAMILY. SAVE FOR HIS OLD, ADDLED MOTHER, HE'S UTTERLY ALONE.
THE TIME HAS COME, ZHILAN!
NOW WE SHALL REMOVE THE FIVE WEAPONS SOCIETY'S HEAD!
NEXT: Secret Origins!

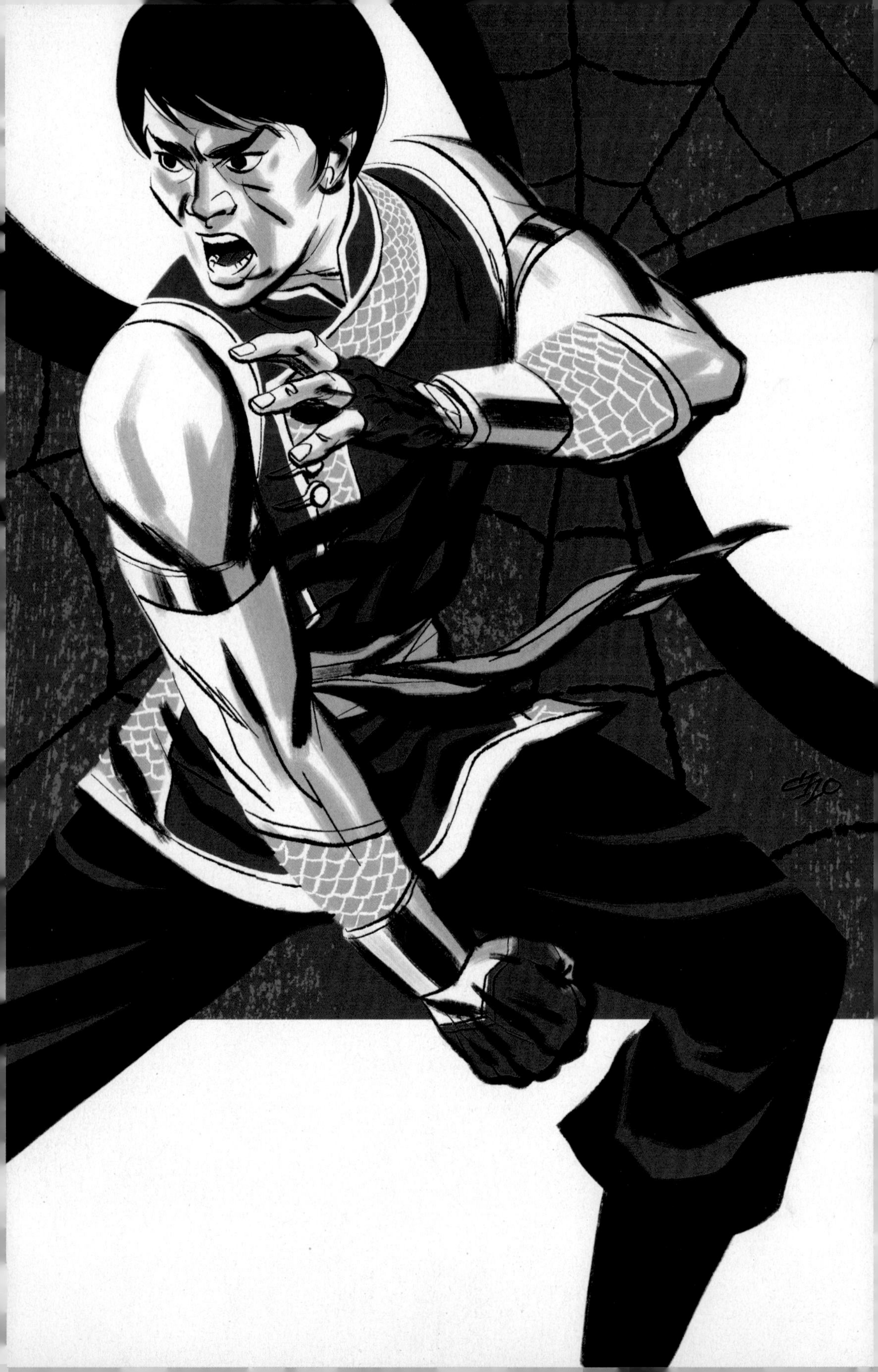

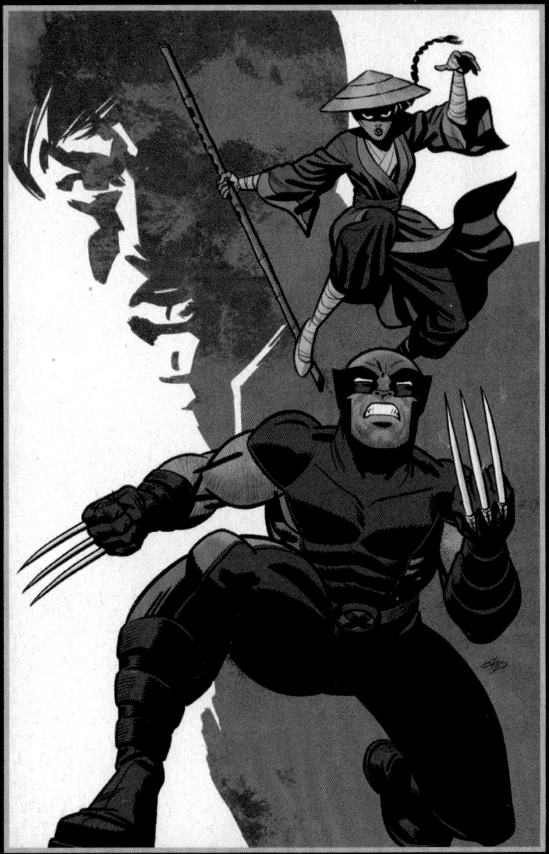

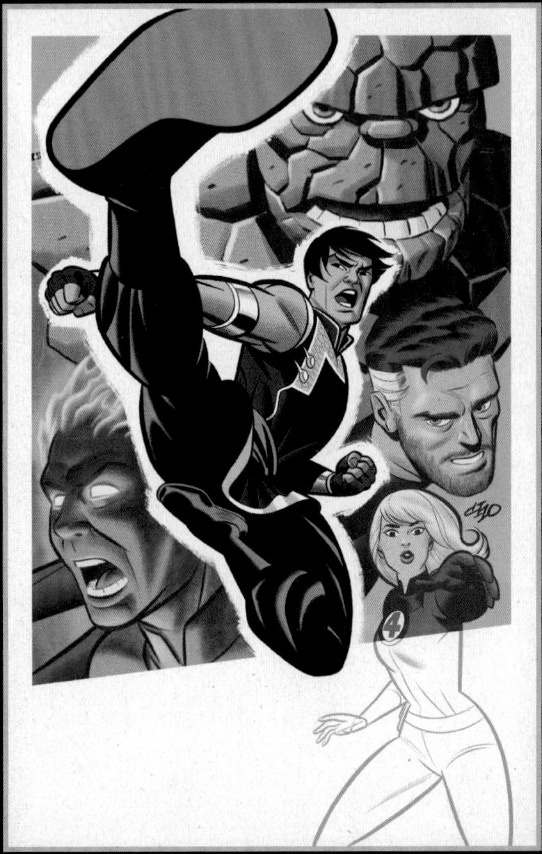

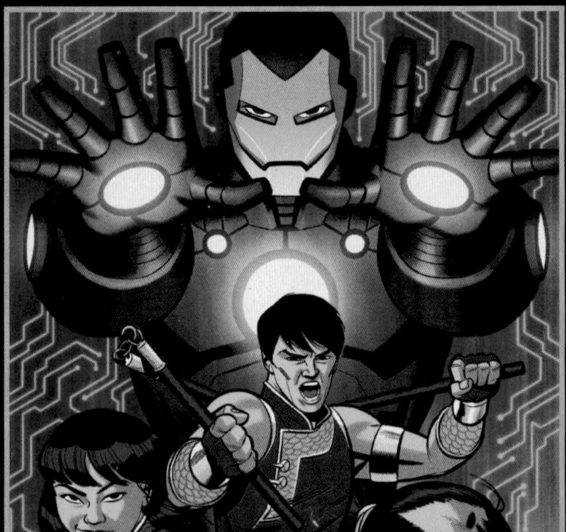

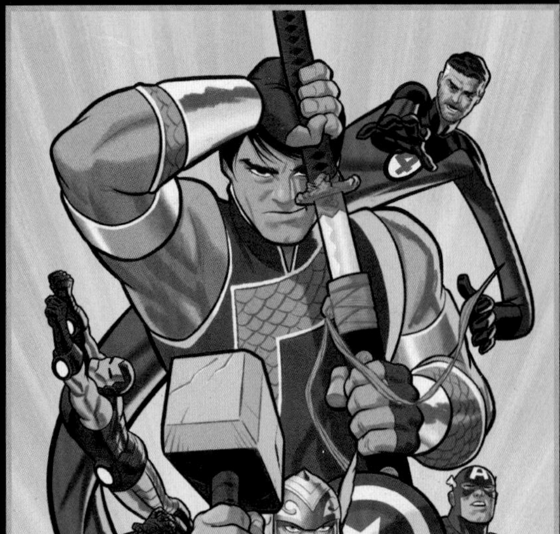

#3-6 VARIANTS BY

MICHAEL CHO

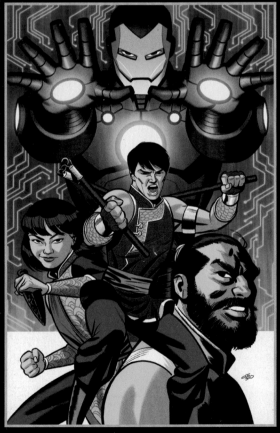

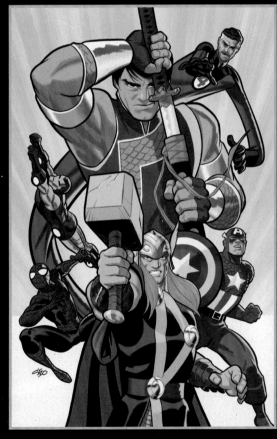

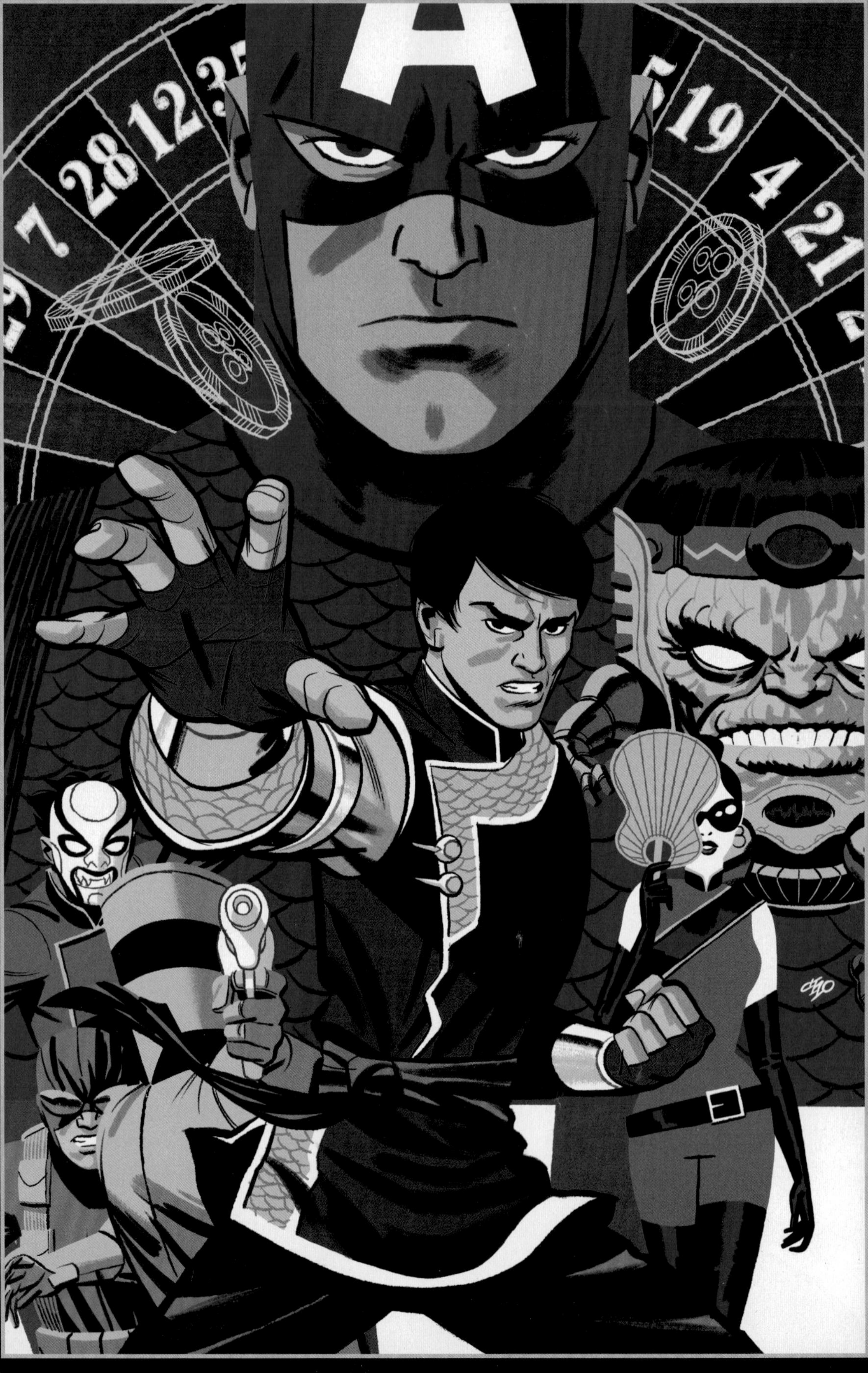
7
28
12
19
4
21

#2 VARIANT BY
MICHAEL CHO